MW01384028

Baseball
Explained

Baseball Explained

PHILLIP MAHONY

McFarland & Company, Inc., Publishers
Jefferson, North Carolina

LIBRARY OF CONGRESS CATALOGUING-IN-PUBLICATION DATA

Mahony, Phillip.
Baseball explained / Phillip Mahony.
p   cm.
Includes bibliographical references and index.

ISBN 978-0-7864-7964-1 (softcover : acid free paper) ∞
ISBN 978-1-4766-1587-5 (ebook)

1. Baseball—Rules.   I. Title.
GV877.M265 2014   796.357—dc23   2014021263

BRITISH LIBRARY CATALOGUING DATA ARE AVAILABLE

© 2014 Phillip Mahony. All rights reserved

*No part of this book may be reproduced or transmitted in any form
or by any means, electronic or mechanical, including photocopying
or recording, or by any information storage and retrieval system,
without permission in writing from the publisher.*

On the cover: Lobby card for the 1950 film
The Jackie Robinson Story (Pathe Industries)

Printed in the United States of America

*McFarland & Company, Inc., Publishers
Box 611, Jefferson, North Carolina 28640
www.mcfarlandpub.com*

With all my love to Marya, my wife, and to
our children, Patrick, Caroline, Phillip and William.
For their help with this book, thank you to Jim Jerome,
author and journalist, to Fred Berowski,
formerly reference librarian with the
National Baseball Hall of Fame and Museum,
presently director of Library Services at Herkimer College,
and to copy editor Kevin Murawinski of sluicebox-media.com.

Table of Contents

Introduction

Two unlikely events led to the writing of this book.

First, on October 15, 2008, on the 17th floor of the Citicorp Building on Manhattan's East Side, the door to my office was suddenly darkened by the glum figures of not one, but two, of my firm's highest ranking partners. This isn't good, I said to myself. It wasn't. I was laid off, and it would be nearly a year before I was able to find work again in what would reveal itself to be the country's worst economic downturn since the Great Depression.

Second, two and a half months later, on December 29, as the rain and the wet snow fell on Birmingham, England, and as the final seconds of a scoreless soccer game ticked away in Villa Stadium, and as 45,000 drenched Aston Villa fans chanted and sang and celebrated the imminent prospect of not losing to mighty Liverpool, from a tangle of players near midfield Liverpool striker Fernando Torres suddenly broke free with the ball, raced down the muddy sideline, veered into the penalty area to the left of the Aston Villa goal and blasted the ball into the net for the win.

I can explain.

It was because I was unemployed that I spent a lot of time on my exercise bike that winter. It was because I spent a lot of time on my exercise bike while watching TV that, out of sheer boredom, and with the baseball season still a long way off, I started sneaking a peek at the occasional soccer game, a sport I had more or less loathed for my entire life. It was because I snuck a peek at that particular Liverpool game and saw Torres' amazing goal that I suddenly, inexplicably, became hooked on soccer. (Within a few weeks I was watching three or four games a weekend and actually calling it "footie.") It was because I became hooked that I began sending my cousins in England long emails asking questions about the Premier League teams and players and its confusing plethora of side tournaments, called "Cups." It was because I was asking them so many questions about soccer that they, in turn, finally asked me a question: Can you explain baseball to us?

No problem, I thought. After all, I'd been a fan my whole life. I'll just write them a few emails. But it was a problem. I wrote five or six emails before I gave up, all but the first beginning with "Forget everything I said in my last email; start with this one instead." No matter where I started my explanation, other explanations were needed first. No matter where I began, I needed to back up and begin again. And again. And again.

No problem, I thought. I'll just find them a book. But, again, it was a problem. I hit the bookstores, and the Internet, and though I found a few books that seemed, from their titles, anyway, to be the basic explanatory book I was looking for, they weren't because they invariably assumed the reader had a great deal of knowledge about baseball even as they professed to be explaining it.

I came to realize that the difficulty in explaining baseball lies in the fact that Americans learn the game like they learn their first language: not consciously, from an independent and unencumbered starting point ("OK, honey, sit the baby over here and let's get started on the present tense!") upon which subsequent learning builds, but through a passive and gradual seeping into the brain of many fragments from many sources over many years.

Fine, but suppose you don't have many years to learn baseball by osmosis. Suppose you are going to visit some cousins in the States and you'd like to know what all the commotion is about, or you are going there on business and you'd like to impress clients by knowing the difference between a ball and a strike. Or, even more urgently, suppose you already live in the States and don't know a darn thing about baseball and you need a quick explanation before your colleagues and friends and neighbors find out the embarrassing truth. Where can you turn?

The goal of this book is to be the book that you can turn to. Nearly six years after the challenge of explaining baseball was first presented to me, I believe I have written a book that someone with no knowledge of baseball can pick up, read in a couple of days and, afterward, not only be able to enjoy a game of baseball but also understand how deeply the sport is ingrained in American history, culture and everyday life. Whether I am correct in my belief will, of course, be your call.

Some points on how this book is set up:

- Baseball, like many vocations in life, is all about the vocabulary. Stick your head into a discussion among bankruptcy attorneys and you'll hear about cramdowns, claims and cash collateral. Do the same with a group of baseball fans and you'll hear about signs, steals and sacrifices. Once you're familiar with the vocabulary, in either case, you can join the discussion. Until then, you can't. In this book I aim to familiarize you with all the baseball terms that you'll need to learn the game and converse capably about it with knowledgeable fans. The first time I use a term, I bold it for emphasis and easy reference.

- Everyone knows you can't drive down the highway backward using your feet to steer the car, but good luck trying to find the statute that forbids it. Likewise, there are many things about baseball that every fan knows to be true, and that have been true since dinosaurs roamed the Earth, but good luck finding the sources. The three basic authorities of the sport are the *Official Baseball Rules*, which provides the on-field rules of the game, the *Major League Rules*, which provides the off-field rules of the game, and the *Basic Agreement*, which is the collective bargaining agreement between team owners and players, renegotiated every five years or so, and which affects both. These are vital resources, and I will refer to them often, but their functions, individually and collectively, do not include offering an even remotely complete account of what goes on between the beginning and the end of a baseball game. By necessity, therefore, this book will also be based on what I've seen in front of me, while munching a hot dog and sipping a cold beverage, on many a field of dreams, on many a balmy summer eve.

- Not counting this Introduction and a brief closing, this book is divided into four parts. We will start out with "Preliminaries," which will explain those aspects of the game that you need to be familiar with before approaching the game itself. You'll need to be familiar with the setup of the baseball field, for example, and how the length of a game is measured. You won't need to know anything about baseball going into this part, but you'll be ready for the game once you come out of it.

In "The Game" we will study the game itself. We will discuss the objectives of the opposing teams and how they attempt to achieve those objectives within a framework of rules that can, at times, be challenging. Or maybe "overbearing" is a better word. "Exasperating" also comes to mind.

There is an old saying that baseball is an island of activity surrounded by an ocean of statistics. In "Statistics" we will learn that, more than just surrounding baseball, statistics are a vital part of baseball, permeating every aspect of it and influencing the decisions and strategies that propel each game forward.

The fourth and final part is an introduction to **Major League Baseball**, the highest level of baseball played in the world. Major League Baseball is also referred to as the **MLB, the Major Leagues, the Majors**, the **Big Leagues**, the **Bigs**, or, sometimes, **The Show**. Understanding the game is one thing, but to really appreciate and be able to follow Major League baseball, you need to familiarize yourself with such topics as the format of the season and the playoffs, the rules for trading and demoting players and the meaning and the magnificence of the Baseball Hall of Fame.

- Finally, this explanation of baseball is complete, but it is only as comprehensive as it needs to be. Books are written on several of the topics I cover here in only a paragraph or two. Furthermore, there are a lot of things about baseball that, even after being a fan for some 40 years, I don't know and I don't need to know. Baseball is complex enough as it is, and I'm not going to bog you down with rules and exceptions to rules that frankly will never come up. If I've needed to know it, then you'll need to know it, and, if I'm successful, then know it you will.

ONE
Preliminaries

Equipment: The Ball, the Bat and the Uniforms

The details of what follows in this paragraph will be fleshed out throughout the course of this book, but by way of a very brief, but necessary, introductory overview, let me say that baseball centers on a defensive player from one team, called the **pitcher**, throwing a small hard ball, the **baseball**, to another defensive player, called the **catcher**, while a player from the offensive team standing near the catcher, called the **batter**, does his best to hit the oncoming ball with a long piece of wood, called a **bat**, and propel it into the field of play. The act of throwing the ball is called **pitching**, with each thrown ball being a **pitch**. The batter who is trying to hit the ball with the bat is said to be **at bat**, **up at bat**, or just **up**, as in "Bryce Harper is up for the Washington Nationals." The batter will be trying to hit the ball; the pitcher will be trying to pitch in such a way as to make hitting the ball as difficult as possible. This duel between batter and pitcher is at the heart of the game of baseball.

The *Official Baseball Rules* defines the characteristics of a baseball with great specificity: "The ball shall be a sphere formed by yarn wound around a small core of cork, rubber or similar material, covered with two strips of white horsehide or cowhide, tightly stitched together. It shall weigh not less than five nor more than 5¼ ounces avoirdupois and measure not less than nine nor more than 9¼ inches in circumference." Avoirdupois, as we all know, is a French term for a system of weights based on a pound of 16 ounces.

The most significant characteristic of a baseball is only alluded to in passing in the specifications above, which state that the ball must be covered with two strips of hide that are "tightly stitched together." The stitches themselves, by necessity, protrude ever so slightly from the otherwise smooth surface of the ball. This probably completely inadvertent protrusion plays an amazingly important role in how each and every baseball game is played. It is no exaggeration to say that if baseball were to ever replace its current ball with one that was completely smooth, the game would be radically changed.

Here's why. After a ball has been pitched, as it is flying at a very high speed towards the catcher, these raised stitches act like wings on a plane, catching the wind and causing the ball to swerve slightly on its way to the catcher. Whether the ball swerves to the right, to the left, or downward, or a combination thereof, and whether it swerves sharply or gradually, depends on which direction, and how fast, the stitches are spinning.

For example, suppose a pitched ball is flying towards the catcher at 85 mph. In terms of the face of a clock, imagine that the ball is spinning on an axis that runs from 3 o'clock to 9 o'clock and that the top of the ball is spinning down and forwards toward the catcher and the bottom of the ball is spinning up and backwards away from the catcher.

In this case, the stitches on the top of the ball that are spinning toward the catcher are spinning *against* the wind and will generate a greater amount of wind resistance than the stitches on the bottom of the ball, which are spinning away from the catcher and *with* the wind. This unequal distribution of resistance on the ball—the fact that there is higher resistance on the top of the ball—eventually will act to push the ball downward, resulting in a sudden disproportionate loss of altitude as it approaches the catcher.

Well, you might be thinking, all that is very interesting, but what's the point? What's the purpose of making the ball drop so suddenly as it approaches the catcher? Well, remember the batter that's trying like heck to blast that thrown ball with his bat? Imagine you're the batter. Here's the pitch. The ball is coming right in, belt high, looking as fat as can be. I got this one, you think to yourself, and you let forth with a mighty swing of the bat. Then, suddenly, halfway through your swing, that ball that was belt high a millisecond ago suddenly drops like a stone down toward your ankles. In the words of the immortal New York Yankees slugger Babe Ruth, you wind up swinging "where the ball ought to be—but ain't." Your swing goes wildly over the top, missing the ball by a mile and making you look darn pretty silly in the meantime. *That's* the point.

A pitch that drops as it approaches the catcher is called a **curveball**. The best curveballs are sometimes known as a **nose-to-toes curveball** or a **12-to-6 curveball** because their drop is so drastic.

Now here's the million-dollar question: how does the curveball get the spin or the rotation that results in the drop? Here's how: grip + release + velocity. If a pitcher wants to throw a curveball, he will *grip* the ball in a certain way (he will place his middle finger along a seam on the baseball with his index finger next to it providing support, and he will place his thumb under the ball directly opposite the middle finger) and *release* the ball in a certain way (he will snap his wrist and rotate his fingertips over the top of the seams just as he is about to release the ball). This combination of grip and release will cause the ball to spin in the above-described manner as it comes away from the pitcher's hand. To complete the equation, by throwing the ball with enough *velocity*, the desired amount of wind resistance will be generated, and it is that wind resistance, pushing against the uneven, spinning surface of the ball, that will cause it, in the case of the curveball, to drop suddenly as it nears the batter and the catcher.

Repositioning the hand for a different grip and executing a different type of release will result in a different spin and a different pitch. A pitched ball, for example, that moves more in a lateral direction, rather than swooping downward like the curve, is called a **slider**. A **backdoor slider** is a slider that appears to be arcing wide of the catcher, but then, at the last moment, it moves laterally back in towards him.

There are several types of pitches in a Major League pitcher's arsenal, but the formula for all of them is the same:

1. Manner of grip plus manner of release causes pitched ball to spin in a pre-determined direction and speed.

2. Velocity of pitched ball generates wind resistance.

3. Wind resistance flowing over the uneven surface of the spinning ball causes the ball to slightly change direction as it nears the catcher.

It's simple physics, really. Well, truth be told, maybe not *that* simple. Robert K. Adair, Ph.D., a professor of physics at Yale University, wrote an excellent book called *The Physics of Baseball*, which describes in scientific terms why a thrown baseball, with its spinning uneven surface, behaves the way it does, and William Blewett, engineer and science

The curveball grip. "Your hand should form a little 'C.' Pretend you're holding a glass of juice." That's the advice star pitcher Doc Gooden's father gave him when he taught the seven-year-old Doc how to throw the curveball (Spectruminfo\123rf).

writer, followed with the equally commendable *The Science of the Fastball*. We're talking "drag coefficients" and "Magnus forces" and "fluid dynamics" here. Challenging, yes, but to be honest, it is a source of great comfort to me that baseball has, at its core, basic and timeless principals of physics. The Jumbotron scoreboard behind the pitcher might be exploding with instantaneously updated statistics and scores of ball games 3,000 miles away, but if the apple stops falling from Newton's tree, that pitcher's curveball is not going to curve.

Backing up a bit, there are two overarching categories of pitches: **fastballs** and **breaking balls**.

Fastballs are pitches that are thrown as hard as a pitcher can throw them. They can reach speeds of a 100 mph, and take less than a second to reach the catcher. Fastballs are sometimes called **hummers** because of the sound they make slicing through the air. One of the best pitchers of all time, Walter Johnson, was nicknamed "Big Train" because his fastball sounded like a speeding locomotive. In 1907, when the 19-year-old Kansas farm boy made his Major League debut with the Washington Senators, the great Ty Cobb, on the opposing Detroit Tigers, initially dismissed him as "a tall, shambling galoot with arms so long they hung far out of his sleeves." But then Cobb stepped up to the plate, and his opinion of Johnson quickly changed. "The first time I faced him, I watched him with that easy windup— and then something went past me that made me flinch. I hardly saw the pitch, but I heard it. The thing just hissed with danger."

The most popular variation of the fastball is the **4-seam fastball**, which is intended as a pure power pitch. There's not much movement on a 4-seam fastball. There's just blinding speed, pure power, coming **right down the pipe** straight at the catcher. Other types of fastballs have maybe a touch less speed but a little more movement. The **2-seam fastball**, sometimes called the **tailing fastball**, moves laterally a bit toward the same side of the catcher as the side from which the pitcher throws: the pitch tails to the left side of the catcher for a left-handed pitcher; the right side of the catcher for a right-handed pitcher. The **cut fastball**, or **cutter**, moves the opposite way: to the right for a left-handed pitcher, and to the left for a right-handed pitcher.

The **changeup** can best be described as a fake fastball, meaning that the delivery is the same as a fastball—same arm movement, same release point by the pitcher—and it looks like a fastball as it comes straight down the pipe to the batter, but by gripping the ball differently (more palm, less fingertips), a pitcher is able to generate a bit less velocity. The batter, anticipating and reading fastball, swings at a pitch that hasn't even reached him yet.

Breaking balls have less speed than fastballs—thrown usually in the area of 85 mph—but more movement. The most popular breaking balls are the aforementioned curveball and slider.

No two pitchers are physically identical, and therefore neither are their pitches. The size of a pitcher's hands, the length of his arms or legs and his weight, will all play into his grip and release, thereby affecting the spin and movement of the pitch. Nolan Ryan, one of the great pitchers of all time, theorized that "most hard throwers are tall guys with big hands." Bigger hands meant more leverage, and more leverage meant greater velocity. And then there's Mariano Rivera, the esteemed pitcher for the New York Yankees, whose genius was at least partially attributed to his long fingers and unusually supple wrist.

So, again, what's the point of all this curving and dropping and cutting and backdooring? Just imagine being a batter. Imagine a pitched ball flying at you at 98 mph. Blink an eye and it's past you. Now imagine the next pitch flying at you a little slower, but suddenly just as it reaches you, just when you think you have a chance at it, it veers sharply to the left, or to the right. Imagine the third pitch flying at you, apparently at 98 mph again, then *not*, as suddenly it seems to slow down in mid-flight. Imagine the fourth pitch coming right at you then suddenly dropping down to your shoe tops. Imagine the fifth pitch... I think you get the idea.

With all that going on, it might seem near impossible to hit a pitch at all. But what you have to keep in mind is that the batters are every bit as clever and talented as the pitchers and are every bit as determined to hit the ball as the pitchers are to throw it, untouched, past them.

Hitters study pitchers. They look for little ticks, little giveaways, little tip-offs that might tell them what kind of pitch might be coming next. Pitchers, even the best of them, sometimes inadvertently telegraph their pitches with certain body movements or mannerisms prior to the pitch. Warren Spahn of the Milwaukee Braves (now the Atlanta Braves), when throwing a fastball, gripped the ball in such a way that the white of the ball showed through between his index and middle fingers as he brought his arm back to throw. A batter who saw that white space knew what was coming. In the case of Spahn's blazing fastball, knowing it was coming didn't automatically mean that the batter could hit it, but it certainly increased his odds a bit. Opponents noted that Jerry Augustine of the Milwaukee Brewers, in preparing to pitch, brought his hands to his chest when he threw a curveball, to his chin when he threw a fastball. As a rookie, Yankees pitcher Whitey Ford allowed his wrist to lay flat against his stomach when he was about to pitch a fastball, bent against his stomach when he was about to pitch a curveball. In the 2011 World Series, the Arizona Diamondbacks were able to shellac Yankee pitcher Andy Pettitte because they discovered that before he threw a breaking ball, he brought his hands to his belt in a high, looping manner. Before he threw a fastball, however, the route was more direct. Even Babe Ruth, in his pitching days, tipped off his pitches by sticking out his tongue whenever he was about to throw a curveball.

Another thing batters look for are patterns. There are several types of pitches, but most pitchers are only very good at two or three of them, and virtually all have their favorite pitch that they will go to when they are in a jam. Furthermore they often precede or set up their favorite pitch with their favorite secondary pitch. Slugger Barry Bonds, just before he stepped up to bat against a certain pitcher, once confided to a teammate exactly what the pitcher would do. "This guy's gonna start me with a little doo-doo fastball. Then he's gonna throw a little changeup down and away. I'm gonna sit on both those pitches and then he's gonna try and sneak a fastball by me. I'll take him out on that pitch to left field." The teammate watched in amazement as the pitcher did just that: fastball, changeup and fastball again. Bonds didn't swing at the first two but, as predicted, he smashed the third a country mile.

It is said that a good pitcher has command of three things: movement, velocity and location. If the pitcher has mastered the physics of the pitched ball, if he has mastered the grip + release + velocity formula, he will have the movement. If he has developed a good fastball, he will have the velocity. A mix of those two alone can be deadly. And we haven't even started discussing location yet! We'll get to that when we talk about the Mighty Casey, the most famous baseball player that never was, when we resume our discussion of the batter-pitcher duel later on.

But before moving on, a word about cheating.

As discussed, the raised stitches on the baseball help generate movement of the pitched ball. It makes sense, therefore, that if the surface of a ball were altered in any other way, that alteration would also affect movement. For example, suppose a pitcher were to surreptitiously scrape a baseball against his belt buckle, digging a groove on one side of the ball. Even that small amount of unevenness on the surface of the ball will affect the flow of wind resistance over the ball, just as do its raised stitches.

Also as discussed, the manner in which a pitcher releases the ball helps generate spin on the ball. It makes sense, therefore, that if the ball's surface were tampered with in such a way as to enhance that release, that tampering would also enhance the spin. For example, suppose a pitcher were to hide a dab of Vaseline on, say, the underside of the brim of his hat and, on occasion, when he needed a little extra "oomph" on a pitch, suppose he were to transfer that Vaseline to his pitching hand while ostensibly adjusting his hat. Any kind of tobacco juice or spit (hence the infamous **spitball**) would do the trick just the same, as any of these on the surface of the ball would help the pitcher squeeze off his release with more authority.

Tampering with the surface of a baseball in any way is against the rules and can result in a pitcher getting ejected from the game. Nevertheless, pitchers, over the years, have tested the ability of the system to actually catch them in the act. In 1987, when **umpires**—called **umps** for short, and called referees in most sports—suspected Joe Niekro of the Minnesota Twins of scuffing the ball, they halted the game and asked him to empty his pockets. As he did so, Niekro took an Emory board out of his back pocket and tossed it behind him, hoping the umpires wouldn't notice. They did. Niekro also had in his possession a small piece of sandpaper, "contoured to fit a finger" as one of the umpires described it. Niekro, who was ejected from the game and suspended for ten days, said later that he used the sandpaper and the Emory board not to scuff the ball, but to file his nails between innings. Right.

As far back as 1925, the aforementioned Ty Cobb complained about "trick ball pitching" and pitcher's doctoring balls by scraping them with rough-edged rings, by slitting them with razors, by raising a "corrugation on the surface" of the ball through repeated manual irritation of a small area of the ball between pitches, and by purposely having infielders and catchers return a hit or pitched ball to them on a bounce, thus allowing the ball to pick up moisture and dirt.

Actually, in fairness, the Joe Niekro case might not have been all that clear cut. Niekro, you see, was a **knuckleballer**, meaning that he was one of those very rare pitchers—there usually are only two or three at a time in all of baseball—who practice the mysterious and nearly mystical art of the knuckleball pitch, or, for short, the **knuckleball**.

Normally, pitchers try to master at least three different types of pitches so that over the course of a game they can vary their attack and keep the batters off balance as to what might be coming next. Knuckleballers, however, throw almost nothing but knuckleballs, hence the term "knuckleballer." There are no "fastballers" or "curveballers" because to throw only those pitches, pitch after pitch, would be foolish. Batters, anticipating the movement and the speed of the pitch, would make adjustments and be ready for it.

Knuckleballs, in contrast, are anticipation-proof, because no one, not even the pitcher and catcher, can be sure what they are going to do once they leave the pitcher's hand. They can rise, fall, move to the left, move to the right, or all of the above. Observed one umpire, "Not only can't pitchers control it, hitters can't hit it, catcher's can't catch it, coaches can't coach it, and most pitchers can't learn it." Joe Niekro's brother Phil Niekro, also a knuckleballer and in fact one of the best of all time, said that when throwing the knuckleball, all he could do was aim for the catcher's mask and cheer for it on its way in.

Here's the secret: When a pitch, let's say a curveball, flies through the air towards the catcher, the spin that was created by the pitcher's grip and release forces the air in front of the ball to spin off toward the sides and back of the ball, carried along by the spinning stitches. This interaction between the spinning stitches and the wind resistance, as discussed, determines the ball's movement once it leaves the pitcher's hand. The knuckleball, in contrast, *doesn't spin*. The knuckleball is gripped and released in such a way as to perform less than half of one rotation on its way to the catcher. The result? Aerodynamic chaos. As it meanders to the catcher at speeds that can be as slow as 60 mph—only two-thirds as fast as your average fastball—air glances off the uneven (because of the stitches) top, bottom and sides of the knuckleball, creating a pocket of air in the ball's wake that has the same effect on the ball as turbulence has on a plane. The end result is a remarkably slow pitch that twists and turns and never does the same thing twice. New York Mets pitcher R.A. Dickey throws a knuckleball that was described by one writer as "an unimposing pitch that flutters towards the batter like a drunken moth." In 2012, batters had an extremely hard time hitting that drunken moth, and Dickey was one of the most effective pitchers in baseball. "You can throw two knuckleballs with the identical release, the identical motion, in the identical place," Dickey wrote, "and one might go one way and the second might go another way. It's one of the first things you have to accept as a knuckleballer: the pitch has a mind of its own."

And that brings us back to Joe Niekro. The unique grip that creates the knuckleball involves one finger on each side holding the ball in place while two or three fingernails dig into the ball from above and prevent it from spinning on release. Fingernails, therefore, are key. Fingernail maintenance, therefore, is also key. Tim Wakefield of the Boston Red Sox, the premier knuckleballer of the last 15 years, had a pregame ritual that utilized both nail clippers and an Emory board to shape his fingernails "with the precision of a sculptor." Once, while warming up for a game, R.A. Dickey broke a fingernail and had to be driven, in uniform, to a nearby neighborhood nail salon for repairs that cost him all of $7.

The knuckleball grip. "Everything I do starts with nails that grip the ball," Mets knuckleballer R.A. Dickey wrote. "If the nails aren't right I can't grip the ball right, and bad things ensue" (Spectruminfo\123rf).

Knuckleballer Joe Niekro may therefore have had a perfectly reasonable explanation as to why he had an Emory board in his pocket the day the umpires approached him on the mound. Unless his fingernails were made of plywood, however, the sandpaper seems a little harder to explain.

Getting back to spitballs for a moment, pitchers are allowed to blow on their pitching hand during cold weather, and under certain conditions they are allowed to moisten their pitching hand by touching it to their mouths or lips during the game, but they must then clearly dry their pitching hand off before touching the ball again. One way they can dry their hand is with something called a **rosin bag** which is placed on the pitcher's mound by the umpires as part of their pre-game housekeeping duties. A rosin bag is a small, soft, hand-sized cloth pouch full of rosin, which is a powdery drying agent.

Like the baseball, the specifications of baseball bats are dictated by the *Official Baseball Rules*: "The bat shall be a smooth, round stick not more than 2.61 inches in diameter at the thickest part and not more than 42 inches in length. The bat shall be one piece of solid wood."

Unlike baseballs, which are provided by Major League Baseball, players have bats made to order from private companies according to their preferences as far as bat length, bat weight, and type of wood. The bats are stamped with the player's name, usually their signature, which makes them identifiable. The rules require wooden bats, but do not require any particular kind of wood. Ash and maple are most popular, though maple bats have been under scrutiny for their tendency to break on impact with the ball. The rule is also silent as to how much a bat can weigh, but generally bats used in the Majors weigh between 32 and 36 ounces.

Some players prefer a heavier bat because they feel that it gives them a better chance of hitting a ball farther. "The heavier the bat, the longer the drive, that's what I think," wrote the ever eloquent Babe Ruth. Others prefer a lighter bat, which they feel can be swung faster (called greater **bat speed**) thus giving them a better chance of making contact with the ball. Too much bat speed, however, may not always be a good thing. Yankees outfielder Alfonso Soriano, for example, in response to a spell where he felt he was overeager at the plate and swinging too soon at pitched balls, switched to a heavier bat to slow down his swing and correct his timing.

Roughly the top one-third of a bat is tubular and uniform in thickness, and as such it is also the thickest and heaviest part of the bat. Batters will try to hit the ball with the middle area of this thickest part of the bat, the so-called **sweet spot** of the bat, to generate the most power. The bat tapers down to a thinner bottom, and at the very base of the bat, although not required by the rules, bats have knobs that help a batter place and measure his grip on the bat without having to look at it. The knobs also prevent the bat from slipping out of the batter's hands when he swings. Some batters prefer their bottom hand to be touching the knob when they swing. Others feel they have more control over the bat when they place their bottom hand an inch or two above the knob, which is called **choking up.**

Players can be very particular about their bats. Ted Williams of the Red Sox, who is considered one of the best hitters who ever played the game, cleaned his bats with alcohol every night and periodically took them to the post office to weigh them. "Bats pick up condensation and dirt lying around on the ground," he wrote. "They can gain an ounce or more in a surprisingly short time." Ichiro Suzuki, who spent over 11 years with the Seattle Mariners before being traded to the Yankees in 2012, and who is one of the greatest hitters of the modern era, also takes great care that his bats do not accumulate moisture and thus gain weight: he stores his bats in humidors, one in the club house and another, a portable one, for the road. Legendary second baseman Rod Carew fought moisture by storing his bats in a box full of sawdust in the warmest part of his house. "The sawdust acts as a buffer between the bats and the environment," he explained, "absorbing any moisture before it can seep into the wood."

Many players **bone** their bats, meaning that before games, they rub their bats repeatedly with a hard object, believing this closes the pores on the wood and hardens the bat. Animal bones are a popular boning material, but rolling pins, soda bottles and the edge of a porcelain sink have also been used. Pete Rose, one of the most prolific hitters in the history of the game, had his own way of hardening his bats: he soaked them in a tub of motor oil in his basement then hung them up to dry. Did that really harden the wood? I don't see how, but who am I to argue with Pete Rose?

And here too, a word about cheating. The *Official Baseball Rules* forbid tampering with bats, requiring that they be "one piece of solid wood," and that they not be altered in such a way as to "improve the distance factor or cause an unusual reaction on the baseball." Some players have ingeniously found that by drilling a hole in the top of the bat, inserting various foreign materials or objects into the hole and then capping off the hole again, the ball travels farther when hit. Cork is a favorite among cheaters, hence the term **corked bat.** Other players preferred more colorful material. In one game in 1974, Yankees batter Graig Nettles' bat burst open when he hit the ball, sending six tiny superballs flying all over the field. Nettles pled ignorance, saying "some Yankee fan in Chicago" had given him the bat. Right.

As a final word on bats, players are permitted by the rules to put a sticky substance on the handle of the bat to improve their grip, but the sticky substance cannot extend more than 18 inches up from the base of the bat. One of the sticky substances commonly used by batters is a wood preservative called **pine tar**.

The 18-inch rule seems innocent enough, but Billy Martin, then manager of the Yankees, put it to infamous use in 1983 in what came to be known as the **Pine Tar Incident**. In a game at Yankee Stadium against the Kansas City Royals, Royals great George Brett hit a home run that appeared to put the Royals ahead late in the game. We'll discuss home runs at length later on, but for now suffice it to say that it's a very good thing when your team hits one and a very bad thing when the other team hits one. Billy Martin protested that the pine tar on the bat Brett used to hit his home run measured over 18 inches, and therefore the bat was illegal and therefore the home run that Brett just hit with it should be disallowed. The umpires measured the bat, found that Martin was correct, and disallowed the home run. A furious Brett raced from the Royals dugout to protest and a melee nearly ensued.

The lords of baseball eventually overturned the umpires, saying that the violation of the rule—which was originally put in place just to save on the amount of baseballs that had to be removed from the game after coming in contact with the sticky stuff—did not warrant the nullification of the home run. Nearly a month after Brett hit it, his home run was reinstated, the game was replayed from that point on, and the Royals won the game after all.

The 18-inch rule is still a part of the *Official Baseball Rules*, but an addendum has been added that if the rule is violated, the umpires will simply remove the bat from the game until the excess pine tar is removed. Violation of the rule "shall not be grounds for declaring the batter out, or ejected from the game."

Moving on, a discussion about baseball uniforms is a fairly short one. The uniforms, though attractive, are uneventful. Players have shirts, they have pants, they have shoes, and they have a hat with a long brim in front that has come to be universally called, believe it or not, a **baseball hat** or **baseball cap**. It's useful to know that when a team is playing at home, its uniform is traditionally white, and when it's playing away, it's anything but white. Furthermore, the away uniform usually has the name of the team's *city* emblazoned across the front, while the home team usually has the team's *nickname* or some kind of team symbol on the front. You can tell which team is the home team within seconds of turning on the television, just by looking at their uniforms.

Actually, there is one facet of a ballplayer's uniform that is somewhat interesting, and that is, oddly enough, their socks, or, more accurately, the stirrups that loop under the socks and stretch up the player's legs. You may notice while watching a game that some players wear stirrups up over the outside of their pants, nearly up to their knees. Others don't wear stirrups at all, opting instead just to wear their pants pulled down to the top of their shoe. There is no significance to the fact that some players wear them and some don't. The pulled-up stirrups evoke a more historical, traditional look and add color to the uniform, and I guess this appeals to some players, but not to others.

The *Official Baseball Rules* are silent on stirrups, but the fact that some players on a team wear them while others do not seems to be in violation of the rule which states that

David Wright of the Mets, in the foreground, prefers the high stirrups look, while his teammate behind him apparently does not. Question: Are the Mets playing at home or away? (shutterstock.com/David W. Leindecker).

"all players on a team shall wear uniforms identical in color, trim and style" as well as the rule that states "no player whose uniform does not conform to that of his teammates shall be permitted to participate in a game." The freedom to wear high stirrups or not is remarkable considering how uniformity is otherwise so tightly regulated in the MLB. For example, during a 2007 game against the Yankees, with the Yankees threatening to score, Red Sox head coach (called the **manager** in baseball) Terry Francona was suddenly called away from the game and questioned by a league executive as to whether he was wearing the required uniform jersey beneath his blue pullover. Terry wasn't pleased.

Every player, when he is at bat, must wear a protective helmet called a **batting helmet** and when players are playing defense in the baseball field, they wear rather large, odd-looking leather gloves that enable them to catch a hit baseball without breaking their hands. These gloves have come to be universally called, believe it or not, **baseball gloves**, usually referred to as just **gloves**.

Only the catcher in baseball wears unique and fairly interesting equipment. Seeing that someone is throwing a rock hard projectile at him all day long at incredible speeds, it is not surprising that a catcher, like a goalie in hockey, is pretty much covered head to toe with protective padding. He also uses a special type of baseball glove, called a **catcher's mitt**.

Soccer fans might be interested to know that the baseball rules state that no part of a baseball uniform shall include commercial advertisements. Soccer has no stoppages in play at all except for a moment or two to get everyone in position for a corner kick or a throw-in or to tend to a player faking an injury (sorry, I couldn't resist), but even then the game clock continues to run. This lack of stoppages in play makes it impossible to have TV commercial breaks during a soccer game. Sponsors, therefore, simply buy advertising space on teams' jerseys instead. Not so in baseball. In some baseball stadiums it seems that everything that doesn't move has an advertisement fastened to it but so far anyway, players' uniforms do not.

The Field

Many team sports, including soccer, basketball, ice hockey, rugby and lacrosse, have a free-flowing format where one minute a team is moving forward on offense, trying to score, and the next minute that same team is moving backwards on defense, trying to prevent the other team from scoring. There is no break in the play to formalize a team's transition from offense to defense. It just happens: the movement of the teams is constant, and the transition from offense to defense is seamless.

Baseball, like cricket and American football, has a more structured format: the offensive and defensive functions of teams are separate, and there is a break in the play when the teams switch from one to the other. Unlike American football, however, baseball does not have different players for defense and offense. In a baseball game there are nine players playing at a time for each team, and with the one exception caused by the Designated Hitter rule, which we will discuss later, all nine play both offense and defense.

The aforementioned batter trying to hit the ball represents the offensive function of a team. During the course of a game all nine players on a team will take their turns batting. When they are not on offense—when they are not batting or waiting their turn to bat—all nine players will all go out onto the field and assume defensive positions. Again, the Designated Hitter will provide the lone exception to these rules.

We will discuss the nine defensive positions a little later on. First, we need to talk about the field itself.

Baseball fields are beautiful. That's all there is to it. I have been to hundreds of baseball

This view of beautiful Busch Stadium, home of the St. Louis Cardinals, shows the diamond shape of baseball fields. It also shows the iconic Gateway Arch in the background. According to the team's website, during an average 81-game season at Busch, fans enjoy 540,000 hot dogs, 181,000 pounds of nacho chips and 32,000 gallons of nacho cheese. They also go through 15,373,600 feet of toilet paper (Gino Santa Maria\123rf).

games and I can honestly say that to this day the beauty of the baseball field still turns my head. Three things strike you. First, the colors: the acres of perfectly manicured, painfully green grass are set off against sections of an impeccably groomed tan mixture of clay, sand and silt that is commonly, though incorrectly, referred to as dirt. Second, the purity: the field is almost completely devoid of the lines and numbers and circles that crisscross most sports fields. And third, the shape: unlike the boring rectangles of nearly every other sport I can think of, the baseball field is shaped like, of all things, a diamond.

THE PITCHER'S MOUND AND HOME PLATE

Even if you don't know a thing about a particular sport, you can learn a lot about it just by studying its field of play. Take a soccer field, or an ice hockey rink. On either end, you have goals with nets. OK, easy enough: it's the goal of one team to put the ball or whatever in this net here, and the goal of the other team to put it into that net there. The presence of a series of lines and circles on the field or rink most likely indicates limitations on player movements. The same can be said of a basketball court.

Baseball fields, on the other hand, reveal very little about what goes on in the game. There are no goals. Instead, at the base of the diamond-shaped field, you have five small

This view of Target Field, home of the Minnesota Twins, shows the pitcher on the pitcher's mound in front of the partially-obscured pitcher's plate, having just pitched the ball to the batter, who stands at the ready in the batter's box. The catcher is crouched behind home plate, and partially visible behind him is the home plate umpire. The pitcher is throwing with his right hand; the batter is batting from the left side of the plate. As will be discussed, the side the pitcher pitches from versus the side the hitter hits from plays an amazingly important role in baseball strategy (Mark Herreid\123rf).

white markers, surrounded by the tan-colored dirt which is then surrounded by grass. And then at the top of the diamond, you have more grass: lots and lots of grass. If I had to guess, I'd guess that most of the action takes place at the base of the diamond, just because it looks busier than the top of the diamond, but other than that....

I would be right that the base of the diamond is the busiest part of the field and where most of the action takes place. I'm going to start my discussion of the field, therefore, with the busiest part of the busiest part: two areas at the base of the diamond called the pitcher's mound and home plate.

Located at the outlet of the baseball diamond is, to use the magnificent language of the *Official Baseball Rules*, "a five-sided slab of whitened rubber" that looks like a triangle attached to a square. It is 17″ in width at its widest point and 17″ long at its longest point. This slab of white rubber is called **home plate**, or just **home.**

Directly in front of home plate is a circular, slightly elevated mound of dirt called the **pitcher's mound,** sometimes called **the hill.** At the center of the pitcher's mound is another slab of white rubber, this one smaller and rectangular, measuring 24″ by 6″. This is called the **pitcher's plate** or the **pitcher's rubber.** The pitcher's plate is exactly 60 feet, six inches away from the back of home plate.

The area from the pitcher's mound to home plate comprises a very small part of the baseball field, but for three very good reasons, I would guess that 90 percent of the time you are watching a baseball game, you will be watching what goes on in this area.

- First, you already know about the duel between pitcher and batter that is at the heart of the game of baseball. That duel takes place here. The pitcher will be standing on and pitching from the pitcher's mound, the catcher will be crouched down behind home plate while he catches the pitches, and the batter will be standing just to the side of home plate while he bats, Specifically, there is a rectangular box outlined in chalk on the field directly on both sides of home plate. These boxes, which are 6' × 4', are each called a **batter's box**. A batter must stand within one of these two boxes when attempting to hit a pitch with the bat. A hitter can't hit unless and until both his feet are in a batter's box. Behind home plate is another rectangular box, called the **catcher's box**, where the catcher is stationed.

  A batter who holds the bat near his right shoulder, with his right hand above his left hand, is called a **right-handed batter**, a **righty batter** or a **righty,** and he will stand in the box to the right of the plate, looking in from the pitcher's mound. A batter who holds the bat near his left shoulder, with his left hand above his right hand, is called a **left-handed batter**, a **lefty batter** or a **lefty,** and he will stand in the box to the left of the plate, looking in from the pitcher's mound. Generally, just as people are born writing with their left or right hand, batters are either lefty or righty batters by nature. Some batters, however, are ambidextrous in the sense that they can bat comfortably either lefty or righty. They are called **switch hitters** and they can choose which batter's box they stand in depending on whether they choose to bat lefty or righty against a particular pitcher.

- Second, points are scored by the offensive team in this area. And we might as well get this out of the way now: a scored point is called a **run** in baseball. As the *Official Baseball Rules* succinctly puts it: "One run shall be scored each time an offensive player legally advances to and touches first, second, third and home base." We'll talk about first, second and third base in a moment, and a large part of this book is devoted to just how an offensive player goes about the business of "legally advancing" around those bases, but for now just know that another reason this area of the field is so central to the game is that after certain prerequisites are met, runs are scored when an offensive player steps on or otherwise touches home plate.

- Third, since most of the action takes place in this area, it should not be surprising that the **umpire-in-chief** is stationed there. There are four umpires assigned to regular season Major League baseball games, and the umpire-in-chief, the umpire who, among other things, has the power to call rain delays and approve substitutions, is stationed at home plate behind the catcher, and is therefore also called the **home plate umpire**.

While one batter is standing at the plate, the next offensive player who is scheduled to be a batter stands or kneels in a chalk circle behind and off to the side of home plate, where he can warm up and await his turn at bat. This warm up area is called the **on deck circle.** There is one for each team, on either side of home plate. Batters who are scheduled to bat next and are therefore warming up in the on deck circle, are said to be **on deck**. The batter due up immediately *after* the batter on deck is said to be **in the hole**, which means he's waiting to come out to take his place on the on deck circle once the batter's turn is over and the on deck batter moves to the plate to take his turn. Thus you might hear an announcer say: "The Los Angeles Angels are coming to bat: Mike Trout is up first, Eric Aybar is on deck and Albert Pujols is in the hole. Tampa Bay Rays pitcher David Price certainly has his work cut out for him!"

THE INFIELD

Baseball is so ingrained in American culture that many baseball terms are used in everyday American life to describe loosely corresponding non-baseball situations and events. A business deal might have a second lender "on deck" in case the first lender backs out. Something which occurred very quickly is said to have happened "right off the bat" as in "Right off the bat, the boss rejected my request for a raise." When a difficult situation calls for someone—an elected official, for example—to show some fortitude and confront that difficulty, it might be said that that official was forced to "step up to the plate." For reasons to be explained later, "Who's on first?" is an expression commonly used when people working together are confused about what their functions are. For example, when asked who is in charge, a response might be "Nobody knows. It's chaos. It's a case of 'Who's on first?'" And just the other day, in court, after an attorney delivered an admiringly comprehensive summary of a complex legal issue, the judge complimented her for having "covered all the bases."

The infield, as centerpiece of the game, has inspired my absolute favorite baseball metaphor, but before we get to it, let's be clear as to what exactly the infield is. About sixty-four feet to the left of the pitcher as he looks in to home plate is a 15″ square white canvas bag, attached to the ground. This is the aforementioned **first base**. At the same distance directly behind the pitcher is another, called **second base**, and to his right is the last, called **third base**. First base, second base and third base are often referred to as just **first**, **second** and **third**. Together, first, second, third and home form a diamond around the pitcher's mound, and each side of the diamond measures ninety feet. In other words, it is ninety feet from home to first, from first to second, from second to third, and from third to home.

Collectively, the area that encompasses home, the pitcher's mound and the three bases—the area we referred to before as the busiest part of the baseball diamond—is the **infield**.

And now for my favorite metaphor. When I was a young man and still playing the field (another baseball expression), the progression around the bases in baseball—the process of legally advancing from one base to the next—was often used as a vague metaphor for sexual, let's say, achievement. If your friend came to you and said that he got to "second base" with a girl the night before, it was kind of unclear what he meant, but you knew that he had gotten further than first base, so it couldn't have been bad.

In the late 1970s, the musician Meat Loaf became very popular thanks in large part to a song called "Paradise by the Dashboard Light," an excellent song about a young man's earnest attempts to achieve intimacy with a young lady in that most exclusive of locations: the back seat of a car. As sounds of passion begin to rise, the voice of none other than Phil ("Scooter") Rizzuto—the former Yankees player who went on to become one of the best baseball radio announcers in the game—suddenly breaks into the song and describes in hilarious detail a ballplayer's progress around the bases from first base, to second base, to third base and on towards home plate. Just as the ballplayer is about to cross home plate and score

This view of an infield shows, from right to left, home plate, first base, second base and third base. At home plate are the batter, catcher and home plate umpire, and at the center of the infield is the pitcher's mound and the pitcher. The two white chalk lines emanating outward from home plate are the first base foul line and the third base foul line. All infields in major league baseball conform to league-mandated measurements and specifications. Outfields, however, vary from stadium to stadium (shutterstock.com/Eric Broder Van Dyke).

a run, however, the young lady's voice interrupts and demands that her suitor "stop right there" and promise that, before they go any further, he will love her forever and marry her. After some initial hesitation, he succumbs to the exigencies of the moment and agrees.

Where was I? Oh yes, the baseball field.

There is a long chalk line running directly from home plate, past first base and on out beyond the infield to the far edge of the baseball field. This is the **first base foul line**. On the other side of home plate, you'll see there is a corresponding line running from home to third and on out beyond third. This is the **third base foul line**. The space outside the foul lines (to the right of the first base foul line and to the left of the third base foul line) is called **foul territory,** which is the equivalent of the out-of-bounds areas in other sports. The space within or between the foul lines, which includes the infield and the outfield, which we'll discuss in a moment, is called **fair territory**. A ball hit into fair territory is **fair** or a **fair ball**; a ball hit into foul territory is **foul** or a **foul ball**. The foul lines themselves are considered part of fair territory.

The first and third base foul lines terminate at the walls which border the far edge of the baseball field, but actually, behind those walls, the function of the foul lines is continued in the form of two tall yellow poles. These are called the **foul poles**, or, more specifically, the **left field foul pole**, beyond third base, and the **right field foul pole**, beyond first base.

This photograph of the "friendly confines" of Wrigley Field, home of the Chicago Cubs, shows the right field foul line running from home past first base into right field, where it merges into the yellow right field foul pole. Also visible are the first base coach (at far right, partially obscured by the batter) in his coach's box, the first base umpire and the two-line, first base running lane. Note in the background the seating that has been built on the roofs of nearby houses (photograph by John W. Iwanski).

In case a ball is hit in the air by a batter and it travels in the air over the wall in the vicinity of one of the foul poles, the umpires can use the foul poles to help them judge whether the ball left the park in fair or foul territory: outside the foul poles is foul; inside the foul poles is fair. Just as the foul line is considered part of fair territory, so too the foul pole is considered part of fair territory. If a ball hits a foul pole, it is a fair ball, so from time to time you'll hear announcers wondering out loud why they are not actually called fair poles, instead of foul poles.

Just one word about umpires here. We know about the home plate umpire, stationed behind home plate. There are three more umpires, collectively called the **field umpires**, and they are stationed at and assigned to judge plays in the area of the three bases. The **second base umpire**, for example, will oversee plays made at second base. The **first base umpire** and the **third base umpire**, however, not only monitor their respective bases, but also have the added task of judging whether a fly ball landed on the fair or foul side of, respectively, the right field foul pole and left field foul pole. In postseason playoff games two additional umpires are added whose main function is to judge whether fly balls are fair or foul, and they are stationed out along the foul lines on either side of the outfield so as to get a closer look at the ball as it travels over the fence.

As we will discuss shortly, the walls at the farthest end of the baseball field are often called **fences**, even if they are, in fact, walls. Coming down to the sides of the baseball field, the walls that separate the spectators from the playing field are called **sidewalls** and, in the area behind the catcher, the **backstop**.

By the way, when a baseball is hit into the stands, the lucky spectator who catches it can keep it. When the ball has some historical, statistical or sentimental importance, it can have tremendous resale value on the sports memorabilia market, and catching it can be like hitting the lottery. In 1998, Mark McGwire of the St. Louis Cardinals hit an unprecedented 70 home runs in one season. Again, we will discuss home runs at great length later, but for now suffice it to say that home runs, by definition, involve a baseball being hit out of the ballpark in fair territory, usually into seats populated by fans. When a batter hits a home run, he and every offensive player already on base, if any, automatically comes home and scores a run, so a home run is usually an important and dramatic event. Believe it or not, the fan who caught McGwire's 70th home run ball in 1998 sold it at auction for $3 million.

AT&T Park, home of the San Francisco Giants, is located just off the San Francisco Bay. When Barry Bonds was closing in on Hank Aaron's career home run record in 2007, it was standard fare to see enterprising fans in canoes and kayaks jostling for position in the bay just past the right field stands so as to be in position to catch a potentially lucrative Bonds home run ball should it happen to clear the stadium wall, which many of them did. The fortunate fan who caught Bonds' 756th career home run ball was sitting in the stands, not floating in the Bay, and one news source reported that he came away with the

Just outside the right field stands of AT&T Park, enterprising Giants fans wait for a potentially valuable Barry Bonds home run ball in this 2006 photograph (photograph courtesy City Kayak).

ball only after prevailing over other fans in a "violent scrum." He sold it at auction for $752,467.

A more recent example of a valuable caught baseball occurred on July 8, 2011, when Derek Jeter of the Yankees hit a home run for his 3,000th career hit, a milestone shared by only 27 other players in the history of the game. The lucky fan in left field who caught Jeter's home run ball shocked the baseball world by returning it directly to Jeter and asking for nothing in return. "Mr. Jeter deserved it," said the good-humored fan, named Christian Lopez, "I'm not going to take it away from him." The Yankees rewarded Lopez with a meet-and-greet with Jeter, an assortment of bats and jerseys, and box seats for the rest of the season. Nevertheless, in the weeks that followed, the ramifications of Lopez's financial sacrifice began to receive nearly as much publicity as Jeter's accomplishment, especially when it was revealed that Lopez was not only heavily in debt with student loans, but might even have to pay taxes on the gifts the Yankees gave him. The issue was settled when Yankee sponsors volunteered to pay off not only any tax bill he might incur, but his student loans as well.

Since we are on the subject of baseballs hit into the stands, it should be noted that in many ballparks it is customary for an opponent's home run ball to be **rejected**, or thrown back out onto the field, by the fan who catches it. Every ballpark I know of has a policy that a fan throwing anything onto a field will be ejected from the stadium, but the rejection of an opponent's home run ball is widely immune from punishment.

Now let's talk about the bases. In the words of the *Official Baseball Rules*, "the offensive team's objective is to have its batter become a runner, and its runner advance" around the bases. When an offensive player is standing at home plate with the bat in his hand trying to hit a pitch with his bat, he is, as we have said, called the batter. However, as soon as that batter begins the business of legally advancing around the bases, he is called a **runner**. Same guy, different title.

A batter gets on base and thereby becomes a runner by either hitting a pitched ball with his bat into fair territory without making an out, which will be discussed later, or by being awarded free passage to a base by other means, which will also be discussed later. For now, the important thing to remember is that once a runner advances around each of the three bases then steps on or otherwise touches home plate, he scores a run for his team.

Runners cannot run loop-de-loops around the infield while legally advancing from one base to the next. They are guided by the **base lines**, which are straight lines that run from one base to the next. The portion of the foul line that runs from home to first, and, on the other side, the portion of the foul line that runs from third to home, also serve as base lines. From first base to second base, and from second base to third base, there is no chalk line in the dirt to indicate the base line, but it is understood that there is an imaginary straight line running from first to second, and another from second to third.

Base lines do not represent strict paths which runners must adhere to while legally advancing around the bases. A runner who intends to advance more than one base is not expected to run to the initial base, step on it, turn on a perfect right angle, then head to the next. Instead, such a runner will **round** the initial base, meaning that, while running as fast as he can, he will step on the initial base some half-way through a wide turn that, both before and after, can take him several feet off the base lines. Thus, you might hear an announcer say, "Adam Jones of the Baltimore Orioles steps to the plate. Here's the pitch. Jones slams a shot down the right field line! The ball is rolling into the corner! Jones is rounding first, he's heading to second!"

Within that generous context, there are two rules that specifically define the route a runner can take from one base to the next.

The first rule of base running states that a runner, while advancing, cannot take evasive action in relation to a defensive player trying to make a defensive play against him. In other words, while rounding first and heading to second, for example, it's fine for a runner to make a big wide turn off the base lines, but once a defensive player tries to make a defensive play on that runner, that runner's movements are restricted as far as trying to avoid that player. A runner can try to dive headfirst or slide feet first *under* the defensive player, but he cannot veer more than three feet to his left or right should he try to go around the defensive player.

The second rule holds that a batter running from home to first base must stay within the double lined, three feet wide **running lane** between home and first, but only if by running outside of the running lane, he would interfere with the defensive player who is responsible for defensive plays in the area around first base. The purpose of this rule is to limit collisions and injuries around first.

While the runner is legally advancing around the bases, he is advised and guided by two coaches from his team who are stationed along the first and third base foul lines, just outside of fair territory. Like the manager in soccer, they are limited in their movement by a chalk box on the ground. They generally have to stay in that box, called a **coach's box**, while giving advice and guidance to the runners. These coaches are called, respectively, the **first base coach** and the **third base coach**. Other coaches include the **pitching coach**, the **hitting coach**, and the **bench coach**, the latter being a kind of second-in-command who discusses strategy with the manager during the course of the game. Only the first and third base coaches, however, are stationed on the field of play.

Finally, in foul territory more or less behind the third base coach and the first base coach are the two **dugouts**, one for each team. A dugout is a covered, enclosed area where the manager of a team is stationed, along with any immediate assistant coaches, as well as players (except certain pitchers) who either are not playing that day or who are not playing at that moment. A fixture in each dugout is the **bat boy** or **bat girl**, a lucky lad or lass whose summer job consists of running out on the field during stoppages in play to retrieve dropped bats and to bring extra balls to the umpire and to perform various other housekeeping chores over the course of the game.

As will be discussed, the manager, with the help of his assistants, will dictate offensive strategy from the dugout by sending hand signals to the first and third base coaches. To avoid detection, the first and third base coaches will then translate those hand signals into their own set of hand signals and then send them on to the batter and runners. For that reason, pitcher Christy Mathewson wrote that the dugout "is the place from which the orders come, and it is here that the battle is planned and from here the moves are executed. The manager sits here and pulls the wires, and his players obey him as if they were manikins." Mathewson wrote that in 1912, and though sensitivities may have changed a bit in the past hundred years, what goes on in the dugout has not. Dugouts are so named because they are usually a few steps lower than the surface of the playing field. Players and coaches in the dugout are protected against foul balls by a protective screen.

Sometimes battles are not only planned in the dugout; sometimes they actually take place there as well. In 2007, I was at a game in Chicago's Wrigley Field where fiery Cubs pitcher Carlos Zambrano, upset at the sloppy play of his teammates, got into an argument in the dugout with his catcher, Michael Barrett, which escalated into an all-out brawl that ended with the much smaller Barrett being sent to the emergency room. A few seasons later Zambrano got into another dugout argument, this time with teammate Derek Lee. Zambrano did a lot of yelling and screaming, but this time stopped well short of initiating fisticuffs. You can call Zambrano passionate or you can call him disruptive, depending on how you look at it, but apparently you can't call him stupid. Derek Lee is 6'5" and weighs 240 pounds.

Baseball, by the way, is the only sport I know of where managers wear the team uniform, just like the players. In the old days, managers played as well as managed, and though baseball hasn't seen a player-manager in many years, the tradition of the managers wearing uniforms has stuck around. Baseball, you will find, is big on tradition.

THE OUTFIELD

The large grassy area beyond the infield is called the **outfield**. There are no markings dividing the outfield—it is just one vast expanse of green grass—but it is considered divided into **left field** (the area beyond third base), **center field** (the area beyond second base) and **right field** (the area beyond first base). These are sometimes referred to just as **left**, **center** and **right**. The areas between are sometimes referred to as **left-center** and **right-center**.

As we have seen, the rules of baseball have a very tight rein on the infield. Everything, from the size of the batters boxes to the distance between bases to the color of the pitcher's rubber is tightly controlled and narrowly defined. These measurements and specifications are identical in every ballpark throughout the MLB.

Outfields, however, are just the opposite. First, the rules of baseball merely suggest sizes of the outfield. On the aforementioned fences that mark the outermost limits of the outfield is printed the distance, in feet, of that particular fence from home plate. The rules only say that it is "preferable" that the fences by the left and right field foul poles be at least 320 feet from home plate, and the fence in center field be at least 400 feet from home plate.

This flexibility has resulted a wide variety of outfield sizes. Boston's Fenway Park, the oldest ballpark in the Majors, was built in 1912. Its outfield measures only 310 feet to left and 302 feet to right, but 420 feet to center. In contrast, baseball's newest stadium, Target Field, home of the Twins, is significantly longer to left (339 feet) and to right (328 feet) but has a shorter center field fence at 404 feet. The center field fence at Minute Maid Park, home of the Houston Astros, is the longest in the Majors at 435 feet; the center field fence at Petco Park, home of the San Diego Padres, is the shortest at 396 feet. Minute Maid Park's center field fence, therefore, is a full 9 percent farther from home plate than Petco Park's.

The rules are also silent as to the color, size, shape and makeup of the outfield fences, and as a result, there is a great diversity in their appearance as well as their distance from home plate. For example, the walls in Wrigley Field, home of the Chicago Cubs, are made of brick and are famously covered in Ivy. The left field fence in Fenway Park, at 37 feet, is much, much taller than any other outfield fence in baseball, and because of its size and green color, it is called the "Green Monster." I said that Fenway's center-field fence was

420 feet from home plate, but actually, only part of it is. The center-field stands and the left field stands meet at an uneven angle, creating an indentation (called "the triangle") that angles sharply back into the stands. In both Citifield, the home of the Mets, and the aforementioned AT&T Park, part of the right-field fence juts unevenly into the outfield as if the builders were trying to create a ricochet effect for balls hit against it.

In addition to the flexibility in the makeup of the outfields and the outfield fences, there is also no regulation size for foul territory. Exact measurements are not easily available for foul territories, but in some stadium, the distance between the foul lines and the sidewalls, or the foul lines and the backstop, is clearly much bigger than it is in others.

Don't forget: we're not talking about different seating capacities or tier structure or parking lot configurations; we're talking about a sport where the actual playing surfaces themselves vary from stadium to stadium. These differences are obviously more than just charming cosmetic idiosyncrasies. They have a very important effect on games, as managers for each team must cope with those differences and their effects on the game must be anticipated and planned for in advance. In simplest terms, a ball hit 325 feet down the left-field line at Fenway, unless it is very high, will hit off the Green Monster and ricochet back onto

This view of Fenway Park shows the left field fence, the famous "Green Monster" and the warning track, the thin strip of dirt between the fences and the outfield grass. Note that under the Sports Authority sign there is a ladder running up the length of the wall. In the old days groundskeepers used to climb the ladder to retrieve home run balls that landed in a net on top of the wall. The net has been replaced by the extremely hard-to-get Green Monster seats, but the ladder remains (Christopher Penier\123rf).

the field; a ball hit 325 feet down the left-field line at Target Field, however, will land somewhere in the grass far short of the outfield fence. The ramifications to both offensive and defensive strategies are obvious.

But to some extent, however, these differences *are* charming cosmetic idiosyncrasies, and in large part because of them, every baseball stadium has a distinctive character and an appeal all its own. That's why so many baseball fans go on what are called **baseball pilgrimages** in which they visit different parts of the country to attend games in different stadiums. I know of no other sport where the venues play such an important part in the sport's popularity. I mean, my son Patrick and I are big hockey fans. Between his house league games and our following the New York Rangers around the East Coast a bit, we've been to 50 ice hockey rinks if we've been to one. I love ice hockey, but let's face it: outside of the center-ice team logo and the color of the seats, if you've seen one rink, you've seen them all. That is far from the case with baseball fields.

It would be nice if we could say that the flexibility in the makeup of Major League outfields was the brainchild of some long ago baseball marketing genius, but it wasn't. In the 1920s and 1930s, before the explosion of the automobile, teams were forced to build their stadiums in crowded city centers and had to fit them into whatever limited space was available. It was not uncommon, for example, for stadiums to be shoehorned into rectangular, and fairly small, city blocks. In the old Griffith Stadium in Washington, D.C., for example, part of center field had to be built around some apartment house buildings and the result was a rather large angular indentation in left-center field. Again, within all these stadiums, the infield could be tightly controlled, but the outer perimeter of the park, and therefore the outfields, varied a great deal from stadium to stadium. The lords of baseball have been wise, in the years to follow, not to tinker with the flexibility that was once imposed on them by necessity.

A few other things you should know about the outfields:

- The **bullpens** are the areas where pitchers hang out when they are not pitching, and where they warm up when they are called into a game. There is one for each team, and they are located just beyond the outfield fences in right and left fields, cut into the stands. In a few stadiums, however, including Wrigley Field and O.co Coliseum, home of the Oakland Athletics (usually called the Oakland A's for short), there is no bullpen, and, instead, reserve pitchers sit in chairs up along the foul lines with their backs to the crowd. If they are needed, they warm up right there in foul territory.
- The scoreboards in today's baseball stadiums, usually towering over the outfields, contain not only the usual amazing crystal clear video screens to show instant replays, but also during the game they virtually bombard the audience with a relentless flow of statistics, out-of-town scores, advertisements and quirky side-show diversions. We'll take a more in depth look at scoreboards later in this book.
- The **warning track** is the last 15 feet or so of the outfield closest to the outfield fences. Although the outfield is grass, the warning track is dirt. A defensive player, running full speed and looking back and up to catch a ball rapidly descending from great heights, knows, without looking, that he is getting close to the outfield fence when he feels the dirt beneath his feet.
- In most stadiums in Major League Baseball, there are no seats in the lowest rung of the

center-field stands. The reason is that in the old days the batter often would lose sight of a pitch against the backdrop of white or light shirts worn by fans seated there. For the safety of batters, the seats in dead center were taken out of commission and simply roped off and painted black or a dark color. As new stadiums are built, that space—often referred to as the **batter's eye** area—has been more economically or esthetically put to use, so that now, for example, there is a restaurant with smoked windows in center field in Yankee Stadium, and in both the Globe Life Park in Arlington, home of the Texas Rangers, and in Busch Stadium, home of the Cardinals, there is a section of downward sloping grass that blends visually into the grass in the outfield. Coors Field, home of the Colorado Rockies, is famous for its batter's eye: a large blue wall—it looks to be a few stories high—that is nearly covered with ivy, and at the foot of which is a beautiful section of landscape featuring an assortment of trees, rock formations and waterfalls. The different ways that batter's eye areas are utilized adds to the uniqueness of the various stadiums.

The Fielders

As noted earlier, when a team is playing defense, it sends nine players out into the field. They are collectively referred to as **fielders**, and their act of catching the hit ball is sometimes referred to as **fielding** the ball. Each fielder is assigned a certain area of the field to defend or **cover**. The fielders assigned to cover the infield are collectively referred to as the **infielders**, and individually, the names of their positions align with the base they are covering: the **first baseman**, **second baseman** and **third baseman** stand near and are responsible for defensive plays in the vicinity of those bases. The **shortstop** is the only player whose name isn't self-explanatory. He stands at and covers the area between second base and third base. We already know where pitchers and catchers are stationed.

Pitchers and catchers, by the way, are technically infielders but they are often spoken of as if they were off on their own. An alternative term often used to describe them is that together they comprise a team's **battery**.

Since we are on the subject of infielders, I have to take a little break here and advise you that you can't be a true baseball fan unless you are familiar with the hilarious "Who's on First?" skit by the 1940s comedy team Abbott & Costello. In the skit, Abbott has taken a job coaching a rather odd baseball team and Costello, curious about the players, asks him the infielders' names. Abbott answers, matter of factly, that Who's on first, What's on second and I Don't Know is on third. Costello, taken aback, asks for clarification:

COSTELLO: That's what I want to find out. I want you to tell me the names of the players on the team.
ABBOTT: I say Who's on first, What's on second, I Don't Know is on third.
COSTELLO: You don't know the fellows' names?
ABBOTT: Yes.
COSTELLO: Then who's playing first?
ABBOTT: Yes.
COSTELLO: I mean the fellow's name on first base.
ABBOTT: Who.
COSTELLO: The fella playing first base.
ABBOTT: Who.

COSTELLO: The guy on first base.
ABBOTT: Who is on first base.
COSTELLO: What are you asking me for?
ABBOTT: I'm not asking you, I'm telling you. Who is on first!
COSTELLO: I'm asking YOU who's on first.
ABBOTT: That's the man's name.
COSTELLO: That's who's name?
ABBOTT: Yes.
COSTELLO: Well go ahead and tell me.
ABBOTT: Who.
COSTELLO: The first baseman.
ABBOTT: Who is on first.
COSTELLO: Do you have a first baseman on first?
ABBOTT: Yes
COSTELLO: Then who's playing first?
ABBOTT: Absolutely.
PAUSE
COSTELLO: When you pay off the first baseman every month, who gets the money?
ABBOTT: Every dollar of it. Why not? The man's entitled to it!
COSTELLO: Who is?
ABBOTT: Yes.
COSTELLO: So who gets it?
ABBOTT: Why shouldn't he? Sometimes his wife comes down and collects it.
COSTELLO: Who's wife?
ABBOTT: Yes. After all, the man earns it.
COSTELLO: Who does?
ABBOTT: Absolutely.
COSTELLO: All I'm trying to find out is what's the guy's name on first base.
ABBOTT: No. What is on second base.
COSTELLO: I'm not asking you who's on second.
ABBOTT: Who's on first.
COSTELLO: That's what I'm trying to find out!
ABBOTT: Well, don't change the players around.
COSTELLO: I'm not changing nobody!
ABBOTT: Take it easy, buddy.
COSTELLO: What's the guy's name on first base?
ABBOTT: What's the guy's name on second base!
COSTELLO: I'm not asking you who's on second base.
ABBOTT: Who's on first.
COSTELLO: I don't know.
ABBOTT: He's on third.

There's more, and it gets funnier and funnier.

Players are said to **play** or be playing their assigned position. For example, you might hear that Roy Hobbs will be playing shortstop tonight for the New York Knights, though shortstop is often abbreviated to **short**, as in "Hobbs will be playing short tonight for the Knights."

The fielders assigned to play the outfield are collectively referred to as the **outfielders**. Individually, the names of their positions align with the part of the outfield they are covering: the **left fielder**, **center fielder** and **right fielder** stand in and are responsible for defending those areas.

Together, the infielders and outfielders are sometimes referred to as **position players**. Position players are all players except pitchers.

Infielders are pretty much spread out evenly across the infield for the sake of better coverage. The first baseman, for example, does not stand on first base all game long. He covers the area around first base, and goes directly to first base only when necessary.

Fielders are not anchored to one place on the field when playing defense. Before a defensive play is made, if it enhances their defensive strategy in dealing with a certain situation, fielders (except pitchers and catchers) can station themselves a bit more to the right or left, or closer to home or further away from home. In contrast, pitchers, at the start of a play, must be on the pitcher's mound, and catchers must be behind home plate in the catcher's box. Once a defensive play is in progress, however, any fielder—pitcher and catcher included—can go to any part of the field necessary to make a defensive play or to assist one of their teammates in making a defensive play.

By the way, in case you don't know it, the aforementioned Roy Hobbs is a fictional player and the New York Knights is a fictional team, both featured in my favorite baseball movie of all time, *The Natural*. In that movie, which is based on a 1952 novel of the same name by Bernard Malamud, Hobbs, a middle-aged ballplayer whose career was sidetracked a tad when he was shot and nearly killed, is attempting a comeback in a world full of rude, obnoxious 25-year-olds who have no respect for his age and experience and no appreciation for his talents. In the end, he outperforms and outsmarts them all.

I wonder why I like it so much?

The Format of the Game

THE LENGTH OF THE GAME: NINE INNINGS

Unlike most team sports, the length of a baseball game is not measured in time. The units of measurement, instead, are the turns the teams take on offense, meaning, the turns the teams take at bat. One turn by each team at bat, taken together, is called an **inning**. In other words, in one inning, Team A takes a turn at bat, then Team B takes a turn at bat. A baseball game is normally comprised of nine innings.

Innings are referred to by their numbers, as in **first inning, second inning, third inning,** or sometimes just by their ordinal numbers, as in **first, second, third**: "The Padres scored three runs in the second and now they have added two more here in the sixth."

Since both teams must take a turn at bat for one inning to be complete, innings are thought of in halves, with Team A's turn thought of as half an inning, and then Team B's turn thought of as the other half of that inning. The two half innings together, not surprisingly, make up one whole inning.

The **visiting team**—the team that has traveled all the way from another city to play in the game—is compensated for their troubles by getting their half inning turn at bat first. The **home team**, the team whose city and stadium the game is being played in, will graciously start out the game playing defense, and they will be at bat second.

A quick terminology break. You'll remember that the player who is trying to hit the ball with the bat is said to be at bat, up at bat, or just up, as in "Chris Davis will be up first for the Orioles." Those terms are also applied to his team as a whole when it is their turn on offense. Thus, you might hear an announcer say, "The Pittsburgh Pirates are at bat and Andrew McCutchen will be the first batter up for the Pirates."

Baseball announcers will refer to the halves of an inning as **the top half of** an inning (visiting team's half) and **the bottom half of** an inning (home team's half). More likely, though, they would simply say **the top of** an inning, or **the bottom of** an inning, as in "The Toronto Blue Jays scored three runs in the top of the third."

THREE EXCEPTIONS

I said above that a baseball game is "normally" nine innings long because there are two occasions when a game could be shorter, and one occasion where a game could be longer.

The first time a game can be shorter than nine innings is when the visiting team has come to bat in the top of the ninth and, after their at bat is over, they are losing. For example, suppose Home Team is leading Visiting Team by the score of 6–2 after eight innings. Suppose Visiting Team doesn't score in the top of the ninth, or scores only one, two or three runs. In this case, after the top of the ninth is over, there would be no need for Home Team to come to bat in the bottom of the ninth because they would have already won the game. The bottom of the ninth is, in effect, cancelled as unnecessary.

Likewise, suppose the game is tied or Home Team is losing going into the bottom of the ninth. If, in the bottom of the ninth, Home Team scores enough runs to take the lead and win the game, then at the point they take the lead, the game will end even if Home Team has not technically completed its inning. Again, the rest of the bottom of the ninth is, in effect, cancelled as unnecessary.

The second time a game can be shorter than nine innings is when it is cut short by rain. A game will often start in and continue through a light drizzle, but if during the game the rain increases to the point where the game cannot continue, the umpire-in chief will announce a **rain delay**, which means the game will be halted, a protective rubber tarp will be pulled out over the infield and everyone, the fans and the players alike, will just wait to see if it stops raining. A rain delay can last for hours. Eventually, either the rain will let up and the game will be resumed, or, if it does not look like the weather will improve, the umpire-in-chief can **call** the game, which means he declares the game to be over, at least for that day. A game that has been halted because of rain is said to have been **rained out**, and the game itself is sometimes referred to as a **rainout**. Whether a rained-out game counts as an official game, or whether it must be played over again from scratch at a later date, depends on the **rainout rules**.

The rainout rules are important to know because there will be times when dark clouds will gather over a game in progress and a few scattered drops will begin to fall. Depending on how your team is doing, you will be forced to make a difficult choice: should I root for rain? Or should I root against rain? If you are misinformed about the rainout rules and wind up rooting for the wrong option, the consequences to your team could be disastrous. Really.

Before I go any further, I would like to pose a problem that you should be able to solve after we have finished our discussion on rainouts. There is a very famous and very amusing painting by artist Norman Rockwell called *Three Umpires*. The 1948 painting depicts a scene in a game between the old Brooklyn Dodgers and the Pirates. Google it and take a look. In the foreground, as you can see, three umpires are looking up to a sky that is partially clear and blue and partially cloudy and ominous, as drops of rain fall around them.

The problem I pose to you is this: in the painting, is the rain beginning? Or is it ending?

To solve the problem, let's wring out the four possible outcomes of a rainout. But before we get our feet wet with the rainout rules, let me say this: given the fact that precipitation is a fairly common natural phenomenon, you would think that baseball, an outdoor game after all, would have come up with a simple set of guidelines to deal with it. But "simple" and "baseball" are two words that rarely co-exist in the same sentence. For whatever else their value might be, the rainout rules offer a valuable introduction to baseball's curious mindset. I think it's important, therefore, to try to wade through them.

Rainout Outcome # 1: A rainout will be considered a **regulation game,** meaning the game will count as an official game and the team that was winning at the time play was called will be declared the winner, only if the losing team has had at least five full innings at bat. In other words the home team, if ahead at the time the game was called, can only win if the visiting team had a full turn at bat in the *top* of the fifth, and the visiting team, if ahead at the time the game was called, can only win if the home team had a full turn at bat in the *bottom* of the fifth. Let's call this "the Minimum Innings Requirement."

Example: Home Team is leading 3–2 after seven innings. The game is rained out in the top of the eighth while Visiting Team is up. The game is official and Home Team wins because Visiting Team, the losing team, has had five full innings at bat.

Rainout Outcome # 2: A rainout will not be considered a regulation game if the game lasted less than the innings needed to fulfill the Minimum Innings Requirement. It will be as if the game never happened, and it will be replayed in its entirety at another time.

Example: Home Team is leading 3–2 after two innings. The game is rained out in the top of the third inning. The game is not official and will be rescheduled and replayed in its entirety because Visiting Team, the losing team, did not have five full turns at bat.

Rainout Outcome # 3: A rainout will be considered a **suspended game,** meaning it will be halted, placed "on hold" and completed at a later date, if the game lasted longer than the number of innings needed to fulfill the Minimum Innings Requirement, and either (i) the game is tied when called or (ii) the Visiting Team takes the lead in the top of a subsequent inning and the game is called before Home Team has a chance to complete a full turn at bat in the bottom of that same inning. In other words, when Visiting Team takes the lead in the top half of an inning in a regulation game, Home Team must have "last licks" in the bottom half of that inning or the game will be suspended and finished later on.

Example: After seven complete innings, Visiting Team and Home Team are tied 2–2. In the top of the eighth, Visiting Team scores a run and goes ahead 3–2, and then the rains come and the game is called. The game will be completed at a later time, because Home Team did not get a chance to get their last licks in the bottom of the eighth.

Rainout Outcome # 4: All post-season playoff games that are rained out are considered suspended, regardless of the inning or the score when the game was called, and are picked up from where they left off and finished in their entirety at a later time.

OK, now let's get back to our Norman Rockwell. The question was whether, in the picture, the rain was beginning, or was it ending. To find the answer, look closely at the background.

Behind the umpires, to their left, are two elderly gentlemen, presumably the managers of each team, engaged in discussion. The Dodgers manager, identifiable by the hat in his hand, is pointing to the sky and smiling. The Pirates manager, in contrast, is scowling at him and is clearly is not happy.

Behind the umpires, to their right, the scoreboard shows the Dodgers are the home team, it is the bottom of the sixth inning and the Pirates, the visiting team, are leading 1–0.

Per Rainout Outcome # 1, we know the game is official because the losing team, the Dodgers, already had their required five innings at bat. If the game is rained out now, the Pirates will be the winners. Presumably, therefore, if the rain was *beginning*, the Pirates manager would be cheered by the possibility of an imminent rainout preserving his lead and ensuring his victory. On the other hand, if the rain was *ending*, it would be the Dodgers manager who would be cheered by the prospect of the game continuing and his team, coming to bat in the bottom of the sixth, having the chance to catch up. Now look at the managers. Again, the Dodgers manager is pointing to the sky with a big smile on his face, while the Pirates manager looks like he's ready to explode with anger. The rain, therefore, is ending.

Experts in the evolution of the rainout rule may, at this point, want to raise a hue and cry because I have used contemporary baseball rules to analyze the Rockwell painting, as opposed to the rules that existed in 1947, when the painting was made. True, the 1947 rules were slightly different, but the differences are inconsequential to the situation at hand. Specifically, in some cases, a regulation game called because of rain in mid-inning reverted back to the score at the end of the most recent complete inning, meaning the last inning where both teams came to bat. In this case, if the game were called because of rain halfway through the sixth inning, the score would have reverted back to what it was at the end of the fifth, and the Pirates would have enjoyed a 1–0 win. But, again, since the Dodger manager, not the Pirate manager, is the happy one, we can be confident that no such reversion is taking place, because, again, the rain is ending.

I'll use this occasion to speak briefly about a nearly extinct species called the **doubleheader**, which, in the old days, meant two games played in one day, between the same two teams, back-to-back, for the price of one ticket. Originally, doubleheaders were included in the schedule to keep the season short, enabling baseball to condense its schedule into a briefer time period and finish everything up before cold weather blew in. The problem was that doubleheaders gave away one game for free, which, obviously, isn't the best way to turn a profit for any business.

The scheduled, two-for-the-price-of-one doubleheader may be a thing of the past, but you will hear the term used when a rained-out game is rescheduled to a day when another game is already scheduled. If, for example, a game between the Cleveland Indians and the Astros, at Houston, gets rained out, the game will be rescheduled for the next time that the Indians visit the Astros. To accommodate the additional game, a night game might be added to a date when a day game was already scheduled. Thus, on the same day, you will have the regularly scheduled day game, a pause of a few hours, then the rainout make up will be played at night. This will sometimes be referred to as a **day-night doubleheader**, or a **twi-night doubleheader**, but make no mistake about it, these are two separate games, and if you want to see them both, you'll have to buy tickets for each of them.

The third exception to the nine-inning rule concerns a game lasting longer than nine innings. Unlike soccer, there are no ties in baseball. If a game is tied after nine innings, the teams play **extra innings** until a winner is decided. Extra innings consist of additional whole innings (two halves) until, at the end of a whole inning, one team has more runs than the other. Suppose, for example, that after nine full innings have been played, Visiting Team and Home Team are tied 2–2. The game will now continue into an extra inning, a tenth inning. Let's further suppose that in the top of the tenth, Visiting Team scores a run and has a 3–2 lead going into the bottom of the 10th. One of three things will happen next:

- If Home Team doesn't score in the bottom of the 10th, Visiting Team wins 3–2 and the game is over. After 10 full innings, Visiting Team will have scored more runs than Home Team.
- If Home Team scores two runs in the bottom of the 10th, *they* win and the game is immediately over, just as in a nine inning game, regardless of how many outs are registered when the winning run scores.
- If Home Team scores one run in the bottom of the 10th and the game is thus still tied after 10 full innings, the game will go to an 11th inning, and the game will keep going until, after a complete inning is played, one team has more runs than the other.

Extra innings, the equivalent of overtime or stoppage time in other sports, are a time of great suspense. In fact, one of the most exciting baseball games I've ever attended involved extra innings. A lot of extra innings.

First, to set the scene, I don't like the Boston Red Sox. I'm a New York Yankees fan. I don't like the Red Sox, I think Fenway Park is overrated and ugly, and when I see people on the street with one of those blue baseball hats with the stupid red "B" in front, I cringe. Especially if I see it in New York.

It's OK. Red Sox fans undoubtedly feel the same way about me, my team, my stadium, and my blue hat with its interlocking "N" and "Y." The Yankee-Red Sox rivalry has lasted decades, and no doubt will last as long as baseball itself.

I'll talk about the rivalry again later, but for now, getting back to extra innings, in the 2009 season, the Red Sox beat the Yankees the first eight times they played. As August rolled around, the Yankees were in first place in the Eastern Division of the American League, and the Red Sox were a close second. Finally, on Thursday, August 6, in a game at Yankee Stadium, the Yankees broke through and beat the Red Sox for the first time that year, scoring eight runs in the bottom of the fourth and winning by the score of 13–6.

My three sons and I went to the game the following night, a Friday night game that Yankees fans considered very important. If the Red Sox won, they would resume their assault on first place. If the Yankees won, perhaps it would be a sign that the tide was turning and their grip on first solidifying.

The game went on for 15 long innings. It was an exciting game, a game of one missed opportunity after another for both teams, but some-how, going into the bottom of the 15th, neither team had yet to score a run. The game started at 7 p.m. It was now close to 1 a.m. The stadium was still packed—it seemed almost no one had gone home—but it was quiet. Everyone was exhausted by both the late hour and the ongoing suspense of he game.

In the bottom of the 15th inning, Alex Rodriguez, the mighty Yankees third baseman, stepped up to the plate. He had been stymied so far that night by the Red Sox pitchers, but A-Rod, as he is called for short, was one of those offensive powers who could change a game all by himself. Born in Upper Manhattan, abandoned by his father at a young age and raised by his mother in the Dominican Republic and Miami, blessed with enormous talent and matching good looks, a millionaire several times over, a constant companion both to beautiful women and, it seems, to controversy, A-Rod was all New York, all the time. Now, in the bottom of the 15th, he stepped to the plate with the hopes of 50,000 fans in his hands. The Red Sox pitcher reared back and fired the ball.

I can still remember the sound of the ball being hit by A-Rod's bat. It was such a loud "crack," heard clearly all across the vast expanse of the quiet stadium, that I knew instantly that the ball was hit squarely and, given A-Rod's power, had a chance to carry out of the park. And there it went. As I held my breath, as 50,000 fans held their breath, the small white ball travelled quietly in a breathtakingly high arch across the night sky, and, as fifty thousand fans let out a roar, it settled gently into the right field stands. Home run. Ballgame over. The Yankees win.

Patrick, Philip, William and I still talk about that long night in Yankee Stadium. I think we'll remember that home run, and being together to see that home run, for the rest of our lives.

Some final notes about the format of the game:

- A few hours before the game starts, teams will take turns warming up by taking **batting practice**, also called **BP**, on the field. During batting practice, players will take turns practicing their swing in the in the **batting cage**, a large cage set up around home plate that is closed off on three sides to protect other ballplayers and coaches from foul balls. As players taking BP smack soft pitches tossed to them by a member of their own team, other players jog and stretch in the outfield, and, hopefully, find time to sign a few autographs for fans leaning over the sidewalls.
- Immediately preceding the game, someone, often a celebrity, will sing the National Anthem. When the song is over, the umpire yells "Play Ball!" and the game begins.
- Between halves in the seventh inning, there is a pause called **the seventh inning stretch**, where fans are urged to get out of their seats, stretch a bit, and sing along to the old, classic baseball song, "Take Me Out to the Ballgame." Since the terrorist attacks on 9/11, a patriotic song, such as "America the Beautiful," is often sung as well.
- OK, I have a confession to make. I don't really think Fenway Park is overrated and ugly. It's unique and quirky and very, very old and full of surprises and it's just a heck of a lot of fun. I highly recommend it. But don't tell anybody I said that.

The Lineup

THE LINEUP CARD

You've done well, pilgrim. You know about spitballs, stirrups, Green Monsters, baseballs worth millions of dollars, the 1947 rainout rules and, most importantly, little doo-doo fastballs (whatever they are). Clearly, you are nearly ready for the game to begin.

Something important happens first. Before the game, the managers of both teams meet at home plate with the home plate umpire and each manager provides him with two copies of something called a **lineup card**.

The lineup card is a sheet of paper that has a team's **lineup** for that game written on it. The lineup is a list that shows: (i) what players will be playing for a team in that particular game, (ii) what defensive positions they will be playing and (iii) what order they will be batting in when taking their turn on offense (called the **batting order**).

The batting order is the center of a team's offensive game. Previously, we noted that nine players play for a team in each game, and we have just discussed where those nine players are stationed when playing defense. The role of these nine players while playing offense is simple: as described previously, with the exception of the modification caused by the Designated Hitter rule, each of them comes to bat, one at a time, and they try to put themselves in a position to legally advance around the bases, mainly, though not exclusively, by hitting the pitched ball with the bat. The players come to bat in the order they are listed on the lineup card. When, over the course of a few innings, all nine players have had their turn at bat, the player listed first on the list goes again and the batting order is gone through a second time. In most nine-inning games, each team's batting order will be rotated through about four times.

As an example, let's look at the lineup card for the 2012 World Champion San Francisco Giants. Their lineup for the first game of the 2012 **World Series**—the best-of-seven postseason playoff series between the American and National League champions to determine the championship of the Majors—looked like this:

1. Angel Pagan, Center Field
2. Marco Scutaro, Second Base
3. Pablo Sandoval, Third Base
4. Buster Posey, Catcher
5. Hunter Pence, Right Field
6. Brandon Belt, First Base
7. Gregor Blanco, Left Field
8. Brandon Crawford, Shortstop
9. Barry Zito, Pitcher

The lineup will also be referred to as the **starting lineup**, and the players the **starting** players or **starters**, meaning they started the game. As the game progresses, any starting player can be taken out of the game and replaced by a substitute if, for example, a starting player is injured or the manager feels that utilizing the strengths of a particular substitute might be strategically beneficial.

In the case of the 2012 Giants, when the game started, Angel Pagan was up first, then Marco Scutaro was up second, and so on. If, say, the first four players in the lineup come to bat in the first inning, then, come the second inning, the player listed fifth, Hunter Pence in this case, would be the first one up. Again, after the ninth batter has his turn, we would start all over with Angel Pagan.

The teams' lineups will also be posted on the scoreboard so that fans can follow along and anticipate what batters will be up next. On the scoreboard, however, the lineup is usually very condensed, with the position abbreviated to two letters and with just the players' uniform numbers substituting for their name. Thus, the scoreboard lineup for the above 2012 Giants lineup would look like this:

GIANTS
1. 16, CF
2. 19, 2B
3. 48, 3B
4. 28, C
5. 8, RF
6. 9, 1B
7. 7, LF
8. 35, SS
9. 75, P

As will be discussed in greater length later, the order of a lineup, the choice to put certain players at the top and others at the bottom, the choice to put a certain player immediately ahead of or behind another player, is the result of the manager's careful study of each player's offensive strengths and weaknesses, and how the batting order can best be used to enhance those strengths and downplay those weaknesses.

The first player listed in a lineup is called the **leadoff hitter** or **leadoff batter**; the fourth player is called the **cleanup hitter** or **cleanup batter**. Although the term cleanup hitter will only apply to one player in the lineup (Buster Posey, in the Giants lineup) throughout the game, the term leadoff hitter is used interchangeably as far as batting order in the lineup overall and batting order in a particular inning. Since Angel Pagan is listed first in the lineup given above, you will hear an announcer say that Angel Pagan is the **leadoff** batter, he is **leading off**, he is **batting first**, or that he is **up first** in the lineup and for the game generally. But suppose, again, that the first four players in the lineup come to bat in the first inning, and in the second inning the player listed fifth in the lineup, Hunter Pence, is the first scheduled batter. Pence, since he is the first one up for that particular inning, would be spoken of as being the leadoff batter, leading off, batting first, or being up first *for that inning*. Thus, you might hear an announcer say, "The leadoff batter, Angel Pagan, appeared to have hurt his ankle last inning. We'll see whether he'll remain in the game. And now, leading off the second inning for the Giants will be Hunter Pence."

THE DESIGNATED HITTER

An important presence in at least some of the lineups in modern Major League baseball is the **Designated Hitter**, also referred to as the **DH**.

In the game's original form, baseball teams played nine players at a time. All those nine players played a position in the field when their team was on defense, and then all those nine players eventually got a turn at bat when their team was on offense. This is the way baseball was played in both leagues, in *all* leagues, from clipper ship days right up until 1973.

The problem with this traditional arrangement was that, also since clipper ship days, pitchers couldn't hit. By this I mean that when pitchers took their turn batting, they were almost universally terrible offensively. As far back as 1929, National League President John Heydler complained: "Practically all pitchers are weak hitters and weaker baserunners. When they come to bat, they literally put a drag on the game. No one expects them to do anything, and they ... suspend the action of the play." The main job of pitchers, after all, was pitching.

As the good President Heydler pointed out, offensive skills were not expected of them, and whatever offensive skills they had were by and large not developed.

Interestingly enough, the ineptitude of pitchers offensively was, by necessity, at the heart of several strategic decisions made each game by managers who did their best to isolate this ineptitude so that it did the least amount of damage in a game, and who also, at times, actually tried to get some small, sneaky benefit out of it, usually employing the element of surprise. How well a manager responded to the many challenges posed by a pitcher's lack of offensive skills could very well decide a victory or defeat on the field, and to many purists, those challenges contributed to the allure and sophistication of the game.

To other fans, however, it was simply the most boring thing in the world to see a pitcher at bat.

When its attendance dropped in the early 1970s, the American League, one of the two Major Leagues, decided that it could inject more excitement into the game and generate more fan interest if, every time a pitcher was due up to bat, someone else batted for him instead, someone who could actually hit the ball with a bat. This player wouldn't play the field at all during the game. Their sole function would be to hit in place of the pitcher; they would be designated to hit in place of the pitcher. Hence, they were called the Designated Hitter.

The National League, the other of the two Major Leagues, was against changing the time-honored way of playing a baseball game, and therefore they were against implementing the Designated Hitter rule. The result of the debate was that in 1973 the American League was allowed to utilize the Designated Hitter rule, while the National League was allowed not to. For the first time, the two leagues operated under significantly different rules, and it's been that way ever since.

Some American League teams have a steady DH, meaning the same player plays DH game after game. In these cases, the DH Rule has prolonged the careers of many an aging ballplayer. The steady DH is usually a player who is an offensive powerhouse, but who is usually a bit past his prime, an older guy whose knees, maybe, won't allow him to play the field with the dexterity he used to have. Some steady Designated Hitters, such as David ("Big Papi") Ortiz of the Red Sox, have made enormous contributions to their teams and added a great deal of excitement to the game.

Other managers don't have a steady DH. They use the position instead to give different ballplayers "half a day off." This comes in handy when a player is recovering from a minor injury or when a player is getting long in the tooth and needs to rest his weary bones now and then by not playing the field. The 2012 Yankees, for example, rotated five players through the DH spot during the season, all of them over 34 years old.

CHANGES TO THE LINEUP: POSITION PLAYERS

As discussed, before a game begins, each manager gives the home plate umpire two copies of his team's lineup card. The home plate umpire keeps one copy of each lineup and gives the other copy to the opposing manager. Once the home plate umpire gives the lineup cards to the opposing managers, the lineups are final and the manager can only change his lineup by substituting one player for another under the rules that we will discuss in this section.

Like soccer, once a player is taken out of a baseball game and replaced by a substitute, he cannot come back in the game. But unlike soccer, there is no limit to the amount of substitutions a manager can make in baseball. If the manager has six or seven reserve players in the dugout he can substitute them all in during the course of a game if he feels it would be beneficial, provided that, while doing so, he can keep all defensive positions covered (i.e., if he takes a shortstop out of the game, he has to make sure that position is covered either by a substitute shortstop or by another player moving over to short while the substitution takes their position).

Here's how it works.

Question: Suppose you're the manager. Suppose it's the seventh inning, your team is losing by two or three runs, and right now you badly need some offense. Suppose the third baseman who started the game for you is coming to bat. Suppose he's in a horrible offensive slump. What's a manager to do?

Answer: Before your slumping third baseman comes to the plate, you notify the home plate umpire that you are making a substitution. Then you take your slumping third baseman out of the game and substitute in another third baseman to bat for him, one that hopefully is having a little more luck at the plate. The substitute third baseman will come into the game, bat in the place of the original third baseman, and when your half inning is over, the substitute third baseman will go out into the field and play third.

Question: Suppose the substitute third baseman is slumping offensively as well, or just isn't that good at offense? But suppose your reserve catcher, sitting down at the end of the dugout bench blowing bubbles, is an offensive powerhouse? You can't substitute the catcher in for the third baseman because the catcher never played third base in his life and you sure don't want him to start learning in the middle of a game. Still, he's an offensive powerhouse and right now you badly need some offense. What's a manager to do?

Answer: Again, before your slumping third baseman comes to the plate, you notify the home plate umpire that you are making a substitution, you put the reserve catcher in to bat in place of your starting third baseman, then, after your half of the inning is over, and before your team takes the field to play defense, you take the reserve catcher out of the game too, and put in the substitute third baseman to finish the game at third. So, in effect, you've make two substitutions instead of one: starting third baseman out, reserve catcher in; reserve catcher out, substitute third baseman in. The advantage is that you have gotten your offensive powerhouse reserve catcher up to bat; the disadvantage is that there are now two players (the starting third baseman and the reserve catcher) that you cannot use for the remainder of the game. Suppose you only have two catchers on your team? Now that your reserve catcher is done for the day, you better hope your starting catcher doesn't get hurt!

When a player is substituted in for another solely for the purpose of taking a turn at bat—in this case the reserve catcher—that substitute batter is called a **pinch hitter**.

Basically, the same substitution procedures are followed when a manager wishes to substitute a good defender in for a poorer defender (called a **defensive replacement**), or a fast baserunner in for a slow baserunner (called a **pinch runner**).

When substituting one player for another, a manager cannot change the order of the lineup. If the leadoff hitter, for example, is taken out of the game, his substitute can only be put in that same leadoff spot in the lineup. There is one exception. If a manager makes two substitutions at once, he can put either substitute in either vacated slot in the lineup. This is called a **double switch**.

The double switch is most often used in the National League when the pitcher is coming to bat. If, for example, the pitcher is scheduled to come to bat, and if, like most pitchers, he can't hit worth a lick, and if the manager needs some offense at that point, the manager can take out the pitcher and also take out one of the other position players at the same time. He can then put the substitute position player into the pitcher's spot in the lineup (so that he not only gets to bat right away but also gets to stay in the game afterwards), and he can put the substitute pitcher into substituted-for position player's spot (so that, hopefully, he won't be scheduled to come to bat for another two or three innings).

PLATOONING

A manager's decisions as to what players to put in a starting lineup, what order to put them in in a starting lineup, when to take them out of the starting lineup and substitute in another player, and what player to substitute in, are all heavily influenced by what side of the plate a batter hits from, and what hand the pitcher opposing him throws with. Now pay close attention, because this gets a little strange, but for now just trust me on this: this practice of matching up batters and pitchers based on what side the batter hits from and what side the pitcher pitches from, called **platooning**, is without question the driving force behind the vast majority of substitution decisions made by managers during the course of a modern baseball game.

Let's start off by using a righty batter as an example to illustrate what platooning is all about.

A righty batter, as discussed, is a batter who holds the bat with his right hand on top and who stands to the right of the plate looking in from the pitcher.

When a pitcher who pitches with his right hand (also called a **righty**) pitches the ball to a righty batter, he is throwing from the side of his body that is on the *same side* as the side of the plate where the righty batter is standing. That means that the righty pitcher's hand, with the ball in it, is coming forward from directly in *front of* or even slightly *behind* the righty batter.

In contrast, when a pitcher who pitches with his left hand (also called a **lefty** or a **southpaw**) pitches the ball to a righty batter, he is throwing from the side of his body that is on the *opposite side* of the side of the plate where the righty batter is standing. That means that the lefty pitcher's hand, with the ball in it, is coming forward from slightly *across* from the righty batter.

It is by now an indisputable fact, born out by years of statistical evidence, that because of this opposite side presentation, a righty batter can pick up a pitch coming out of a lefty pitcher's hand sooner than he can coming out of a righty pitcher's hand. By "pick up a pitch" I mean he can see it sooner, assess it sooner, take measure of it sooner, and therefore he has a better chance of hitting it with his bat. The same, in reverse, holds true when lefty batters face righty pitchers.

In today's game, pitchers can throw the ball up to 100 mph. A pitch can takes less than a second to get to the catcher's mitt. When I say that a righty batter can pick up a pitch coming out of a lefty pitcher's hand sooner, we're talking about a fraction of a second sooner. Maybe even a fraction of a fraction of a second sooner. Nevertheless, when the base line we are using is less than a second, then a fraction of a second—even a fraction of a fraction of a second— is *a lot*.

Taken together, these photographs bring to life the importance of platooning. In both, the batter is a righty. Notice how, in the top photograph (Thomas Barwick/Getty Images), the ball thrown by the right-handed pitcher comes from a point that is almost behind the batter and at least initially appears to be coming right at him, while in contrast, the ball thrown by the left-handed pitcher, in the bottom photograph (vladyc\123rf), comes from across his body, giving the batter a better perspective as the ball approaches him.

The statistical evidence (which we will discuss later in the section on statistics) is so over-whelming, and the advantage for the offense of having a righty hitter bat against a lefty pitcher, and a lefty hitter against a righty pitcher, is so well recognized, that managers on offense will do their best to structure their lineup and their pinch hitters in such a way as to get as many righty-lefty and lefty-righty **platoon matchups** as possible. Meanwhile, the managers on defense are, of course, doing just the opposite: structuring their pitchers and substitute pitchers in such a way as to get as many righty-righty and lefty-lefty matchups as possible.

With the platoon system now in mind, let's return to our bubble-blowing pinch-hitting offensive powerhouse catcher and discuss how his entry into the game as a substitute would really unfold in today's MLB.

OK, once again, your offensively weak third baseman is scheduled to come to bat. You want to bring up a pinch hitter. You scan your dugout for a pinch hitter and you see your offensive powerhouse reserve catcher at the end of the bench.

But stop right there, and rewind. Actually, what would really happen now is that before you scanned your dugout, you'd look first at the opposing pitcher. Suppose he was a righty. You would now scan your dugout not just for any pinch hitter, but for a *lefty* pinch hitter, so that you would take advantage of that statistical edge that a lefty-righty matchup would bring. Fine, suppose for the sake of argument your powerhouse reserve catcher is in fact a lefty. You notify the home plate umpire, and your reserve catcher is announced as a pinch hitter over the stadium loudspeaker.

End of story? Not at all. The opposing manager sees your lefty-batting offensive powerhouse reserve catcher in the on deck circle. Hells Bells, he exclaims, I'm not going to let them get a platoon advantage over me! So what does he do? He asks for a time out of his own and calls for a replacement pitcher, a lefty, to face your lefty catcher, thus nullifying the advantage you thought you had just cleverly created.

End of story? Still no. Because you, as the offensive manager, can now, in turn, take the lefty-batting offensive powerhouse reserve catcher out of the game *even before he gets up at bat* and you can send in a righty pinch hitter to regain the platoon advantage.

End of story? Yes, but only for a while. Once in a game, a pitcher must pitch to at least one batter, so the offensive manager gets the last word here and the substitution tit-for-tat has to end at this point for at least this batter. It could resume on the next batter, and the opposing managers could go back and forth all day long making offsetting substitutions if they wanted to. But they don't want to. And the reason they don't—the only reason they don't—is that there are only so many players available to them. Once the offensive powerhouse catcher was announced as being in the game, for example, he was considered to be officially *in* the game, and so if you then turn around and take him *out* of the game, he can't come back *into* the game even if he never actually got *in* the game in the first place. Makes sense? Like any other player who was officially in the game, once he's taken out of the game, he's done for the day.

If you think platooning makes the game strategies more complicated, you are correct, but if you factor in switch hitters, it gets even crazier. Switch hitters, as we mentioned previously, can bat comfortably and effectively from either side of the plate. How can a manager defend against a switch hitter? It seems that no matter what kind of pitcher you use against him, he'll just preserve the platoon advantage by switching to the other side of the plate.

That's true to some extent, but the fact is that most switch hitters are stronger from one side of the plate than the other, and managers will take advantage of this by inserting a substitute pitcher that will **turn the batter around** to the side of the plate he is weaker from. For example, if a switch hitter's personal statistics shows he is much more potent offensively batting righty, the opposing manager might send in a righty to pitch to him, thus forcing him to bat lefty, which, lefty-righty advantage notwithstanding, may be his weaker side.

As a final note on platooning, let me just reemphasize that this strategy is most often used in regards to substitutions. A manager can take platooning into account when choosing his starting lineup too, of course, but starting lineups are usually comprised of a team's best players *overall*. If one of those players is less adept at, say, hitting lefties than he is at hitting righties, it just might be something the manager is willing to put up with given the other talents that the player brings to the table. That's why a platoon-based pinch-hitting substitution of a starter is most likely to occur late in the game and when a team is behind. At that point, a starting player's other tools may be less important than his ability to hit the ball and generate offense.

Still, you will occasionally see teams who have starting positions shared equally during the season by two **platoon players**, one starting against lefties, while the other starts against righties. I'm thinking of the 1986 World Champion Mets, who played the entire season with lefty-batting players splitting starting duties with righty-batting players at third base, second base and center field. It worked for them!

As a final, final note on platooning, in the interests of full disclosure, let me put on the record that in their efforts to get and then keep a platooning advantage, opposing managers these days will often, between them, change pitchers several times during the course of a game. Manager Tony La Russa once used four pitchers to throw just eight pitches. In 1992, the Mariners used 11 pitchers in one nine-inning game. When a pitcher is changed between innings, and a new pitcher starts off a new inning, the change is seamless and unobtrusive. But when the change is made in the middle of an inning, the interruption to play can be significant and the game can be slowed considerably. Every time a new pitcher is brought in in the middle of an inning, the whole game stops while the manager or a coach goes out to the mound to take the ball from the departing pitcher, and while the new pitcher trots in from the bullpen, and then while the new pitcher takes his place on the mound and throws his allotted eight warm-up pitches. When this happens four or five or six times during the course of a game, well, frankly, it can be just a wee bit boring to sit through.

In the National Hockey League, if a team wants to change goalies during the game, the old goalie skates off, the new goalie skates on, and the game resumes within seconds. Baseball should learn something from this. Before a pitcher is brought into a game, he warms up by throwing practice throws in the bullpen. To then give a pitcher eight more warm-up throws from the pitcher's mound is, in my opinion, a luxury that an already slow game can't afford.

CHANGES TO THE LINEUP

Starting Pitchers

What a pitcher does with his throwing arm is truly unnatural and almost painful to watch. To freeze-frame a pitcher during the middle of a pitch is to find a man with an arm, as one writer put it, "almost hideously contorted." It's as if pitchers are trying their hardest

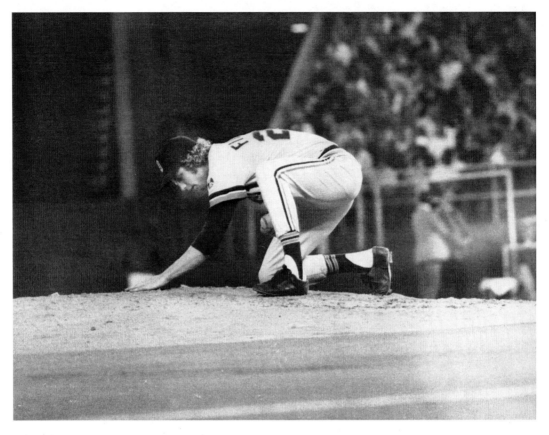

Mark Fidrych in his prime, tending to his office (National Baseball Hall of Fame Library, Cooperstown, New York).

to tear apart the tendons in their pitching arm or dislocate their pitching shoulder with each and every pitch. During the course of a baseball season, it is almost a routine occurrence that pitchers succumb to season-ending or even career-threatening arm injuries.

One such potentially career-ending injury is so common that the surgery to repair it is named after a pitcher. The injury involves ligaments in the pitching elbow becoming worn out through years of repetitive throwing motions and eventually just "popping" off the elbow. The surgery—called **Tommy John Surgery** after the first pitcher to have it done in 1974— replaces the ligament with a tendon taken from another part of the body and then secured by looping it through a series of holes drilled into the bones around the elbow. If a pitcher heals correctly, the tendon "learns" to become a ligament and in about a year the rehabbed pitcher is back pitching in the Major Leagues. The operation has an 85–90 percent success rate. As of this writing, about fifty active Major League pitchers, or about one out of every seven, have undergone Tommy John Surgery.

The best way to prevent injuries to a pitcher is to avoid overuse of that pitcher, and the best ways to avoid overuse are to limit a pitcher's use within each game, and make sure a pitcher gets enough rest between appearances.

Pitchers can be classified into one of two groups. **Starting pitchers** begin games for a team, and **relief pitchers** come in later on in games to replace the starting pitcher if he is losing effectiveness, if the manager wants to take him out of the game to prevent overuse, or, as we have discussed, if the manager feels the need to take him out to get a platoon advantage at some critical point in the game.

The problem of overuse is especially pressing for starting pitchers because so much of a game's outcome depends on their performance. Generally, starting pitchers are expected to pitch into the sixth or seventh inning, and not get tired and lose effectiveness until they have thrown about 100 pitches. These 100 pitches, of course, don't include probably as many warm-up pitches thrown before the game and before each inning. It is not uncommon to see starting pitchers sitting in the dugout with ice packs on their arms and shoulders while their team is at bat.

To make sure they get enough rest between games, starting pitchers are put in a **pitching rotation**, which is kind of like a batting order for starting pitchers. Normally, a team's pitching rotation consists of a team's five best pitchers. Each pitcher in the rotation will take a turn starting a game, one after another, so that each of them will get at least four days rest between starts.

Two asides about pitching rotations: First, reverting back to the discussion about platooning for a moment, a pitching rotation will ideally have a mixture of left-handed pitchers and right-handed pitchers, the better to keep opposing teams off balance. Second, a pitcher's position in the rotation will usually reflect his worth to the team. The first pitcher in the rotation will be the best and most dominant pitcher on the team, which is why he is often referred to as the **ace** of the pitching staff.

To prevent overuse of a starting pitcher within any given game, a manager might employ a **pitch count**, meaning, he will put a loose limit to how many pitches his starting pitcher will be allowed to throw per game. Pitchers, again, generally throw about 100 pitches a game, which normally would bring them into the seventh inning or so. If things are going well, meaning, the pitcher is effective and is efficient with his pitches and the opponents are cooperating with quick and unproductive turns at bat, and if the pitcher insists he is feeling good and pain free, the manager may go as far as, say, 120 pitches, especially if it will enable the pitcher to pitch a complete, nine-inning game.

Aside from being a coveted personal achievement, for a starting pitcher to pitch a **complete game** has the added value of allowing the team's relief pitchers to rest and save their arms for another day. Complete games, however, have become more and more rare over the years as in the late innings of a game managers tend more and more to **go to the bullpen**, meaning, they tend to bring in a relief pitcher, or a sequence of relief pitchers, to finish the game.

If this sounds to you like a whole lot of pampering for starting pitchers, you're not alone. Old-time pitchers love to tell tales of how they used to pitch with three days rest (a four-pitcher rotation was once common) and often threw over 150 pitches in a game.

A great story from those old days concerns a pitching duel that took place on the evening of July 2, 1963, in the old Candlestick Park in San Francisco. That night, a 25-year-old pitcher named Juan Marichal, in his fourth year in the Majors, pitched for the Giants. Warren Spahn, 42 years old and in his 18th year in the Majors, pitched for the Braves. Both pitchers would go down in history as two of the greatest pitchers ever, and that night, they would compete in a game that some have called the greatest game ever pitched. Both pitchers pitched every inning of a scoreless tie that went to the bottom of the sixteenth inning before Willie Mays won it for the Giants with a home run. Spahn threw 201 pitches that night and Marichal threw no less than 227. "If that happened today," Marichal speculated years later, "they'd fire the manager and general manager—everyone but the players!"

Marichal and Spahn later exchanged stories about why they forced themselves to pitch that entire game, or, as they say, to **go the distance**. It turns out that the thing that drove them to keep pitching that day, was each other. Marichal, when his manager tried to take him out of the game, said: "You see that man pitching over there? He's 42 and I'm 25. And nobody gonna take me out of here while that man stays on the mound." Spahn, as it turned out, was telling his manager the corresponding equivalent: "As long as that little kid is still pitching in there, nobody is going to take me out!"

The other side of the coin, though, would probably be the sad story of Mark "The Bird" Fidrych, a starting pitcher for the Tigers in the late 1970s. Fidrych, a tall, lanky kid with a long mane of curly blonde hair, was as goofy a character as he was a great pitcher. At the start of an inning, he often would get down on his hands and knees and not only smooth out the pitcher's mound with both hands, but he would actually *talk* to it. Not stopping there, he would then talk to the ball before throwing a pitch. Sometimes, to make sure the baseball knew exactly where he wanted it to go, he would close one eye, hold the ball in front of his open eye as if it were a dart, and whisper to the ball as he lined it up with home plate.

In 1976, his rookie year, Fidrych was incredible. I won't cite statistics—they wouldn't mean anything at this point anyway—but suffice it to say that that year "The Bird" was not only one of the two or three best starting pitchers in baseball, but he was a wildly colorful cult figure among Tigers fans and hugely popular among baseball fans everywhere. He drew huge crowds wherever he pitched, and, perhaps as a result, he was allowed to pitch way more innings than any rookie, whose arm was still developing, should have been.

After that one phenomenal year, The Bird was never the same. In 1977 he was plagued by a series of arm injuries that kept him out of action most of the year. In 1978 and 1979 he barely pitched at all. After the 1980 season, at the age of 26, he retired.

During the 2012 season, the Washington Nationals, perhaps with pitchers like Fidrych in mind, made a controversial decision regarding Stephen Strasburg, their young superstar pitcher. Following a sensational college career, Strasburg was chosen by the Nationals as the first pick in the 2009 college draft. After being brought up to the Majors at the end of the 2010 season, however, Strasburg underwent Tommy John Surgery and did not play for almost the entire 2011 season. He returned in 2012 and was one of the game's most dominant pitchers right through to September, at which point, much to the disappointment of Nats fans, General Manager Mike Rizzo decided that Strasburg, although healthy, would not pitch again that year.

Even before the season started Nats management had decided to limit the amount of innings Strasburg would throw that year. Considering that he was still so young, still so early in his career, and still only one year removed from major reconstructive surgery, the decision seemed a wise one. The problem was that in large part because of Strasburg, the Nats had made the postseason playoffs for the first time ever. Would they really now keep him out of the playoffs, even though he was not injured? The Nats stuck to their guns. "When we signed Stephen," Rizzo explained, "I made a promise to him and his parents that I would take care of him and that's what we are going to do. We are looking at not only competing for the playoffs this season, but also in '13, '14, '15 and beyond. Stephen is a big part of those plans and I will not do anything that could potentially harm him down the road."

The Nats, without Strasburg, were eliminated in the first round of the playoffs by the Cardinals.

Relief Pitchers

Unlike starting pitchers, relief pitchers do not work on a rotating basis. Rather, they are put into one of the following three categories and then called into a game as their category is needed.

Middle relievers or **long men** are normally called into a game anytime before or during the seventh inning. If a starting pitcher goes down to injury in the third inning, for example, or is completely ineffective beginning in the fifth inning, a middle reliever (or two, or maybe even three middle relievers, depending on game conditions) will come into the game and just try to prevent further damage until the eighth inning or so. While the later inning relief pitchers tend to be specialists, meaning that's all they do, middle inning relievers are usually a mixed bag of pitching types. It might be cruel to say it, but it seems that middle relievers are generally those pitchers good enough to be on a team, but not good enough, or at least not *yet* good enough, to be either a starting pitcher or one of the late-inning relief specialists.

Setup relievers or **setup men** generally pitch only the eighth inning, and possibly some of the seventh as well. Setup relievers are specialists—they *set up* the game for the relief pitcher who follows them and who will finish the game. Teams usually carry one setup reliever, and he will be the second best reliever on the team.

Finally, the **closer** generally pitches only one inning, the ninth. There is only one closer per club. The closer is the best relief pitcher on the team, period. In a close game, with your team ahead by three runs or less, your closer will pitch the last inning to nail down the win.

The setup man and the closer are usually only used to preserve small leads. If the manager needs a relief pitcher in the late innings, and if his team is already up or down by a substantial amount, he won't waste his setup man or closer. After all, he might need them the next day. So he might just bring in one of his middle relievers to finish the game.

Closers are among of the biggest stars in the game. They are the macho men of relief pitchers. When closers are playing at home, and when they are called into the game for that last crucial inning or last couple of outs, many of them trot in across the outfield grass from the bullpen to the pitchers mound accompanied by a theme song of their choice.

Mariano Rivera of the Yankees is widely regarded as the best relief pitcher of all time, a reputation at least partially founded on the longevity of his excellence: he was every bit as masterful a pitcher in 2013, when he retired at the age of 43, as he was in 1996, when he was first assigned to relief pitching duties at the age of 27. But what really made Mariano so unique is that throughout this long career, he threw virtually the same pitch time after time: a nasty cutter that looked like a straight fastball until at the very last fraction-of-a-second it broke to the left—meaning it broke in on the hands of a lefty batter, or away from the flailing bat of a righty batter. No curveballs, no sliders, and very few fastballs: just, basically, cutter after cutter after cutter after cutter, with slight variations on the sharpness of the cut created by variations in the amount of pressure on the ball applied by the fingertips. The general rule is that predictability is fatal to a pitcher, because if a batter knows what's coming, they can plan and prepare and be ready. Mariano's cutter, however, was nearly supernatural in its late-breaking sharpness and its accuracy.

I can honestly say that Mariano's entry onto the field at Yankee Stadium was about as dramatic a moment as you would find in sports. Imagine: it's the ninth inning, the Yankees are ahead but their lead is being threatened, the manager walks slowly out to the pitcher's mound, looks toward the bullpen and taps his right arm, a signal to send in a righty relief pitcher. The crowd begins to buzz in anticipation. Suddenly, Metallica's "Enter Sandman" comes booming over the loudspeakers and the crowd erupts, because they know that is Mariano's entrance song (because, they say, he put even the best opposing batters to sleep). After a dramatic pause, as the music reaches its crescendo, the bullpen door swings open, and after another dramatic pause, Mariano comes trotting slowly out onto the field. It was sheer theater. Each and every time, the fans in Yankee Stadium went absolutely nuts.

A similar scene played out for years in San Diego and, later, in Milwaukee, when AC/DC's "Hells Bells" preceded the entrance of Trevor Hoffman, one of the greatest relievers ever, and at Fenway Park, where, until he was traded to the Philadelphia Phillies after the 2011 season, the sounds of the Dropkick Murphys' "I'm Shipping Up to Boston" over the loudspeakers meant only one thing: Jonathan Papelbon was coming in to close the game down. One Boston fan told me the scene gave him goose bumps every time.

To be clear, even when the manager does elect to bring in a relief pitcher, he only needs to bring in the ones required for the situation. If the starter gets bombed early, the manager might bring in the middle reliever first, then, if his team takes the lead, the setup man, then the closer. If the starter makes it through to the seventh inning, the manager might only bring in the setup man and then the closer. If the starter makes it all the way to the ninth, the manager may go straight to the closer. But, again, the setup man and closer will normally be used only to preserve a small lead.

Relief pitchers usually only pitch an inning or two at a time, maybe three, so a one-game pitch count is irrelevant. On the other hand, they may be called in to pitch two nights in a row, maybe even three nights out of four. Thus, managers tend to judge their use or overuse over the course of a few games, rather than on a single game.

Just a quick note on terminology to end our discussion of relief pitchers. During a game, starting pitchers who are not pitching that day will spend their time hanging out in either the bullpen or on the bench with the rest of the non-playing position players. All relief pitchers who are not currently pitching, however, will hang out in the bullpen, because they could get the call at any time to start warming up. The term "bullpen," therefore, has become synonymous with the team's relief pitching corps as a whole. Thus, you might hear an announcer say something like "The Mets' bullpen has been especially strong so far this year, appearing in 10 games and giving up only one run."

THE DESIGNATED HITTER, CONTINUED

Now that you know about platooning, pinch hitters, starting pitchers and relief pitchers, you can appreciate a little more the problems that National League managers have to deal with in the absence of the DH rule. Every time the pitcher is scheduled to come to bat, the National League manager has to ask himself a series of questions:

1. First, am I behind in the game and do I need offense here?
2. If the answer is yes, then do I need offense, do I need a pinch hitter, more than I need the skills of this particular pitcher for the rest of the game?
3. If the answer is yes again, then do I have a pinch hitter available who matches well against the opposing pitcher as far as a lefty-righty or a righty-lefty matchup?
4. If the answer is yes again, then I am willing to use that pinch hitter once and then not have him available again for the rest of the game, or, in the alternative, is the double switch an option?
5. If the answer to either question is yes, then what are the chances that the opponents might change pitchers to nullify the platoon matchup once I commit and announce my pinch hitter into the game, and how will I react if they do?
6. Finally, if I take this pitcher out of the game, what relief pitchers do I have available? Do the relief pitchers I have match up well against the opposing lineup? If we're in the early innings, do I have enough relief pitchers available to get me through the rest of the game? Am I willing to use them today and possibly not have them available tomorrow?

Clearly, in the American League, the choices are much simpler. Since the pitcher doesn't bat, the manager only needs to think about replacing him if he begins to tire or lose effectiveness. At that point the American League manager has to make the same decisions as the National League manager as far his relief pitchers go, but, in effect, he only has to worry about the sixth question above, but not the first five. Obviously, the DH rule simplifies things greatly, and that's exactly why many fans don't like it. To them, it's as if someone playing chess were to say: pawns are boring, queens are exciting, so let's replace all the pawns with queens!

Two
The Game

Objectives of the Defensive Team

Three Outs

Your baseball knowledge is growing exponentially. Now you also know about pitchers talking to baseballs and tendons learning to become ligaments and first basemen named Who. It's time to play ball, my friend.

When discussing the infield, we learned that according to the *Official Baseball Rules*, the offensive team's objective is to "have its batter become a runner, and its runner advance around the bases." The defensive team's objective, predictably, is "to prevent offensive players from becoming runners and advancing around the bases." It may seem counterintuitive, but through trial and error (actually, several trials and several errors), I've determined that the most effective way to explain baseball is to start by discussing the defensive team's objective, so we'll begin with that.

The defensive team prevents an offensive player from becoming a runner and advancing around the bases by forcing, or inducing, him to instead get or make an "out." An **out** is essentially an instance where a batter or a runner is unsuccessful in his attempt to advance to a base. Once three offensive players have **made out**, their team's turn on offense is over, their half-inning is over, any runs they have scored during that half-inning are finalized on the scoreboard, and the opposing team comes in to take its turn at bat.

You may have noticed by now that baseball is a game of threes and multiples of threes: nine innings, nine players in a lineup, three bases, three outs in a half-inning, the three-feet limit on taking evasive action while base running. So you probably won't be surprised to learn that there are three ways for a batter to make an out. Those three ways are: by a fly out, ground out, or a strikeout.

Fly Ball Outs

If a batter connects with a pitch and hits a **fly ball**—a ball that is hit in the air and does not touch the ground—and a defender, *any* defender (infielder, outfielder, pitcher or catcher), catches it before it hits the ground (also known as **catching it on the fly**), the batter is out. Whether it's in foul territory, or fair territory, whether it's a **pop up** or a **pop fly** that travels more *up*, staying in the infield, than *out* to the outfield, or whether it's a blazing **line drive** rocketed by the batter "sharp and direct," as the *Official Baseball Rules* say, into the playing field, or whether it's a lofty wallop that travels across the sky to the deepest part of the outfield—in all these cases, if a fielder catches the ball on the fly, it's a **fly ball out,** also called a **fly out.**

Once a batter flies out, he will leave the field, return to the dugout, an out is registered against his team, and the next batter in the lineup will take his turn at bat.

By the way, if there is some dispute as to whether the fly ball was caught before it touched the ground—in some diving catches, it can be hard to tell if the fielder actually caught the ball before it hit the ground or merely **trapped** it between his glove and the ground before quickly scooping it up—the closest umpire will determine whether the ball was caught on the fly or not.

GROUND BALL OUTS

Fly balls are easy: if a defender catches a hit ball before it hits the ground, it's an out. That's all there is to it. A **ground ball,** also known as a **grounder,** is a hit ball that strikes the ground at least once before it is caught, regardless of where on the field it hits the ground. A ball that is hit and bounces along the infield 15 times before it is caught by the shortstop is a ground ball; a ball that is hit and travels 400 feet and hits the ground once in the warning track before it is grabbed by the center fielder, is, for purposes of this discussion, also a ground ball. Grounders are a little more complicated than fly balls, because there are two ways to get an out on a ground ball, called a **ground ball out** or a **ground out.**

The Key Concept: Force vs. Tag

I'm going to go out on a limb here, and say that the concept I'm about to discuss in relation to ground ball outs—the concept of a force out versus a tag out—is the key to understanding the entire game of baseball. It is a concept that will go beyond our discussion of ground ball outs and underlie every offensive strategy we discuss. Therefore, it will also of necessity underlie every *defensive* strategy as well.

As essential as it may be, the authors of the *Official Baseball Rules* have opted not to explain this concept in clear, concise terms that would make it easier for a beginner to understand. I think I've identified the force out/tag out sections of the *Official Baseball Rules,* but I can guarantee you that if you didn't *already* know what they were talking about, there is no way you would know what they were talking about just by reading them.

I have, therefore, reordered and rewritten those rules into what I call the Ground Ball Rules. These five rules govern how an offensive player legally advances around the bases when either, as the batter, he hits a ground ball, or, as a runner, he is already on base when the batter hits a ground ball. These five rules are, of necessity, preceded by three Basic Baserunning Rules, which transcend ground ball situations and will apply to other aspects of the offensive game as we go forward.

I know what you're thinking: I'm talking about baserunning rules and you don't even know yet how a batter becomes a baserunner in the first place. You're right, but now I'm just going to ask you to trust me. Although we will be getting just a tiny but ahead of ourselves here, it won't be anything you can't handle, and a host of fun-filled examples will follow to bring all these rules to life.

First, a terminology break: the ball is said to be **in play** when the opportunity exists for the batter and/or runner(s) to advance. The opportunity that puts the ball in play could be created by any one of a dozen or so events on the field, and we will cover the main ones throughout the course of this book, but the opportunity-creating event that concerns us at the moment is the batter hitting a ground ball.

OK, here we go...

Basic Baserunning Rule # 1: When a runner is advancing around the bases, he must touch first, second, third and home in that order. In other words, there are no shortcuts.

Basic Baserunning Rule # 2: Two runners cannot occupy the same base at the same time.

Basic Baserunning Rule # 3: Runners must advance around the bases in the order in which they get on base. In other words, a subsequent runner cannot pass up a runner already on base just because he runs faster.

OK, that was the easy stuff. Now fasten your seat belts, because this is where it gets interesting.

Ground Ball Rule # 1: If the batter hits a ground ball into fair territory, that batter must run to first, meaning he is **forced** to run to first by the *Official Baseball Rules.*

That wasn't so bad, was it? What it means is that when a batter hits a ground ball, it's not up to him whether to advance or not. He can't say: Maybe next time, or, I like the view from home plate better. He has to advance, and, per Basic Baserunning Rule # 1, he has to advance to first base first.

Ground Ball Rule # 2: If the batter hits a ground ball into fair territory, he is **forced** to go to first, and he can just stop there if he wants, but he can also immediately **choose** instead to run beyond first and advance to second, third, or even all the way home if the opportunity presents itself and in his judgment the potential rewards for doing so outweigh the risks.

Again, not so bad. Now we are going to kick it up a notch and place an imaginary runner or two on base when the batter hits his ground ball.

Ground Ball Rule # 3: If, when a batter hits a ground ball into fair territory and is running to first, there is already a runner on first, then, per Basic Baserunning Rules #2 (two runners cannot occupy the same base at the same time), and #3 (the original occupier of the base must be the one who leaves), the runner who is already on first is **forced** to run to second. He has no choice. He has to go. And when that runner on first runs to second, if there already happens to be a runner already on second as well, then that runner on second, by virtue of the same rules, is now in turn **forced** to run to third. And when that runner on second runs to third, if there already happens to be a runner on third as well, then the runner on third, again by virtue of the same rules, is now in turn **forced** to run home.

Pretty simple, really. It's kind of like bumper cars. A batter arriving at first base bumps a runner already on first to second base, and that runner can bump a runner already on second to third, and so on. Now let's make it even more interesting.

Ground Ball Rule # 4: If, when the batter hits a ground ball into fair territory and is running to first, there is *not* already a runner on first, but instead there is a runner on second, third, or on both second and third, then Basic Baserunning Rules #2 and #3 will not apply to them because the batter is not forcing them off their bases. After all, the batter is running to first, a base which is not occupied. As a result, if the batter runs to first and *stops at first,* any runner(s) already on second, third, or both second and third can just stay right where they are. But, again, they can also **choose** to advance if in their judgment the potential rewards for doing so outweigh the risks.

Again, not so bad. If a runner is advancing to first and there is not already a runner on first but, instead, there is a runner on second, the bumper-car analogy doesn't apply. That runner on second isn't forced to advance by the runner going to first, but he has the option of trying to advance if he thinks he can do so successfully. And now for the grand finale:

Ground Ball Rule # 5: If when the batter hits a ground ball into fair territory and is running to first, there is *not* already a runner on first, but instead there is a runner on second, or third or both second and third, and if the batter *does not stop at first* and **chooses** to advance further, the runner(s) ahead of him now have to advance because of Basic Baserunning Rules #2 and # 3. But here's the twist—and the importance of this will be revealed in a moment—because the original runner **chose** to advance past first to second and beyond, the runners that must now advance ahead of him are considered to have advanced by **choice** as well.

And now for the wrap-up:

In these five rules, you'll notice that two terms were highlighted: "force" and "choice." Sometimes a runner will be **forced** to advance to the next base because of the rules of baseball; sometimes a runner will **choose** on his own to advance to the next base.

With that difference in mind, here is the key concept to understanding not only ground ball outs, but, to a large extent, the game of baseball itself:

1. If, when the ball is in play, the batter or a runner is advancing to a base because he is **forced** to, the defense gets him out when a fielder simply gets the ball and steps on or otherwise touches that particular base before the runner gets there and touches it. This is called a **force play** or **force out.**

2. If when the ball is in play, the runner is advancing to the next base because he **chooses** to, then his ambitiousness and competitive zeal is rewarded by making it significantly more difficult for the defense to get him out: instead of getting the ball and just stepping on or otherwise touching that base before the runner does, the fielder actually has to tag the runner with the ball before the runner touches the base in order to get him out. This is called a **tag play** or a **tag out.**

Well, that's nice, you might be thinking, but why is the difference between a tag play and a force play so important? For now, suffice it to say that for the defense, tag plays are infinitely less preferable because they are much more difficult and more risky to execute. Tag plays, as you will see, can involve fielder-runner collisions, balls getting jarred from the fielder's gloves, and uniforms getting all dirty. And they're a lot slower. In a tag play you have to wait for the runner to get to you to tag him out. If there are any other runners on base, they could be advancing in the meantime. With force plays, on the other hand, there's no waiting involved. You get the ball, you step on the base before the batter gets there for the out, your uniform stays clean, and you're immediately ready for the next play. Any time a defense can opt for a force play over a tag play, it will. Conversely, any time an offense can opt for a tag play over a force play, it will. Just how each side will attempt to "opt" for one or the other will be covered throughout this book as we discuss the various strategies and counter-strategies for getting runners on base and moving them around the bases to score.

Two quick notes regarding what it means to "tag" a runner with the ball: First, it is sufficient for the fielder to tag the runner with the hand or the glove that is holding the ball. The ball itself does not have to make contact with the runner. Second, a fielder can tag any part of the runner to make an out: his shirt, pants, shoe, head, stirrups ... you get the picture.

It will be the decision of one of the umpires (first, second and third base umpires for plays at one of those bases, or the home plate umpire for plays at home plate) whether a runner arrived safely, or was **safe**, at his respective base. That means that either (i) in the case of a force play, the runner stepped on our touched the targeted base before a fielder with the ball stepped on or touched the targeted base, or (ii) in the case of a tag play, the runner stepped on or touched the targeted base before a fielder tagged them with the ball. If the umpire calls the runner safe, that means the runner has legally advanced to that base. When the next batter comes to the plate, the runner will be standing on that base hoping to legally advance further.

If, however, in the umpire's judgment, either (i) in the case of a force play, a fielder with the ball stepped on or touched the targeted base *before* the runner stepped on our touched that base, or (ii) in the case of a tag play, a fielder tagged the runner with the ball *before* the runner stepped on or touched the targeted base, then that runner is out. These, then, are the aforementioned two ways an offensive player can make an out on a ground ball: a tag out and a force out. Having made out in either of these manners, that player will leave the field, return to the dugout and an out will be registered against his team.

A safe call by an umpire is indicated by the umpire extending his arms outward to the side, parallel to the ground. An out call is indicated usually by the umpire pumping or raising his right fist, or some similar punching-type gesture.

Terminology break: If a batter or runner arrives safely at one of the three bases, it is sometimes said that he **reached** that base, as in "Yadier Molina of the Cardinals reached second in the third inning." Also, when a fielder fields a ball and throws to a teammate covering a base to get an advancing runner out, it is said that the fielder **threw the runner out**, as in "Here's the pitch ... Molina belts a sharp ground ball to Rangers third baseman Adrian Beltre... Beltre scoops up the ball and throws out Molina at first!"

The following examples for the Ground Ball Rules should help bring them to life. As a setting, we'll use Game 1 of the 1951 World Series between the New York Giants and the Yankees, played at Yankee Stadium in the Bronx. Why the 1951 World Series? Because my father came here from Ireland in 1951, and that was his first World Series, and he became a huge New York Giants fan, so this is a little tip of the hat to him, but also because that World Series, and the lead up to that World Series, made the 1951 baseball season part of one of the most interesting, most memorable, and perhaps most notorious, seasons in baseball history.

The 1951 World Series was one of the fabled **Subway Series** of the 1940s and 1950s that featured two New York teams playing against each other. (The term Subway Series referred to the fact that you could ride the subway from one team's stadium to the other.) In the ten World Series played between 1947 and 1956, six featured the Yankees against the Brooklyn Dodgers and one, this one, featured the Yankees against the Giants.

You may have noticed that, in my earlier example of a lineup card, I used that of the 2012 World Champions, the *San Francisco* Giants. The relocation of the Brooklyn Dodgers and the New York Giants to the West Coast after the 1957 season, where they became the Los Angeles Dodgers and the San Francisco Giants, is one of the defining events in the history of American baseball. On one hand, the moves transformed the game to a truly national game by locating teams, for the first time, on the West Coast, but on the other hand this purely business-driven decision broke the hearts of hundreds of thousands of abandoned fans back in New York, my father's included.

The 1951 Series, like the eventual move of the Dodgers and the Giants to the West Coast, signaled a ringing out of the old and a ringing in of the new. This was the last World Series to be played by the great Yankees center fielder, Joltin' Joe DiMaggio, otherwise known as the Yankee Clipper, and the first World Series played by two of the great stars of the modern era: Willie Mays of the Giants and Mickey Mantle of the Yankees.

With that background in mind, let's get on to our Ground Ball Rule examples.

Example: Ground Ball Rule # 1: The Yankees are up. Yankees shortstop Phil ("Scooter") Rizzuto (that's right, the same Phil Rizzuto who later, as Yankees announcer, did the voice over for Meat Loaf's song) is at the plate. There are no other Yankees on base. Here's the pitch. Scooter hits a ground ball towards Giants second baseman Eddie Stanky. As Scooter races down to first base, Stanky fields the ground ball cleanly and throws it to first baseman Whitey Lockman, who catches the ball and steps on first base before Scooter gets there. Scooter is out on the force.

- *This was your basic force out. Having hit a ground ball, Scooter runs to first in accordance with the rules of baseball. Therefore the fielding play at first is a force out, executed when Lockman, having caught Stanky's throw and in possession of the ball, merely stepped on first before Scooter got there.*
- *And by the way, when there are no runners on base, the term used is that the **bases are empty**, or there is **nobody on**, as in "There are two outs and nobody on here in the bottom of the sixth."*

Example: Ground Ball Rule # 2: Scooter steps to the plate. Bases are empty. Here's the pitch. Scooter hits a massive shot over the head of the Giants center fielder Willie Mays. The ball bounces several times and rolls toward the outfield fence. Mays turns and gives chase. Scooter, as he runs to first, realizes he will certainly be able to get to first base safely. After all, he's halfway there and Mays hasn't even caught up with the ball yet, nevermind thrown it in to first baseman Whitey Lockman in time for the force out. Scooter knows he will be safe at first, and if he wants to he can stop right there. But Scooter, being the ambitious and competitive chap that he is, chooses to try for second base. He steps on first, and without slowing down a bit, keeps running towards second. Mays, meanwhile, retrieves the ball and seeing Scooter jetting towards second, hurls a bullet to his second baseman, Eddie Stanky, who catches the throw and slaps a tag on Scooter just before Scooter can step on second. Scooter is out at second on the tag out.

- *This is your basic tag out. Scooter was forced to go to first, but it was his own choice, after that, to try to outrun the throw to second base. Therefore, the fielding play at second was a tag play, not a force play. Stanky tagged him before he reached the base, and Scooter was out.*
- *Scooter, to avoid being tagged by Stanky, could have **slid** into second base. A **slide** looks exactly like a tackle in soccer. But in baseball, a slide is an evasive action designed to give Stanky, in this case, the minimum of Scooter's body mass to tag. If Scooter just ran standing up into second base, Stanky could tag his arm, his chest, whatever part of Scooter's body*

The great Ty Cobb demonstrates the art of sliding. Notice that, in addition to coming in feet-first, Cobb is leaning away from the base in a further attempt to make it harder for a fielder to tag him. Cobb, who was never accused of being a charm school graduate, was known to sharpen the spikes on his cleats to further discourage fielders from getting in his way (National Baseball Hall of Fame Library, Cooperstown, New York).

was closest to him. But by sliding, Scooter is coming into the base foot first, so that the only target available is his foot, which is a much smaller target than his chest and arms.

- *There's another advantage to the slide, and another reason why a tag out is more difficult than a force out. Scooter's foot may knock the ball out of Stanky's glove as the tag is applied. If that happens, and if Scooter can then touch second before Stanky can retrieve the ball and re-tag him, Scooter will be safe.*

Example: Ground Ball Rule # 3: Now we are going to make things interesting again by putting a runner on base. Here we go: Scooter steps to the plate. This time, however, let's suppose that by virtue of a previous play, Joe DiMaggio is already a runner at first. Here's the pitch. Scooter hits a weak ground ball to Giants second baseman Eddie Stanky. Scooter, naturally, sprints toward first. DiMaggio, already on first, has no choice but to dash towards second. Stanky catches the ground ball hit by Scooter and, with the ball in his hand, steps on second base before DiMaggio arrives. DiMaggio is out at second on the force.

- *This too is your basic force out. Having hit a ground ball, Scooter has no choice but to run to first, and DiMaggio, already on first, was forced to run to second. Therefore the fielding play at second was a force out, which was accomplished when Stanky, with the ball, merely stepped on second before DiMaggio did.*

- *You may have noticed that we crossed over into new territory in this example. We opened up by saying there are three ways to get a batter out: Fly out, ground out and strike out. But in the above example we spoke about getting a runner out—DiMaggio—on a force play. An out can be made by either a batter or a runner, and the force out and tag out concepts apply not only to a batter who hits the ground ball and advances around the bases, but also to runners already on the bases when the batter hits the ground ball. As this book progresses, we will see that there are other ways that a runner can make out that are unique to a runner—getting caught stealing or getting picked off, for example.*

- *Let's look deeper into Example # 3. Both Scooter, going to first, and DiMaggio, going to second, were potential force plays. Instead of stepping on second to get DiMaggio on the force, Stanky could have instead thrown to first baseman Whitey Lockman to get Scooter on the force. It's just common sense, however, that, if possible, Stanky would rather force out the runner more advanced on the bases, called the **lead runner**, because he was one step closer to home and a greater threat to eventually score. In this case that lead runner was DiMaggio. In situations like this, when, after fielding a ground ball, instead of throwing to first to get the batter out on a force, the fielder throws to another base to get a more advanced runner out, it's called a **fielder's choice**.*

- *Again, both Scooter, going to first, and DiMaggio, going to second, were potential force plays. Stanky, having chosen to get the lead runner, stepped on second to force out DiMaggio. Fine. But suppose Stanky then took a look down at first and realized Scooter had not gotten there yet? If Stanky, having stepped on second to get DiMaggio out, then threw on to first, and if first baseman Lockman caught the throw and stepped on first before Scooter arrived, then that would be a force out as well. In other words, there would have been two force outs (DiMaggio at second and Scooter at first) on one ground ball. Whenever the defensive team gets two outs on one hit ball, it is called a **double play**. Some expressions used to describe a double play are that the defensive team **turned a double play**, or **turned two**.*

- *Terminology break: The term "fielding play" is often just abbreviated to **play**, as in "the play at second was a force out," with the term **make the play** meaning that a fielder was able to successfully register an out on the play, either by throwing to another fielder (as in "Giants second baseman Eddie Stanky fielded the ball and threw on to Whitey Lockman to make the play at first") or by getting the out himself ("Giants second baseman Eddie Stanky fielded the ground ball and made the play at second to get lead runner DiMaggio")*

- *It just occurred to me that baseball has three (!) separate meanings for the word play. A fielder can play his position, a batter can put the ball in play, and a fielder can make a play on a hit ball. For a player just trying to play the game, that plainly could be confusing!*

- *Well, that's kind of played out. Moving on, in a potential double play situation, the lead runner will often purposely choose to slide into base in an effort, not only to be safe, but also to disrupt the fielder and **break up the double play**. In the above example, if DiMaggio were to attempt to slide safely into second just as second baseman Stanky is stepping on second for the first out and preparing to **complete the double play** by throwing on to first base for the second out, Stanky might have to take evasive action while he is throwing and as a result, his throw to first may to be off mark, thus enabling Scooter to be safe at first.*

Why would Stanky take evasive action? Because when a player slides, he comes in feet first. Players wear cleats, and cleats can injure you, or at least hurt like heck, if they kick into you.

- *In some situations, it will be obvious that the runner sliding into a base has no chance at all to be safe at that base, and he is just using that as a pretense to try to break up the double play. That is perfectly permissible, as long as his slide is going generally toward the targeted base. But if, in this example, DiMaggio's slide is nowhere near second base and is too obviously aimed at the fielder, and, as a result, the throw is disrupted and Scooter is safe at first, the second base umpire may rule that DiMaggio committed interference, and both he and Scooter are therefore automatically out.*

- *A quick tribute here to Joe DiMaggio. DiMaggio became famous for many things, including leading the Yankees to nine World Series championships in his 13-year career, his marriage to Marilyn Monroe and his place of honor in Simon & Garfunkel's "Mrs. Robinson." What baseball fans of his time appreciated most about DiMaggio was the fact that, despite his fame and fortune and myriad of baseball accomplishments, he always played hard, always hustled and was never afraid to get his uniform dirty. "There is always some kid who may be seeing me for the first or last time," DiMaggio said, "I owe him my best."*

In this photograph from the 1955 World Series, as Jim Gilliam of the Brooklyn Dodgers slides hard towards him in an attempt to break up the double play, shortstop Phil Rizzuto of the Yankees avoids him by jumping high and throwing on to first. Gilliam, as you can see, has gone far from second base, his ostensible target, in an attempt to disrupt Scooter's throw on to first, but as long as a runner is in the general vicinity of the base he is sliding toward, he will most probably not be called for interference (National Baseball Hall of Fame Library, Cooperstown, New York).

Example: Ground Ball Rule # 4: Scooter steps to the plate. This time, however, DiMaggio is already a runner on third, not first. Here's the pitch. Scooter hits a weak ground ball to Giants second baseman Eddie Stanky. As Stanky fields the ball, Scooter, naturally, commences running toward first. DiMaggio could stay at third because he is not being forced to go further. But let's suppose the Yankees are one run down and Joltin' Joe chooses to be aggressive and run home to try to tie the game. Now you'll have, simultaneously, Scooter running to first and DiMaggio running home. Stanky could elect to get Scooter out on the force by throwing on to his first baseman, Whitey Lockman. But he will most probably want to keep DiMaggio from scoring. Therefore he will probably throw instead to his catcher, Wes Westrum, to try to nail DiMaggio at the plate. Here's the catch: since DiMaggio wasn't forced home, but chose to run home to try to score, Westrum will have to tag him to get him out, and that might be difficult because DiMaggio will no doubt be sliding full force into home and doing his best to dislodge the ball from Westrum's hands.

This example shows that on one play you can have a force play at one base (Scooter on first) and a tag play at another (DiMaggio at home). Taking it a step further, suppose that when Scooter hit his ground ball, Mickey Mantle was on first *and* DiMaggio was on third. Scooter, running to first, would be a force play, Mantle, bumper-carred to second, would also be a force play, but DiMaggio is still not being forced off third. Therefore, again, if he elects to run home, it would be a tag play at home.

- *Would there ever be a time when Stanky would opt to throw Scooter out at first, rather than throw DiMaggio out at home? Yes. If there were already two outs when Scooter came to the plate, then the force out of Scooter at first would be the third out and would end the inning, and DiMaggio would have been unable to score.*

But wait a minute, you ask. Suppose that by the time Stanky threw to first to get Scooter on the force, DiMaggio had already touched home plate: Wouldn't his run have counted then? Good question, but the answer is no, and here's why: The Official Baseball Rules hold that if the third out is a force out of a runner advancing to any base (Scooter, in this case, advancing to first) then, even if a speedy baserunner (DiMaggio, in this case) crosses home plate before that third out is made, his run does not count.

But wait, there's more: If the third out is not a force out, but a tag out, then if a speedy baserunner (DiMaggio, again, in this case) crosses home plate before that third out is made, his run will count. A quick example: DiMaggio on third, Scooter at bat, two outs. Scooter hits a mighty fly ball over center fielder Mays' head. It bounces several times as it rolls to the wall. DiMaggio runs safely home and easily scores a run. Scooter reaches first, then tries to advance to second. Mays throws him out at second. Since DiMaggio stepped on home plate before Scooter was tagged out at second for the third out, DiMaggio's run will count.

- *A quick tribute here to Willie Mays. In these examples, I have referred to balls being hit over his head in center field. I do this almost tongue in cheek, because Willie Mays didn't allow that to happen too often. Mays, certainly one of the top five or six ballplayers to ever play the game, was a spectacular fielder. He was famous for his thrilling **basket catches,** where, instead of reaching overhead to catch a fly ball with two hands, which was and is most common, he held his glove in front of him, anywhere from belt to mid-chest high and* *allowed the ball to drop into it, as if it were a basket. In the first game of the 1954 World Series against the Cleveland Indians, he made what some describe as the greatest catch of all time. With the game tied in the eighth inning and the Indians threatening with two men on, Indians batter Vic Wertz hit a towering blast to dead center that would have been a home run in any other ballpark, but in the Polo Grounds it fell victim to Mays' glove, which had been called "a place where triples go to die." As Wertz's shot soared through the air, Mays turned around and ran full speed back to the center field fence and, with his back completely turned to home plate, he reached up and made an over-the-shoulder catch that saved the game for the Giants.*

- *Terminology break. We spoke above about a situation where Mantle was a runner at first and DiMaggio was a runner at third. When there are runners on first and third, it is often said that there are **runners on the corners**, as in "Scooter steps to the plate with runners on the corners and nobody out." We also spoke about a double play where the second baseman caught the grounder, stepped on second to get the runner coming from first, then threw on to first to get the batter coming from home. In the same situation (runner on first), when a double play is the result of a ground ball hit to the third baseman, who throws on to the fielder covering second, who throws to the fielder covering first, it is said that it is an **around the horn** double play. Where's the horn? I have no idea.*

- *OK, we are almost home, so to speak. Just one more example to go!*

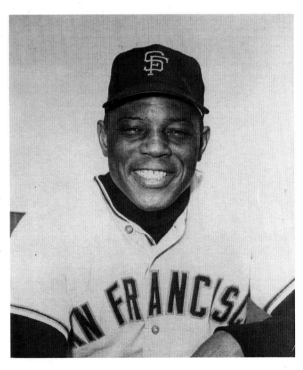

Willie Mays. The so-called "Say Hey Kid" is rated right up there with Babe Ruth, Henry Aaron and Ty Cobb as one of the greatest players of all time (National Baseball Hall of Fame Library, Cooperstown, New York).

Example: Ground Ball Rule # 5. Scooter steps to the plate. This time, the great Yankees catcher, Yogi Berra, is already a runner at second when Scooter comes up. Here's the pitch. Scooter hits a massive shot over the head of Giants left fielder Monte Irvin (we'll give Willie Mays a break this time). The ball bounces several times and rolls to the outfield fence. Irvin turns and gives chase. Scooter, as he runs to first, sees that Irvin still hasn't caught up with the ball, so Scooter, being the ambitious and competitive chap that he is, steps on first base then chooses to keep going to second. Yogi, already on second, has no choice now but to run to third. Irvin retrieves the ball in left and throws a bulls-eye to Giants third baseman Bobby Thomson. Thomson catches the ball and tags Yogi as he slides into third. Yogi is out on the tag out.

- *This is a tricky one because it might seem that Scooter, by not stopping at first, forced Yogi to advance ahead of him, and therefore you might think that Yogi would be a force out at third. But that's not the case. When Scooter chose to advance an additional base, the rules work in such a way that he and all the runners ahead of him, as a unit, are all considered to have chosen to advance an additional base. Put another way, Scooter's ambitiousness and competitive zeal are imputed to all the runners ahead of him, and therefore they all benefit from having the more difficult tag rule apply to them, not the force rule.*

- *In this example, I slowed things down to help make my point, but in real life, of course, Yogi, on second, would not stand around waiting to see if Scooter advanced and bumper-carried him to third. Yogi, like Scooter, would be watching the flight of the ball as it soared over Irvin's head and would have made his own independent assessment (with the assistance of the third base coach) as to how far he could advance and when. Nevertheless, the dichotomy remains that (i) Yogi could not have stayed at second even if he wanted to because of the advancing Scooter, and (ii) despite this, his advance to third would be a tag out situation, not a force out.*

And that's it for the force out/tag out rules. Congratulations! If you've made it through this unscathed, and I'm sure you have, then you've taken a great leap forward in understanding the game of baseball. But before moving on, here are a few final notes on baserunning, nicknames, The Curse, and some other important matters:

- **Overrunning the bases**: A batter, after he hits the ball, and after he runs to first base, can actually keep running straight past first after he steps on first. Like a sprinter after he wins a race, the rules do not require a baserunner to stop on a dime on first base. He is allowed to **overrun** first base. If he's called safe, he can just walk back to first and stand there waiting for play to resume. A runner can also overrun home plate in the same way. If he's running home he can just step on the plate and keep on running to his dugout. Again, he doesn't have to stop on a dime on home plate. However, runners *are* required to stop on a dime on second base and third base. If a runner overruns either second or third, once he's off the base, he can be tagged out by a defensive player. This often happens when runners are sliding and their momentum carries them clear past the base. For that reason you'll sometimes see a sliding runner reach out and grab the base, literally wrapping an arm around it, to stop himself from accidentally sliding completely past it.

- **Tagging on a force play**: A fielder on a force play only has to step on the targeted base with the ball in his hand to get the force out, but he also has the option of tagging the runner instead. Suppose Scooter hits a slow ground ball toward Giants first baseman Whitey Lockman, and Lockman has to run in towards home plate to pick it up. Meanwhile, Scooter is on the verge of charging right past him on his way to first. Once he fields the ball, Lockman has three options: (i) he can try to run back to first base before Scooter gets there and just step on first base, or (ii) if the pitcher or another fielder has run over to cover first while Lockman is retrieving the ball, Lockman can toss the ball to them and they can then step on first and get the force out, or (iii) Lockman can just reach out and tag Scooter as Scooter runs by him.

- In case you're wondering, Yogi Berra was not nicknamed after the cartoon character Yogi Bear. In fact, it was the other way around. Yogi's real name was Lawrence Peter Berra. Reportedly, when he was a child, a friend noticed the similarity in appearance between Berra and a snake charming yogi in a movie, hence the nickname was born. After a long and brilliant career as a Yankee catcher (he played in a record ten World Series winning teams) and as a manager, the elder Berra became famous for his often befuddling sayings, called Yogi-isms, such as "The future ain't what it used to be," "You can observe a lot by watching" and probably his most popular: "It ain't over 'til it's over."

- Since we're on the subject of nicknames, the immortal Babe Ruth's real name was George Herman Ruth. George was born in 1894 above the family tavern in a rough, waterfront Baltimore neighborhood and at the age of seven he was placed by his family in the St. Mary's Industrial School for Boys, a reform school, where he spent the next 12 years of his life. While at St. Mary's, George excelled for the school's baseball team, and earned an invitation from Jack Dunn, owner of the local minor league team, the Baltimore Internationals, to try out for the team. (I will discuss the Minor Leagues, the little brother of the Major Leagues, later in this book.) When he was seen on the field for the first time, someone referred to the young George as "Jack Dunn's newest babe." Babe became his nickname from that point on, but other nicknames eventually stuck as well, including "The Bambino" and "The Sultan of Swat."

The Babe Ruth story is an important one in the annals of baseball and warrants a quick digression. After only three months with the Internationals, he was traded and promoted to the Red Sox. Despite being an excellent pitcher and showing enormous potential as a batter, the Red Sox sold him to the Yankees on December 26, 1919, in what was possibly the worst personnel decision ever made in the history of baseball. The Red Sox owner used the money to invest in a Broadway show that failed and closed soon after. Babe, meanwhile, left pitching behind and went on to become a baseball legend as a prodigious home run hitter, leading the Yankees to four world championships and attracting huge crowds wherever he went. His drawing power led to the construction, in 1922, of Yankee Stadium in the Bronx, the first three-tiered sports stadium in America, which was immediately dubbed **"The House That Ruth Built."**

The Red Sox, meanwhile, sunk to the depths of despair. Babe had led the Red Sox to the World Championship in 1918, but once he was gone, decades of championship-less frustration followed. Red Sox fans, among the most loyal and knowledgeable fans in baseball (the so-called **Red Sox Nation** extends far beyond Boston) believed that the selling of Ruth brought **The Curse,** short for **The Curse of the Bambino,** on the team, because surely their subsequent bad fortune could only be explained by supernatural displeasure at the transaction. Life as a Red Sox fan wasn't made any easier by the fact that the Yankees, even long after Ruth was gone, seemed to always be the team that kept the Curse alive. The result? A rivalry that spanned the decades and is the fiercest in American sports. More on the rivalry later.

- Speaking of rivalries, other intense rivalries in Major League Baseball include the Giants and Dodgers (which is still as heated on the West Coast as it was years ago on the East Coast), the Cardinals and Cubs and the Mets and Braves.
- As an example of just how heated the Mets-Braves rivalry can be, perennial Braves star Chipper Jones enjoyed such success against the Mets, especially in their then-home field Shea Stadium, that in 2004 he named his newborn son "Shea." To Mets fans, Chip-

per was for many years the dreaded Mets Killer, and they were fond of derisively chanting (among other things) his real name ("Laaaary! Laaaary!") whenever he came to the plate. Many never forgave him for his below-the-belt suggestion, after he almost single-handedly knocked them out of playoff contention in 2009, that Mets fans could now "go home and put their Yankees stuff on." Chipper changed his story and years later insisted that he named his son Shea because he liked the name, and not as a dig to Mets fans, but I don't know of any Mets fan who's buying it.

Before we move on to the next section, I have decided, after some initial reluctance, to torture you a little with a fun-filled trick question related to the tag out/force out rules.

Ready? OK, here goes. The Yankees are up. They have runners on first and third. Mickey Mantle steps up to the plate. Here's the pitch. Mickey smacks a hard ground ball up the middle that is gobbled up by Giants second

The Babe (National Baseball Hall of Fame Library, Cooperstown, New York).

baseman Eddie Stanky. Stanky steps on second to force out the runner coming from first, then throws on to first baseman Whitey Lockman to force out the batter. Double play, right? Right.

OK, now let's reverse it. Suppose that hard ground ball is smacked instead down the right field line and is gobbled up by first baseman Whitey Lockman. Lockman steps on first to force out the batter, then throws on to second baseman Stanky to force out the runner coming from first. Double play, right? Wrong.

Wait, what did he just say? Wrong?

Yes, wrong, and here's why. If the first baseman, fielding the ball, steps on first base to get the batter out on the force before he throws on to second, the runner, previously on first and heading to second, is no longer forced to run to second. Why? Because when the first baseman stepped on first, the bumper car that would have bumped the runner over to second—the batter—was forced out and was removed from the equation. The result? The play at second is now going to be a tag play, not a force play.

What's the diff, you ask? Either way, you get the second and third out, right? Either way, the inning is over, right? Yes, but since the third out—the out on the runner going from first to second—is now a tag play, not a force play, that means that the runner on third (remember him?) can score a run if he crosses the plate before that tag play is made for the third out.

Yikes! You think to yourself. That's not good! Is there any way we can prevent that? Yes, there is. If the first baseman, Whitey Lockman, upon fielding the ball, does not initially step on first base to get the bumper-carring batter out, but instead elects to first throw on to Stanky to get the runner, he will have **preserved the force** on the runner going to second. Stanky can then quickly throw back to Lockman to get the force out on the batter. The result? Double play, with the final out being a force out, so that the runner on third doesn't score even if he crosses the plate before the third out is made.

Pretty cool, right? Come on, be honest!

STRIKEOUTS

We've now gone over two of the three ways the defense can get a batter out: a fly out and a ground out.

The third way to get a batter out is by a **strikeout**, or by **striking him out.** Unlike a fly out or a ground out, the strikeout does not involve the batter hitting the ball. In fact, it involves him *not* hitting the ball, or, at least, not hitting it into fair territory.

To strike out a batter, the pitcher needs to throw **three** (naturally!) **strikes** to the batter, and there are (need I say it?) three ways to get a strike.

Swinging Strike

The first way to get a strike is easy. The pitcher throws the ball, and the batter swings the bat at the ball and misses it. This type of strike is called a **swinging strike**.

Sounds simple, and it is, with one small catch. There is no definition in the *Official Baseball Rules* of precisely how far a bat has to be swung to count as a swing, and, hence, a strike. Sometimes a batter begins to swing at a pitch and then changes his mind; he **holds up**, or stops, halfway through his swing and does not complete his swing. Does that half swing, sometimes called a **check swing**, count as a swinging strike, or not?

In the absence of a written rule, a home plate umpire must use his own judgment in determining whether a batter swung or not. Some home plate umpires hold that if the top or head of the bat goes past the front of the plate, then it's a swing. Others hold that if a batter **breaks his wrists**, meaning not that he literally sustains a fracture, of course, but that he allowed his wrists to bend or turn as he swung the bat, then it's a swing.

Either way, if a batter begins to swing, holds up on his swing, and if the home plate umpire rules that he did not swing, the pitcher's manager can **appeal** the decision and ask that either the first or third base umpire be consulted with regarding whether the batter actually swung his bat, or **went around** with his bat, or not. The reasoning is that from their angles they may have had a better view on the arc of the swings of, respectively, a righty or lefty batter. Of course, the first and third base umpires do not have the benefit of an official definition of a swing either, so it's still comes down to a judgment call.

Before we go any further, let's state the not-so-obvious: when a batter comes up to bat, no matter what happens, it does not carry over into his next time at bat. Suppose, a batter comes up in the first inning, swings at the first pitch, misses, then swings at the second and misses that again. He has two strikes on him. Then, let's suppose that on the third pitch he hits a lofty fly ball to center field which is caught on the fly by the center fielder for a fly ball out. His next time up, that batter starts with a clean slate. The two strikes he accumulated in his previous at bat do not carry over.

Foul Ball

The second way to get a strike is easy too. If the batter hits the pitched ball and it lands in foul territory, it is a foul ball. A foul ball is a strike, but (and this is a important), a foul ball cannot be a *third* strike. A foul ball with two strikes already on the batter just doesn't count. Suppose a batter swings and misses at the first pitch. That's strike one. Suppose he hits the second pitch into foul territory, or **fouls off**, the second pitch. That's strike two. Suppose he fouls off the third pitch. That's *not* strike three. It's nothing. He can swing at and foul off the next gazillion pitches, it still won't be strike three.

Let's get a little more specific as to how a hit ball becomes a foul ball:

- Ground balls: If a ball hits the ground and then bounces into foul territory *before* it passes first base or third base, it's a foul ball. If, however, a ball hits the ground, bounces past first base or third base and subsequently bounces into foul territory *after* it passes first base or third base, it's a fair ball and the batter can advance around the bases.
- Fly balls: A ball that stays in the air and lands in foul territory is a foul ball. A ball that stays in the air and lands in the stands is judged to be fair or foul by where in the stands it lands. If the ball lands outside the foul poles, it is a foul ball. If it lands inside the foul poles, it's fair.
- Again, the first and third base umpires decide whether a ball is foul or fair, and will indicate their call by either holding both hands above their head (foul ball) or by gesturing dramatically with one hand towards fair territory (fair ball).
- And just for the record, home plate is in fair territory. That means if a batter swings at a ball and drives it directly down into home plate, it's in play. If the ball bounces off home plate across the foul lines to either side of the batter or behind the batter, it will, however, be a foul ball, just like any other ground ball that rolls into foul territory before it passes first or third. But if the ball bounces off the plate and goes straight ahead into fair territory, it is a fair ball and the batter can advance around the bases.

Two more important rules regarding foul balls:

- If it is caught on the fly by a fielder, a foul ball is an out, just like any other fly ball out. But if it is hit on the ground, a foul ball cannot be picked up by a fielder and thrown to a base for an out. If it's hit on the ground, once it **rolls foul** or **goes foul**, it's a dead ball. It's a strike against the batter, as discussed above, but it's dead as far as the fielders are concerned.
- OK, I lied. There is one time when a foul with two strikes can be a third strike and an out. If, with two strikes on the batter, the batter fouls off the ball straight back into the catcher's glove and the catcher holds onto it without dropping it, the third strike counts and the batter is out. A third strike foul that is held onto by the catcher in this manner, resulting in an out, is called a **foul tip**.

- Honestly, the foul tip rule is one of those stray baseball rules that seem to have dropped out of the sky without rhyme or reason. I've tried to figure out the logic behind it, but I can't. If a batter hits a foul ball high into the air, and a fielder catches it on the fly, it's an out, whether that foul ball would have been strike one, strike two or an infinity of subsequent non-strike-threes. For the sake of consistency, you would think that a foul tip into the catcher's mitt would also count as a kind of fly out, regardless of which strike it might have been. But it doesn't. Only a foul tip on the third strike counts as an out. Embrace the mystery, I guess.
- There is actually a third (naturally) important rule regarding foul balls and third strikes, but we'll discuss that later when we discuss an offensive strategy called the sacrifice bunt.

Called Strike

Earlier, we discussed the duel between pitcher and batter which is at the heart of the game of baseball. Truth be told, as complex as that duel might have seemed in our earlier discussion, we only scratched the surface. The time has come now to add a few important brush strokes to our portrayal of that duel. The focal point of these additional details will be that odd-shaped little slab of white rubber located on the ground next to the batter and in front of the catcher: home plate. Sure we know that if a runner steps on home plate, he scores a run for his team, but home plate plays another vital role in the game of baseball, and that role concerns the third way to get a strike, a **called strike**, which we will discuss now.

While a swinging strike and a foul ball both involve the batter swinging at pitches, a called strike involves the batter *not* swinging at certain pitches that are thrown into an imaginary box floating above home plate called **the strike zone**.

A pitch thrown into the strike zone is, basically, a pitch that can be hit. If a pitch is down by the batter's ankles, or over his head, he can't be expected to hit it. But if it's in the strike zone, the lords of baseball have held that the batter can and should try to hit it. And if he doesn't even try, if he doesn't take a swing at a pitch that's inside the strike zone, he's penalized with a called strike.

Terminology break: In baseball, when a batter doesn't swing at a pitch, it is said the batter **takes** the pitch. You might hear an announcer say: "Here's the pitch, Hobbs takes, and it's a called strike one."

The parameters of the strike zone are dictated by the *Official Baseball Rules*. The sides of the strike zone extend up from either side of the plate, and in the words of the rules, the top of the strike zone is "a horizontal line at the midpoint between the top of the shoulders and the top of the uniform pants"—in other words, the top of the strike zone is about mid-chest height—and the bottom of the strike zone is "a line at the hollow below the kneecap." This is probably the first time in all of world literature that the "hollow below the kneecap" has even been acknowledged as existing, never mind been granted such an important role in human affairs. At any rate, the strike zone is measured not when a batter is standing straight up, but when he is crouched down at the ready in the batter's box, in his **batting stance**, preparing for the pitcher's next pitch. The more a batter crouches down in his batting stance, the smaller the strike zone gets.

The imaginary black outline of the strike zone is part of the strike zone, and since a strike shall be called whenever "any part of the ball passes through any part of the strike zone," the entire pitched ball does not have to pass within the strike zone for a strike to be

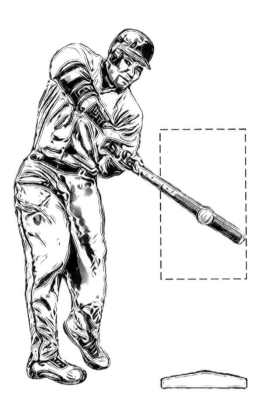

The sides of the strike zone extend upward form the sides of home plate, while the upper boundary is at mid-chest height and the lower boundary is at knee-level (Courtesy PatzImaging).

called. Part of the ball, indeed almost all of the ball, could pass *outside* the strike zone, as long as some small sliver of the ball passes through one of the lines that define its perimeter. In baseball terminology, the lines on the outline of the strike zone are sometimes referred to simply as **the black**, and it is said that the best of pitchers will exploit the outer limits of the strike zone by **pitching on the black**. Another phrase used to describe pitchers who pitch on or close to the black is that they **work the corners** or **paint the corners**.

Pitches in the strike zone are considered pitches that can be hit, but certainly pitches on the black—which, again, are in the strike zone but perhaps too close or too far or too high or too low to be in the batter's ideal comfort zone—are not as easy to hit as pitches thrown right down the center of the strike zone. With that in mind, what do you think batters see more of? "Home plate is 17 inches wide," said Warren Spahn. "I give the batter the middle 13 inches. That belongs to him. But the two outside inches on either side belong to me. That's where I throw the ball."

Earlier, I described a 4-seam fastball as a power pitch coming, at blazing speed, "right down the pipe at the catcher." Let me add now that even the most overpowering of fastball pitchers will work the corners and mix them up from one pitch to the next to keep the batter off guard. Sure, it's coming down the pipe, but which pipe? The pipe that leads to the black on top edge of the strike zone? The bottom edge? The lower right hand corner? The upper left hand corner?

A pitch thrown in the strike zone that the hitter doesn't swing at is referred to as a called strike because the home plate umpire, standing behind the catcher, has the job of making an immediate determination as to whether or not a pitch that the batter did not swing at is in the strike zone. If, in his judgment, such a pitch is in the strike zone, he will holler very loudly "Strike!" or some stylized version thereof (i.e., "Steeeeeeeee-rike!!!") usually accompanied by a fanciful fist punch. Since the home plate umpire is *calling* the pitch a strike, it's therefore called a called strike.

Think of a called strike as one of baseball's moral judgments. Just as the ambitious runner choosing to try for that extra base is rewarded with having the more difficult tag out rule apply to him as opposed to the easier force out rule, the slovenly batter who squanders the opportunity of swinging at a pitch in the strike zone suffers the wrath of a called strike.

So what does the "called strike" mean during the course of a game? Here's what. You're the batter. Here's the pitch. It's coming right down the pipe, looking very fat. You're thinking: I'm going to blast this pitch a country mile. But hold on. Something is fishy here. You remember that this pitcher throws a lot of curveballs. There's a chance this pitch coming right down the pipe toward you is going to drop suddenly, is going to **fall off the table,** just as it reaches you and wind up down around your ankles somewhere, way below the strike zone. So if that might be the case, why swing at it at all? *Now* you know why: because if you don't swing, if it turns out that it's *not* a curve, and if it sails right by you into the strike zone, belt-high, without dropping, it will be a called strike. **Three strikes, you're out**, my friend. You don't have a heck of a lot of leeway here. If this pitch looks like it's going to be in the strike zone, you will be hard pressed not to take a swing at it.

A final word on called strikes. My youngest son William played in the local **Little League**, or youth league, for I guess five years or so, starting at the age of eight, and for most

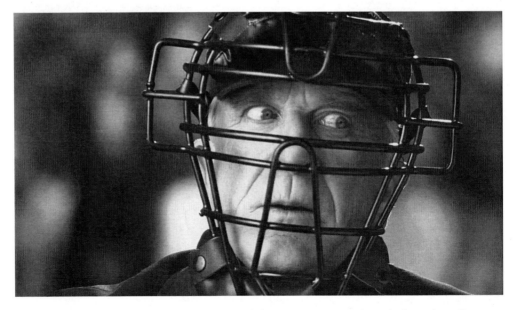

Strike? Leslie Nielsen as the accidental home plate umpire in *The Naked Gun* (1998).

of them he was a catcher, and a pretty good catcher at that. Will, being the bright lad that he is, realized that Little League umpires—just like their Major League counterparts—call pitches based at least in part on where a catcher's mitt is when the pitch is caught. If the catcher's mitt is outside the strike zone: ball. If inside: strike. Will then figured—just like *his* Major League counterparts—that if he could trick the umpires into thinking he caught the ball inside the strike zone, even though he didn't, he just might get them to call a pitch a strike, even though it wasn't.

The practice is called **framing a pitch**. When framing a pitch, a catcher essentially tries to fool the umpire into thinking that a pitch that was just barely *outside* the strike zone, was instead just barely *inside* the strike zone. The way a Major League catcher does it is by catching a pitch midway through a nearly imperceptible sweep of his mitt that brings the pitched ball inside the strike zone a millisecond *after* it is caught.

Like anyone else, umpires don't like to be made fools of, and they have ways of showing their disapproval if they find that a catcher is framing pitches. In Will's case, the Little League umps at the neighborhood field were more amused than irritated that he would mimic his big league idols by trying to frame pitches. However, they were more irritated than amused when he would further mimic his big league idols by shaking his head in exaggerated disbelief when the call didn't go his way. Will, like I said, is a bright lad, and he abandoned the practice after just a few games.

When the third strike is a pitch the batter swings at but misses, the batter is said to have **struck out swinging**. In contrast, when the third strike is a pitch the batter doesn't swing at but is called a strike by virtue of being in the strike zone, the batter is said to have **struck out looking**, since, on some level, the batter just looked at the strike as it sailed by.

Either way, when a batter strikes out, just as the batter who grounded out or flied out, he will leave the field, return to the dugout and an out will be registered against his team.

Again, to state the not-so-obvious: a swinging strike is always a strike regardless of whether or not the pitch is in the strike zone. The strike zone only comes into play when the batter doesn't swing at, or takes, the pitch.

Back to the home plate umpire. Whenever I see a colorfully stylized strike call by a home plate umpire I think of a very funny scene from the movie *The Naked Gun*. Leslie Nielsen plays a bumbling detective looking for bad guys in the middle of a baseball game between the Angels and the Mariners. Trying to get on the field without being noticed, he knocks out the home plate umpire in the locker room and switches clothes with him. He then finds himself on the field, behind the catcher, when the pitcher delivers the first pitch of the game. Nielsen stands there and says nothing. The batter turns and looks at him, the catcher turns and looks at him, because after all, as far as they know he *is* the home plate umpire, and they are both waiting for his call. Finally, Nielsen shrugs and says, softly, "Strike?" The approving partisan crowd erupts in applause. Nielsen looks around, shocked, and, enjoying the instant celebrity, announces the next strike with a little more assertiveness. Again, the crowd goes crazy. Within a few pitches, Nielsen is announcing strikes to the roaring crowd with a combination of moonwalks, splits and cartwheels. Hilarious.

Managers and players are permitted to question or appeal an umpire's decision if there is a reasonable doubt that the decision is in conflict with the rules. However, an umpire can eject any player or manager from the game for questioning a decision that is based on the umpire's judgment. Per that rule, strike calls are not open to debate. The *written* rule, again, says that, as judgment calls, they cannot be questioned under pain of ejection. The *unwritten* rule is that a batter, upset at a called strike, can complain all he wants, but he just can't turn around and complain directly to the home plate umpire. In other words, he can look out at the outfield scoreboard and vent all he wants, curse and swear up a blue streak, but if he turns around and says one hostile word directly to the home plate umpire, there is a good chance he'll be gone.

To illustrate the difference between swinging strikes and called strikes, I'd like to draw your attention to what is probably the most famous strikeout in baseball history: the strikeout of the fictitious Mighty Casey in the poem "Casey at the Bat," written in 1888 by a columnist named Ernest Lawrence Thayer and called by some the most popular poem ever written by an American. In the poem, Casey's fictitious team, Mudville, playing at home, is down by two runs in the bottom of the ninth with two outs and no runners on base. The situation is looking desperate, but the next two Mudville batters somehow manage to get on base, and now, with runners on second and third, mighty Casey, the beloved mighty Casey, steps up to the plate with a chance to tie or even win the game for the adoring crowd.

> *There was ease in Casey's manner as he stepped into his place;*
> *There was pride in Casey's bearing and a smile on Casey's face.*
> *And when, responding to the cheers, he lightly doffed his hat,*
> *No stranger in the crowd could doubt 'twas Casey at the bat.*
>
> *Ten thousand eyes were on him as he rubbed his hands with dirt;*
> *Five thousand tongues applauded when he wiped them on his shirt.*
> *Then while the writhing pitcher ground the ball into his hip,*
> *Defiance gleamed in Casey's eye, a sneer curled Casey's lip.*
>
> *And now the leather-covered sphere came hurtling through the air*
> *And Casey stood a-watching it in haughty grandeur there.*
> *Close by the sturdy batsman the ball unheeded sped-*
> *"That ain't my style," said Casey. "Strike one," the umpire said*

Casey has taken the first pitch, and the home plate umpire has called it a strike. The crowd erupts in anger and threats are screamed at the ump, but the great Casey is able to quiet the crowd.

> *With a smile of Christian charity great Casey's visage shone;*
> *He stilled the rising tumult; he bade the game go on;*
> *He signaled to the pitcher, and once more the spheroid flew;*
> *But Casey still ignored it, and the umpire said, "Strike two."*

Again Casey has taken the pitch; again a called strike. Now, with two strikes, Casey's back is to the wall. One more strike and he's out. Casey quiets the savage crowd, then turns back to the pitcher, this time with a fierce look of determination on his face.

> *The sneer is gone from Casey's lip, his teeth are clenched in hate;*
> *He pounds with cruel violence his bat upon the plate.*
> *And now the pitcher holds the ball, and now he lets it go,*
> *And now the air is shattered by the force of Casey's blow.*
>
> *Oh, somewhere in this favored land the sun is shining bright;*
> *The band is playing somewhere, and somewhere hearts are light,*
> *And somewhere men are laughing, and somewhere children shout;*
> *But there is no joy in Mudville—mighty Casey has struck out.*

A swinging strike, and, since it is strike three, a swinging strikeout. Three outs. Inning over. Ballgame over.

A final note on strikeouts. If, with no one on base, the pitcher strikes out a batter for the first or second out of the inning, the fielders perform what might be called a little on-field celebration by throwing the ball around the infield before giving it back to the pitcher to resume the inning. The catcher, after catching the third strike (be it swinging or called) will triumphantly stand and rifle the ball to the third baseman, who will throw it to the shortstop, who will throw it to the second baseman, who will throw it either to the first baseman or back to the third baseman (it varies), who will then toss it back to the pitcher, who will then resume pitching. It's just one of the thousand little quirky things that make baseball the fun sport that it is.

Pitcher vs. Batter: Casey as Case Study

Although it might seem an unlikely source, a close reading of "Casey at the Bat" reveals a wealth of information about the all-important duel between batter and pitcher. And as we look a little closer at the poem, we'll see many of the things we've been discussing in relation to pitchers and batters start to come together.

Mighty Casey's observation, as he watched the first called strike sail by him, that that particular pitch was just not his "style," is telling. It was the last inning of the game. The opposing pitcher had seen Casey at bat three or four times already, and he probably had a pretty good idea by now of what Casey would, and wouldn't be, swinging at. Furthermore, there is no doubt that in between innings the pitcher and catcher had discussed exactly what Casey's previous at bats had revealed to them about his preferences and "style." Perhaps they had seen him in other games earlier that season as well. If that was the case, there's a good chance that Casey's "style" was the subject of discussion and analysis between the catcher, the pitcher and the manager during a pre-game meeting.

Indeed, if Casey's at bat took place now instead of in 1888, the pre-game meeting would have been enhanced with films of Casey's previous at bats, with complex charts of where in the field Casey tended to hit the ball, called **spray charts**, and with statistics that broke down his "style" in painful mathematical detail: How has he done historically against this particular pitcher? Is he stronger against certain types of pitches and not as strong against others? Can a fastball thrown 95 mph get by him? Is he fooled by a curve? If not, is he fooled by a curve that is **set up** (preceded) by two or three fastballs? Is he over-eager with runners on base? How has he done historically with two outs and runners on base? How has he done historically with the tying or winning runs on base in the ninth inning of home games?

In other words, by the time Casey stepped to the plate in that fateful ninth inning in Mudville, there's a good chance the opposing pitcher knew as much about Casey's style as he knew himself, and was prepared to use that information against him.

Just what *was* Casey's style? Let's look at that first pitch again, the pitch he chose not to swing at: "Close by the sturdy batsman the ball unheeded sped." A called strike, as we know, can be anywhere in the strike zone. A pitch can be on the **inside** of the strike zone (closest to the batter) or on the **outside** of the strike zone (furthest from the batter). This pitch was close to Casey, meaning it was on the inside of the strike zone. Maybe it was even on the black on the inside of the strike zone. Furthermore, there are two reasons to think this pitch was a fastball: first, the narrator twice mentions how fast the pitch was, and second, pitchers often resort to fastballs when pitching inside. A breaking pitch, a pitch with any kind of movement on it, thrown too near to the batter, might result in the pitch accidentally hitting him. I think it's safe to say, then, that the first pitch thrown to the Casey was an inside fastball.

So now we know that an inside fastball is not Casey's style, not his preferred pitch. Welcome to the club, Casey. Inside fastballs are probably nobody's favorite pitch to hit. If a batter hits an inside pitch, chances are it will be a weaker hit than he would have liked because he will not have gotten full arm extension into his swing, and will have hit the ball with a thinner part of the bat lower down than the sweet spot. Casey didn't get the nickname "Mighty Casey" by hitting little doo-doo ground balls, to paraphrase Barry Bonds. So rather than swing at this inside fastball, Casey let it go, preferring to wait to see what the next pitch brought.

Well that's dumb, you might think: if Casey doesn't like inside fastballs, the next pitch is bound to be an inside fastball as well! Not necessarily true. Mighty Casey now knows that the pitcher knows he doesn't like inside pitches, and Casey will, no doubt, make adjustments to guard against the pitcher exploiting that weakness again. For one thing, he might **shorten his swing** by choking up on the bat, meaning, again, he can slide his hands slightly up on the handle of the bat, thereby in effect shortening the bat by two or three inches. Furthermore, he can step back to the outermost rim of the batter's box—the part of the batter's box furthest from home plate—and face the pitcher from there. The effect of these compensating maneuvers is that the next inside pitch will not be as "inside" as it was before. Now, Casey can get a better swing at that inside pitch if the pitcher tries it again.

Casey's situation recalls a story told by pitcher/author/announcer Tom Seaver about the first time he faced his boyhood hero, the great Hank "The Hammer" Aaron, of whom it was said that trying to sneak a fastball past him was like trying to sneak the sunrise past a rooster. In this particular game, the first time Aaron was up, Seaver pitched him inside and induced Aaron to ground out. The next time Aaron was up, Seaver, figuring the inside pitch worked pretty well the previous time, pitched him inside again. Aaron, though, had adjusted by changing his position in the batter's box, as Seaver tells it, "and he hit a home run to left field. And he stopped being my hero that very moment."

And that reminds me of pitcher Juan Marichal's advice on how to pitch to the mighty Aaron: "Throw the ball and close your eyes!" But I digress.

Mighty Casey now knows that the pitcher knows he doesn't like inside fastballs. The pitcher, on the other hand, now knows that *Casey* knows that *he* knows about Casey's aversion to inside fastballs. Throw another inside fastball? Not a chance. Not yet anyway. No, the pitcher might be thinking, let's keep Casey honest and throw the next pitch on the opposite side of the strike zone, the high-outside corner of the strike zone, then maybe come back with an inside fastball for the third pitch.

Casey is certainly not alone in having a "style" or a hitting preference. In his book *The Science of Hitting*, Ted Williams fashioned a diagram which broke down the strike zone into 77 tiny quadrants, and he calculated how well he did with balls thrown in each of them. His style favored pitches that were about belt-high in an area he called his "happy zone." In contrast, the lower outside corner of the strike zone was that place he had most difficulties with, presumably his "unhappy zone." First baseman/author/announcer Keith

Hernandez wrote that he preferred pitches "on the outer three-quarters of the plate." Babe Ruth wrote that his preferred pitch was "a straight fastball and a little below the waist and right up the groove." I can't be sure, nearly a hundred years after he wrote that, what he meant by "right up the groove," but he explained his preference for that type of pitch as follows: "When you catch this ball your upward swing is at its greatest power and if you nail it ... the leverage is there and the blow gets height and distance in the right proportions." If the pitch is any higher than a little below the waist, Ruth noted, "your wallop comes too late to do the best work."

Tom Seaver, in his book *The Art of Pitching*, reconstructed a game he pitched in 1983 against the Cardinals in which his pre-game homework gave him the lowdown on the styles of each of the Cardinals batters. Cardinals second baseman Tommy Herr, for example, was "a dead fastball hitter." Third baseman Ken Oberkfell "liked the ball inside." Left fielder Andy Van Slyke's wallop was most effective with pitches "down and in." The cleanup hitter, George Hendricks, was a pitcher's nightmare who could "cover virtually the entire strike zone with his quick bat" and whose only weakness was a "lower four-inch square of the outside corner."

One of my favorite stories about how extensively pitchers and catchers study their opponent's hitting styles involves then–Dodgers catcher Russell Martin, who, prior to games, was routinely spot-quizzed by his pitching coach, Rick Honeycutt. One day, before a 2009 game against the Cardinals, Honeycutt threw a random name at Martin, that of Cardinals infielder Ryan Ludwick. Martin immediately rattled off the prognosis: "Aggressive first-pitch fastball hitter. If you're going to throw him an off-speed pitch, especially early, you don't want to just throw him a get-me-over strike, you want to make sure it's a good one. The curveball is probably a pitch you want to keep down in the zone, but you can throw that for strikes early in the count. He will chase the sinker that runs into him. Because he has a hitch in his swing, you can beat him with fastballs with good velocity later in counts."

Casey took the first pitch, a called strike. It wasn't his style, we know that, but was there another reason? Did Casey have an ulterior motive in taking the first pitch? Third baseman Wade Boggs, one of the greatest hitters of the modern era, was famous for taking first pitches as a personal policy. Boggs preferred to use the first pitch to analyze the pitcher's movements, release point and speed. He sacrificed the first pitch throughout his career to learn something about the pitcher, the better to prepare him for the pitches that followed. He didn't mind that the pitchers, who eventually caught on to the fact that he would never swing at the first pitch, always, then, threw what amounted to an uncontested first strike. Boggs was confident that what he was learning outweighed the disadvantage he put himself at.

Esteemed second baseman (and also author and announcer) Joe Morgan was in agreement, writing that he learned early in his career that "by swinging at a first pitch you deprive yourself of an advantage that comes from being able to measure a pitcher through his repertoire. The more pitches you take, the more you see what he has. The more you see what he has, the more prepared you are."

What do we suppose was the pitcher's second pitch to Casey? There is a good chance that the pitcher, as discussed, thought it would be wise to lay off the inside fastball for the moment and go to the other side of the plate to keep Casey on his toes. Casey "ignored" the second pitch. The choice of words is important. I would venture to say he ignored it because as he watched it approach, he did not think it would end up in the strike zone. But it did. That Casey was subsequently so angry at himself, not at the umpire, leads me to believe he was fooled, and fooled badly, by a backdoor slider, a pitch that seemed headed outside the far side of the strike zone but then broke back into it at the last moment.

Their deceptive movement is the beauty of breaking pitches like the slider and the curve. "The best pitch in baseball," said the renowned Lew Burdette, "is the one that looks like a strike and then isn't." Note the choice of words: a pitch that looks like a strike and *then* isn't. In other words, a pitch that appears to be a strike while it is en route to the plate but then, somewhere along the way, either drops below or veers away from the strike zone and leaves the batter swinging at a pitch that isn't where he thought it would be. Casey, it seems, was victimized by the reverse: a pitch that looked like it *wasn't* a strike, then *was*.

What would the third pitch be? In a way, it doesn't matter. Down by two strikes, having lost his composure and perhaps even his confidence, facing a pitcher with outstanding control on his fastball and outstanding movement on his breaking ball, Mighty Casey was a dead duck. He couldn't afford to take another pitch. He would now have to **protect the plate** by swinging at anything that was even close to the strike zone. The best he could hope for probably was to **stay alive** by fouling off a few pitches, and maybe in those pitches picking up something helpful about the pitcher's movement or delivery—like Babe Ruth's sticking out his tongue before a curveball.

He didn't. Casey swung mightily at the third pitch and missed: a swinging strikeout. My guess is that the third pitch to Casey was a curveball, which, again, is a pitch that seems headed right into the middle of a strike zone, then suddenly drops and winds up somewhere between the batter's knees and ankles. In Casey's case, watching the pitch sail right toward what Ted Williams called his "happy zone," some part of him, in that fraction of a second before the pitch reached him, must have thought: "Finally, a pitch that is my style, a pitch I can wallop, a pitch I can **get good wood on** and send all these people home happy." To paraphrase Lew Burdette: It was, and then it wasn't.

A three-pitch strikeout that costs your team the game is never a good result, but it might not be the final result. It's very possible that the opposing pitcher was a brand new rookie that neither Casey nor his Mudville teammates had ever seen before. I say this only because Casey was so woefully unprepared for him. Even a great hitter like Keith Hernandez will be the first to tell you: sometimes, the pitcher you know nothing about will be most dangerous. He has no history, no paper trail. Outside of what you've seen so far in that particular game, you have no knowledge of his habits, his preferences, his weaknesses, and his tip-offs.

My guess is that Casey and his manager will get together after the game and start preparing right away, using what they learned in this game for the next time they see this young pitcher. The weapons that he used to obtain the victory this time would be broken down and analyzed in excruciating detail. What was the pitcher's best pitch? What was the pitch he always went to when he was in a jam? Did his curveball break early or late? How fast is his fastball? How lively is it? He used his fastball to set up his backdoor slider against Casey: is this a favorite sequence of his? Did he tip off his pitches in any way? One of the things they will no doubt look into is that, before the first pitch, the inside fastball, the pitcher had "ground the ball into his hip." Was this some kind of habit? Did he ground the ball into his hip before every fastball? Maybe only before inside fastballs? Maybe only before inside fastballs with runners on base?

By the next time they meet, a better prepared Casey would no doubt step into the batter's box to face this pitcher: a better prepared Casey and, dare I say it, a Mightier Casey because of it. I don't know about you, fair reader, but if I were a betting man, I'd wager that after the next encounter between these two ballplayers, the sun will be shining brightly once again on dear old Mudville.

The Dropped Third Strike

OK, one more thing about third strikes. A catcher must complete a strikeout by catching the third and final strike. In that sense, the third-strike-as-out is made consistent with every other type of out, in that the ball must be caught for an out to be made. This is true on fly balls, certainly, but on ground balls as well, where the infielder covering the relevant base must either catch the ball hit by the batter or catch a throw from another infielder before he applies the tag or the force, as applicable.

If the catcher doesn't catch the third strike, if he drops it, the runner can run to first base just as if he had hit a ground ball. The catcher, once he retrieves his dropped third strike, can either tag the batter out, if he's still in the vicinity, or he can throw the batter out as he tries to scamper down to first. If the catcher does either, the out still goes into the books as a strikeout. If the runner is safe at first, it goes into the books as… a strikeout as well, but at the same time it won't count as a third out, and the inning will continue until an official third out is made.

The dropped third strike doesn't happen very often, and it will be uneventful the vast majority of times. But the dropped third strike can have disastrous consequences, as it did for the Brooklyn Dodgers in the 1941 World Series against the Yankees. The Dodgers held a 4–3 lead going into the ninth inning of Game Four when, with two outs and Tommy Henrich at the plate for the Yankees, Dodgers catcher Mickey Owen dropped the called third strike that would have ended the game. Henrich beat Owen's throw to first and started a rally for the Yankees that saw them win 7–4 and take a 3-games-to-1 lead in the Series. The next day, the Yankees won again and claimed the championship.

Signs

As discussed, catchers and pitchers study opposing hitters before each game and formulate a game plan for each batter based on what they've found out to be his tendencies and, hopefully, his weaknesses. Once the game starts, the catcher will proceed to **call the game**, meaning that he will decide what each pitch to each batter will be, in accordance with that game plan. The catcher, as he is squatting behind the plate, will communicate to the pitcher which pitch he wants him to throw by lowering fingers on his ungloved hand between his thighs, near his groin area and sending the pitcher **signs**. One finger might mean: throw a fastball. One finger pointing toward the catcher's thigh closest to where the batter is standing might mean: throw an inside fastball. One finger toward the catcher's thigh furthest away from where the batter is standing might mean: throw an outside fastball. Two fingers might mean a curveball, three a change up, and so on

The catcher, not the pitcher, calls the game because first of all, if the pitcher gave the signs to the catcher, the batter would be able to see them, and if he figured them out he would know what kind of pitch was coming. But there's another reason. The catcher has a better view of and feel for the effectiveness of the different pitches. When a pitcher throws a pitch, he often loses sight of it in his follow through. The catcher, on the other hand, will know exactly how and where a curveball is breaking, for example, or how much "pop" a fastball has. Furthermore, he will have a bird's eye view of how badly a batter is fooled by a pitch, or not.

The pitcher, however, has veto power. If the pitcher disagrees with the catcher's pitch selection and wants him to change it—for strategic reasons or for physical reasons, in the sense that, for example, his arm might suddenly begin to hurt when he twists his hand in his curveball delivery—he can **shake off the sign** simply by shaking his head "no." The catcher will then give him an alternate sign, and when the pitcher and catcher finally agree, the pitcher will give a very slight nod of his head and go ahead with the pitch.

If there is a runner on second the catcher has to be on guard for that runner **stealing signs**. The runner on second, if you can picture it, has a clear view of the catcher. He can see what the catcher is calling for, and if his team has deciphered the catcher's signs, he, in turn, can send a sign to the batter. He can raise his hat, for example, if the catcher has called for a fastball. He can raise his hat with his right hand if it's a fastball inside. He can raise his hat with his left hand if it's a fastball outside.

To prevent a runner on second from stealing signs, the catcher might mix in a bunch of decoy, misleading signs to the pitcher, with it agreed on beforehand that, for example, only the second sign counts. Or the catcher might just jog out to the pitcher and tell him personally what the next pitch should be, all the while covering his mouth with his glove so no one on the other team can read his lips.

There are other, more devious and more inherently dishonest ways to steal signs. Earlier, I used the 1951 World Series between the Yankees and Giants to set the stage for the Ground Ball Rules. I used the word "notorious" in describing the 1951 season. Here's why.

The Giants run to the World Series that year was a classic nail-biter. They came from far behind in the standings, ending the season by winning 42 of their last 48 games and finished tied for first with their archrival, the Brooklyn Dodgers. A three-game playoff series was scheduled to determine which team would advance to the World Series. The Giants won the first game, the Dodgers the second, and the third and deciding game, won by the Giants, involved what is no doubt the most infamous case of sign stealing in baseball history.

The third game was played in the Polo Grounds, home field of the Giants. The Dodgers were ahead going into the bottom of the ninth by 4–1. The Giants scored a run to cut the lead to 4–2, put two runners on base and then Bobby Thomson hit a three-run homer to win the game for the Giants and advance them to the World Series. Considering the fierce nature of the Dodgers-Giants rivalry, and considering what was at stake, and considering also that these three games were the first baseball games to be nationally televised, that home run is considered by many to be one of the most important and dramatic home runs in baseball history. Indeed, it became known as **"The Shot Heard 'Round the World."**

Since then, however, it has been established that Giants batters, most probably including Bobby Thomson, were the beneficiaries of a very elaborate sign-stealing system put in place by their manager, a coach and a local electrician who, ironically, was a Dodgers fan. Here's how it worked. In the Polo Grounds, the Giants clubhouse was located in a small office under the center field scoreboard. The Giants cut away a small part of the mesh wiring protecting one of the clubhouse windows and set up their assistant coach with a telescope just inside that window. From that secret perch, he was able to zoom in with his telescope on the Dodgers catcher and read the signs he sent to the Dodgers pitcher. The electrician had set up a simple buzzer system that ran from that center field clubhouse to the Giants bullpen and dugout, and the assistant coach, reading the sign with his telescope in the clubhouse, used that buzzer system to signal what pitch was coming next to the dugout and the bullpen. One buzz meant fastball, for example, two buzzes meant curveball, and so on. This knowledge was then forwarded from the dugout to the Giants batter by hand signals.

The Giants may have beaten the Dodgers, but their telescope apparently didn't help them, or at least didn't help them enough, against the Yankees in the World Series. The Yankees, with Scooter, Joltin' Joe, Mickey Mantle and Yogi Berra leading the way, won the Series in six games. Sorry, Dad!

As a final word on the three outs necessary to terminate a side's turn at the plate, be aware that announcers have many terminologies for an out that may confuse you, at least initially. A batter who makes an out is sometimes spoken of as having been **retired** by the pitcher. The most common alternative phrases for, say, two outs, are two **away** or two **down**. An inning where three batters come to the plate and all three make out, is often referred to as a **1, 2, 3 inning** or an inning where there was **three up, three down**, or an inning the batters were **retired in order**, or an inning where the pitcher **retired the side**. Thus you might hear an announcer say something like "Justin Verlander of the Tigers retired the Blue Jays in order in the bottom of the first, and now here in the bottom of the second we have one away with Jays shortstop Jose Reyes stepping to the plate."

Objectives of the Offensive Team

OVERVIEW

We just learned that the defensive team's objective is to force or induce the offensive team get three outs, hopefully before they can score a run. We will now discuss the objectives of the offensive team, which are two-fold. The first objective is to put a runner on base, which we will cover in this section. The second objective is to advance that runner around the bases so that, before three outs are made, he crosses home plate and scores a run. We will cover that topic in the next section.

By way of introduction, there are four principal ways a batter can get on base and become a runner: by getting a hit, by walking, by getting hit by a pitch and by reaching base as the result of a fielder committing an error. There are other ways, and we will mention some in passing, and there are still others that are so rare that not only have I never seen them, but I only learned about them when I was researching this book. I haven't needed to know them, you don't need to know them, and we won't cover them.

Three quick preliminary notes:

- While we are discussing the four principal ways of getting on base, keep in mind that once a batter gets on base and becomes a runner, the rules about advancing around the bases and scoring a run are the same regardless of how he got on base in the first place. None of the methods of getting on base are superior or more valuable than the others.

- There is no limit to how many batters can come to the plate during a team's half-inning. One earmark of a very productive offensive inning is that the entire lineup—nine players—comes to bat during an inning, and then the initial batter comes up for a second time during the same inning, all before three outs are registered. This is called **batting around**. Batting around is an unspecific phrase that just means the lineup was gone through once, and then some, during a particular inning. If a team bats around during an inning, it means that they sent up at least ten batters. You might hear an announcer say: "The Rockies batted around in the bottom of the sixth and scored five runs."
- With that in mind, for the record, there is also no limit to the number of runners an offensive team can put on base, by whatever means, during an inning, nor is there a limit to the number of runs a team can score in an inning. Until three outs are made, the offensive team can just keep putting on runners and piling on runs and batting around.

PUTTING RUNNERS ON BASE

Hits

The basic way for a batter to get on base and become a runner is for that batter to get a "hit."

When I was a wee lad playing in the local Little League, I once hit the ball three times in one game. All resulted in ground ball outs, but I was nevertheless very proud of myself. I bragged to my friends that I had gotten three hits. No, they said, you actually had no hits. But I hit the ball three times! I complained. Yes, you did, they said, but you still didn't get any *hits*.

They were right. In baseball, batters hit the ball all the time, but if the hit results in an out, it's not called a "hit." Yes, the announcers will say: "Roy Hobbs *hit* the ball into a double play," but there's a difference between hitting the ball and getting "a hit." A **hit** in baseball is when a batter hits the ball and one of four things happen as a result: a **single** (batter hits the ball and runs safely to first and stops there), a **double** (batter hits the ball and runs safely to second and stops there), a **triple** (batter hits the ball and runs safely all the way to third and stops there) or a home run. That's it. Anything else is not considered a hit. A single is often referred to as a **base hit**. A double or triple is often referred to, respectively, as a **two-base hit** or a **three-base hit**, or, in the alternative, either can be referred to as an **extra base hit**.

The Home Run

Let's start our discussion of hits with the ultimate hit, the definitive and most simple offensive weapon: the **home run,** otherwise known as the **homer** or, less commonly, the **round-tripper** or **four-bagger**. Another expression for hitting a home run is that the home run hitter **took the pitcher downtown**, as in "Buster Posey of the Giants took Dodgers ace Clayton Kershaw downtown in the fifth inning." For the sake of completeness, I must add that a new and rather annoying term for hitting a home run is that a player **went yard**, as in "Buster Posey went yard in the fifth inning." The term "homer" can be used as a verb as well, meaning that a person hit a home run, as in "Posey homered in the fifth inning."

I call the home run the ultimate offensive weapon because when a batter hits a home run, he automatically advances around all the bases, steps on home plate and scores a run, as does every runner on the base when he hits the home run.

A batter hits a home run when he hits the ball out of the park (over the outfield fences) on the fly, in fair territory. It's that simple. When a batter hits a home run, the play is dead. He's awarded the home run automatically, meaning that the outfielder can't climb over the fence and retrieve the ball and try to throw the batter out as he runs around the bases. No, the home run hitter can trot around the bases at a somewhat leisurely rate and enjoy his moment in the sun. In fact, his leisurely run is widely referred to as **the home run trot**. He trots from the batter's box to first to second to third to home. He steps on home, and thus, scores a run for his team.

Again, any runner already on base when the home run is hit also scores automatically. Suppose there is a runner on first when the home run is hit. He trots home and scores a run too, so that in this case, the home run resulted in two runs: the run scored by the batter who hit it, and also by the runner who was standing on first when it was hit.

A home run hit with no other runner on base is called a **solo homer**, because, since no one else was on base, only the batter himself scores a run. A home run with one other runner on base is called a **two-run homer** because that homer resulted in two runs scoring: the batter and the runner on base. A homer with two runners on base is called a **three-run homer**, and a homer with runners on each of the three bases (called **bases loaded**) is the ultimate of the ultimate offensive events, as it results in four runs being scored, and is called a **grand slam**.

The home run, as ultimate offensive event, is also the most dramatic event in the game. Baseball can be exciting for many reasons: a great catch, a great pitching performance, an infamous mistake by a fielder. But years later, it will mostly be the home runs that you remember. I opened this book telling about the soaring home run hit by the mighty A-Rod to end that extra-inning marathon against the Red Sox that I attended with my three boys. A great homer indeed, but when I think of other dramatic home runs I was in attendance for, three come immediately to mind, because I was there, yes, I was, for the fabled Game Six of the 1977 World Series between the Yankees and the Dodgers. In that game, played at Yankee Stadium, Yankee outfielder Reggie Jackson turned in a performance for the ages by hitting three home runs off three different pitchers, all on the very first pitch they threw to him. In fact, I darn near caught the third one.

Here's how it happened. In 1977, I was working for the *Daily News* as a reporter's assistant, called a copyboy, and one of our duties in that pre–Internet world was to go with photographers to sporting events and, after he or she finished shooting a roll or two of film, we would take the film, run outside, jump in a company car, drive back to the office and drop the film off so that it could be developed and the pictures used in the early edition of the next morning's newspaper. Then we would race back to the stadium, rejoin the photographer, and await the next rolls of film.

At Yankee Stadium, the news photographers were located in little booths cut into the wall above the black, vacant seats in center field. From that location, our cameras (like the Giants illegal telescope in the 1951 Polo Grounds) could zoom right in on the catcher and batter, and from there I could see each of Reggie's home runs very clearly. I remember that his third home run of the game was a towering shot, a mammoth blast hit a mile high into the night sky, and I remember thinking, as it started to descend: Wow, that looks like its coming right at me. And then I remember thinking that it was, in fact... *coming... right... at me!* And then I remember thinking: *Help!*

In another moment, however, the falling arc of the ball revealed that, instead of smashing into my tender cranium, it was going to land maybe twenty or thirty feet in front of me, in the blackened center field bleacher seats below. Emboldened, I lowered myself out of the booth and started running-hopping down the black seats toward where I gauged the ball would land. The problem was, I was coming from in from an angle, while another kid from an adjoining photographer's booth (the darn *Times*, probably!) was coming straight down and directly toward the landing zone. I quickly realized he was going to get there first, so I decided to fall in behind him, figuring there was no way he was going to catch the ball, and I would be there to grab it on the bounce. I was wrong. The kid didn't catch the ball, but, as I remember, it landed, bounced up, hit him in the chest, then fell in front of him, and he simply reached down and picked it up.

I may not have caught the ball, but I made it into the highlight films. The official World Series video follows Reggie's third home run into the blackened seats and lingers there just long enough to catch a glimpse of three cloudy figures scrambling madly down the blackened seats towards the ball. I'm the madly scrambling cloudy figure on the right.

Two footnotes to that story: First, I heard later that that kid who caught the ball returned it to the Yankees in exchange for a crisp $100 bill. Seeing what Internet auction houses have done to the price of collectible baseballs like that one, he's probably been kicking himself ever since. Second, Reggie Jackson, because of his clutch hits in postseason games like that one against the Dodgers, went on to earn what is probably the most complimentary nickname ever given to a baseball player: "Mr. October."

I don't think too many people would argue with me that the most famous moments in baseball history are almost all home runs. In the 1932 World Series, Babe Ruth responded to the heckling of the Chicago players and fans by "calling his shot"—pointing to the exact spot over the center field fence where he would deposit the next pitch. Sure enough, on the very next pitch, that's exactly what he did. By the way, some curmudgeons, over the years, have argued that Ruth was in fact only pointing out some unruly fans to the home plate umpire, and that the "called shot" story was just urban myth. But the issue was recently settled by no less an authority than the Supreme Court of the United States, which ruled in favor of the called shot. Actually, I exaggerate, though ever so slightly: on his retirement, Justice John Paul Stevens of the United States Supreme Court was interviewed regarding some of his more important legal opinions, and he revealed that, as a twelve-year-old, he was present at that game and there is no doubt in his mind Ruth called his shot.

We've already discussed "The Shot Heard Round the World," which, for better or worse, is still considered one of the most dramatic home runs of all time, but probably the most dramatic home run of my life time occurred in the first game of the 1988 World Series between the Dodgers and the Oakland A's. Kirk Gibson of the Dodgers had been one of the stars of his team throughout the year despite recurring leg injuries, but come the World Series, those injuries had gotten so bad that he was unable to start the first game, spending almost the entire game in the locker room with ice packs piled on each knee. But with the Dodgers down 3–2 going into the bottom of the ninth, Gibson volunteered to pinch hit and so, with two outs and a runner on first, he limped to the plate. He fouled off the first two pitches, nearly falling over after he swung, barely able to stand up on his injured legs. When he hit a third foul ball up the first base line that he initially ran on, thinking it might stay fair, his limp was so noticeable that the announcers commented: "It's one thing to favor one leg, but you can't favor two." A fourth foul ball kept him alive, then he limped back up to the plate and hammered the next pitch over the right field fence to win the game for the Dodgers. His joyous, repeated fist-pumping as he limped around the bases, is one of the most famous images in modern baseball history.

The Yankees-Red Sox rivalry is full of dramatic home runs. Two good but somewhat less than fearsome Yankees, shortstop Bucky Dent and third baseman Aaron Boone, broke Red Sox hearts by hitting home runs that, respectively, helped win a one-game playoff in 1978 after the two teams finished the season tied for first, and won the seventh and deciding game of the 2003 American League Championship Series to earn the Yankees a berth in the World Series. Since his devastating home run, Boston fans have so often referred to Bucky Dent with an added expletive, that to many, his full name is now simply "Bucky F*cking Dent."

Just as Bucky F*cking Dent's home run might still be a painful memory to many Red Sox fans, the mere mention of the year between 2003 and 2005 makes every Yankees fan cringe. That year, the Red Sox and the Yankees were again playing in the best-four-of-seven American League Championship Series, and the Yankees won the first three games and were even ahead going into the bottom of the ninth inning in game four. Boston rallied, won the fourth game and won the next three to become the first and only team in baseball history to win a seven game post-season playoff series after losing the first three. The Red Sox went on to win the World Series and the Curse, sadly, was dead. Red Sox outfielder Johnny Damon iced the seventh and deciding game with a grand slam in the second inning.

Walk up to any semi-knowledgeable baseball fan and mention the name Joe Carter of the Blue Jays, or Bill Mazeroski of the Pirates, and they'll tell you stories of heart-stopping World Series winning home runs. Walk up to any semi-knowledgeable baseball fan and ask them how many home runs Babe Ruth hit in his career and they won't hesitate: 714. Ask them about Hank Aaron: 755. Ask them about Barry Bonds, the all time leader in career home runs: 762. Ask them who hit the most home runs in a single season: Babe Ruth, 60 in 1927, topped by Roger Maris, 61, in 1961, topped by Mark McGwire with 70 in 1998, and, finally, by Barry Bonds with 73 home runs in 2001. Mention the name Carlton Fisk and they will not only tell you about his dramatic home run that won the sixth game of the 1975 World Series for the Red Sox against the mighty "Big Red Machine," the Cincinnati Reds, but they will also probably be able to imitate his famous celebratory run around the bases. Ask any baseball fan what Ted Williams did on the last at bat of his remarkable career: he hit a home run.

Starting with the 2008 season, certain home runs were subject to opposing team challenges and instant replay review by the umpires. This was the first time the use of instant replays was permitted in baseball, and its use was initially limited to those instances when a controversy exists as to whether the home run ball actually *was* a home run ball.

For example, sometimes a fly ball clears the fence so close to the foul line that it is difficult to tell with the naked eye whether the ball went over the fence in fair territory (a home run) or in foul territory (not a home run). Other times a descending fly run ball drops very close to the fence and suddenly ricochets quickly back onto the field. It can be difficult to tell whether the ball actually cleared the fence and hit something in the stands—a seat perhaps—then bounced back into the field (a home run) or only hit the top of the fence or the outside edge of the fence before bouncing back (not a home run).

Let's take it a step further. Suppose a fly ball is coming down in fair territory just barely over the outfield fence, an apparent home run. But before it drops beyond the wall, suppose the outfielder leaps up, reaches back over the fence and catches it on the fly. Not a home run, right? Correct. But let's further suppose that, just as he is about to catch the ball, a fan in the first or second row of the outfield seats, also intent on catching the descending ball so that he can claim a nice souvenir, inadvertently bumps the leaping outfielder's glove and prevents him from catching the ball and as a result the ball drops uncaught into the stands. A home run? Not a home run? Fan interference with players trying to make a catch on a fly ball has a rich and storied past in Major League Baseball, and the **fan interference rule** warrants a quick digression.

Earlier we spoke about how lucky fans who caught certain record-breaking home run balls made a lot of money on the memorabilia resale market. Most baseballs hit into stands, of course, are not worth more than a few dollars, but almost every one will nevertheless result in fans leaping and reaching and diving over and under each other to try to retrieve them as a souvenir.

Now, if a foul ball is hit deep into the stands, it's no problem: fans can kill each other trying to get the ball without interfering with play on the field. The problem emerges when a fly ball is coming down along the edge of the playing field where both the fans in the front rows, looking for a souvenir, and the fielder, looking to make a catch for a fly out, will wind up getting in each other's way.

And that's where the fan interference rule comes in. The rule states that the fans have a right to fly balls hit into the stands. In other words, if a fly ball is coming down in the stands and a fielder reaches into the stands and makes a catch, fine, it's a fly out. But if a fan, also trying to catch the ball, gets in his way and prevents him from catching it, well, too bad: the result stands. If the ball dropped into foul territory, then, despite the fact that the outfielder would have caught it were it not for the fan, it's a foul ball, and if it dropped into home run territory, then, likewise, it's a home run.

Conversely, the fielders have a right to balls in the field. If in the umpire's opinion, a fielder is clearly prevented from catching the ball in fair territory by an over-eager fan who reaches out of the stands and over the field, thus preventing the fielder form catching the ball for an out, the result will *not* stand. The umpire will rule the play dead and call the batter out, so as to "nullify the act of interference" by the fan.

The difficulty is that it is not always clear whether the ball is coming down in the stands (no fan interference) or fair territory (potential fan interference). I mean, just picture it: a batter hits a possible home run ball a mile high in the air, and as it drops out of the night sky at breathtaking speed in the general vicinity of the bleachers, two dozen fans and one outfielder all jump at once trying to catch it. Was its downward arc going to drop the ball into the outfield? Or one or two feet further out and into the stands? Who the heck can tell? Even instant replay won't always give a clear answer.

Which leads me to a story of the most infamous episode of fan interference—that actually *wasn't* fan interference, by the way—in baseball history. The year was 2003, the place was Chicago's Wrigley Field, and the event was the sixth game of the National League Championship Series between the Cubs and the Florida Marlins (now the Miami Marlins). The Cubs led the seven-game series, three games to two, and led the sixth game by 3–0 in the top of the eighth. The Marlins were at bat. They had a runner on second with one man out, but the Cubs were clearly in the driver's seat. They were five outs away from the World Series.

But first, a little background. As of this writing, the Cubs have not won a world championship since 1908, and their last trip to the World Series was 1945. Like the Red Sox in the good old days, Cubs fans attribute their title drought to a curse. The story has it that in 1945 a fan showed up at the ballpark eager to cheer his team on, but was denied admission because he was accompanied by his goat. Why he brought his goat with him, nobody knows. But he did, he was refused admission, and in his anger he placed a curse on the Cubs. Apparently, the **Billy Goat Curse** was effective. They haven't been to the World Series since.

But in the eighth inning of that sixth game of the 2003 NLCS, the end of the Billy Goat Curse seemed a strong possibility. Cub hearts were soaring. Maybe this would be the year after all. One out in the eighth. A three run lead. It was so close. It was all there, so close....

And then something happened. Luis Castillo, the Marlins batter, lofted a high fly ball down the left field foul line, toward the edge of the stands. Cubs left fielder Moises Alou raced over to the fence, which was perhaps seven feet high, looked up, clearly had a bead on the descending ball, then jumped and reached just over the wall into the stands. If the stands were empty, there is little doubt he would have caught the ball for the second out of the inning. But, of course, the stands were full.

Sometimes, the pure childish joy of catching a major league baseball pushes other considerations out of a fan's mind, considerations like what consequences his or her actions might have on their team's chances of winning the game. This was one of those times. As Alou reached in to make the catch, at least five fans reached to make the catch as well, and at least one, probably two, seemed to get between Alou and the ball, deflecting it away from his outstretched glove and preventing him from catching it for the second out.

Let's stop the action for a moment and review. The ball was coming down in the stands. Not by much. Maybe by a foot or two. But Alou, when he jumped to make the catch, was clearly reaching *in*. Since the ball was in the stands, it was not fan interference, and no nullification of the fans' actions was mandated. Thus, when the ball skipped away from Alou's outstretched mitt and landed in the stands as a foul ball, that was the result that stood: a foul ball, and the situation remained the same: one out and a runner on second. Luis Castillo, the batter, and the Marlins, weren't through yet.

What followed next was a Cubs fan's worst nightmare. And, over the last hundred years or so, Cubs fans have had a *lot* of nightmares. ("I always believed that being a Cubs fan built strong character," one writer opined. "It taught a person that if you try hard enough and long enough, you'll still lose. And that's the story of life.") The Marlins, revitalized by the lucky break in left field, went on to score no less than eight runs in that inning. As stunned Cub fans watched the game spin further and further out of control, there was no doubt in their mind that the Billy Goat Curse was still alive. There was also no doubt in their mind that it was all the fault of the fan whose outstretched hands, in their opinion, prevented Alou from catching the ball for the second out. The Fan, let's call him, became the object of taunts and jeers and chants then, soon enough, shouted threats and thrown objects, including, naturally, cups of beer.

The scene got uglier and uglier. Finally, a phalanx of security guards worked their way down to The Fan and escorted him into hiding in the security office. The next day, in the interests of freedom of the press, the *Chicago Sun-Times* published his picture, his name, the place where he worked and his hometown. No less a luminary than the then governor of the state of Illinois, Rod Blagojevich, stated publically that if The Fan ever committed a crime, he better not ask for a pardon. (The good governor, by the way, was arrested in 2011 and sentenced to jail for fourteen years for corruption. To date, he hasn't received a pardon either.) Eventually, The Fan's home address was found out, and the media swarmed over his neighborhood, interviewing friends and neighbors and kids who, ironically, he coached on a local baseball team. The Fan's face was spread throughout the national media. Cops were stationed outside his house to both control the media and ensure his safety. Somewhere in all of that, the Cubs lost the seventh and deciding game to the Marlins, and the Billy Goat Curse continued, as it continues to this day.

The Fan was forced to move and go into seclusion, and he has never emerged. Nevertheless, Cubs fans still have strong feelings about the event. To this day, the exact seat that the Fan sat in on that fateful night has become something of a tourist attraction, and before games it is not uncommon to see fans taking pictures of each other sitting in that seat and reaching over the wall in a mock (and inaccurate) reenactment of that alleged interference. If you walk up to 25 Cubs fans and ask them The Fan's name, there is no doubt in my mind that at least twenty will know it. Probably more. I'll do my small part by not repeating it here.

Despite the incident with The Fan, I should take a moment to acknowledge that the Cubs are one of the most popular teams in the Majors. Like the Yankees and the Red Sox, their fan base borders on rabid and spans the nation, despite (or, who knows, maybe in part because of) their long championship drought. Part of the allure of being a Cubs fan is their stadium. Wrigley Field, after Fenway Park, is the oldest field in baseball and it didn't even have lights installed for night games until 1988. I can testify from first hand experience that Wrigley Field is baseball heaven. With its ivy-covered outfield walls and turn-of-the-century feel, it's simply beautiful, and hands down it's my favorite Major League ballpark.

I recently read a book about the ultra-devoted Cubs fan base called *Cubs Nation: 162 Games, 162 Stories, 1 Addiction* by Gene Wojciechowski. I recommend that you strictly avoid this book, unless, that is, you can afford to quit your job, leave your family, move to Chicago, rent an apartment within walking distance of Wrigley, go to each and every Cubs game and become fast friends with the ushers, the vendors, the parking lot attendants, the local sports writers and a host of hard-drinking, foul-ball-chasing, Curse-cursing, Cardinals-hating Cubs fans. Because after you read this book, that's exactly what you'll want to do.

Getting back to instant replay for a moment, starting with the 2014 season, the use of instant replay will be expanded to include not only reviews of close home run calls, but other umpire decisions as well, such as whether a ball was fair or foul, or whether a runner was safe or out on a force play. Each manager will have three challenges per game, one before the sixth inning and two after.

And getting back to home runs for a moment, earlier, when discussing the length of a baseball game, I wrote that a game could end before nine innings are complete when the home team scores the winning run in the bottom of the ninth. In that case, I wrote, the game ends immediately when the winning run scores, and the rest of the inning, which is superfluous at that point, is immediately cancelled. The caveat occurs when the game is won in the bottom of the ninth (or in the bottom half of an extra inning) by a home run. When a home run is hit, every run it brings in counts, even if some of them are, in fact, superfluous. For example, if Home Team is down 3–2 in the bottom of the ninth inning and Home Team batter hits a three-run home run, all three runs will count, and Home Team will win, 5–3.

Single, Double, Triple

Home runs are relatively rare. You might get one or two or three in a game, but rarely more than that, and frequently you get none at all. More often than not, therefore, a team will score their runs by getting runners on base via the less dramatic hits—the single, double, triple—then moving them around the bases so that they eventually score.

Let's discuss each type of hit in turn.

A batter hits a single—meaning he gets a hit and advances to first and stops there—by hitting a ground ball and then getting safely to first without being forced out there. Since the play at first is always a force play, to reach base on a single the batter just has to touch first base before a defensive player with the ball does.

There are two ways to hit a single. If the batter is very fast, and if the ball is hit to a spot in the infield that is difficult for an infielder to get to quickly enough to throw that speedy batter out, then a single can be the result of a ground ball that doesn't leave the infield. This is called an **infield single** or an **infield hit**. For example, if a ground ball is hit **deep in the hole**, meaning, it is hit equidistant between either the shortstop and third baseman or first baseman and second baseman so that, instead of moving laterally to get it, they have to retreat diagonally back to snare it before it rolls out of reach into the outfield, a fast runner can beat the throw to first.

More commonly, a single will be the result of a ground ball hit directly into the outfield. The standard single is hit over the heads of the infielders, bouncing once or twice before reaching the outfielder, and though the outfielder cannot retrieve the ball in time to throw the runner out at first, he can retrieve it and return it to the infield before that runner has the chance to advance from first to second. In baseball terminology, the outfielder in this case is said to **hold the runner** to a single.

A quick digression here. Baseball, as you probably know by now, is full of colorful expressions. Here are two more: **Baltimore Chop** and **Texas Leaguer**, wonderful nicknames for certain types of base hits that are, unfortunately, not heard that much anymore. A Baltimore Chop is a hit that is driven down close to the batter and then bounces so high that, by the time it descends, the infielders are unable to throw out the runner and he winds up with an infield single. A Texas Leaguer is a single into the outfield that is weakly hit and just barely manages to drop safety beyond the reach of the infielders. The Baltimore Chop was seen most often on artificial turf infields, but now that, thankfully, its native habitat is largely a thing of the past, so too by and large is the Baltimore Chop itself. The Texas Leaguer is still a thriving species, but now people mostly refer to that type of hit as a **bloop single** which, unlike the term Texas Leaguer, does not require capital letters and is self explanatory. Time is money, after all.

Moving on, a batter hits a double or a triple—meaning he gets a hit and advances to second or third, respectively, and stops there—by hitting a ground ball and then getting safely to second or third without being tagged out there. Doubles and triples are always the result of a ball hit into the outfield that doesn't get caught on the fly. Since the batter will always advance past first to second or third on his own choice, to reach second on a double or to third on a triple the batter has to touch the base before a fielder with the ball tags him out.

The three outfielders cover an immense amount of territory. They are fast and they and their coaches have studied the opposing batters so that they know where any given batter is most likely to hit the ball and, therefore, where best to position themselves. Still their job is clearly daunting: there is a heck of a lot of green grass between, in front of and behind them. The way to get an extra base hit is by exploiting that space and hitting the ball either (i) over an outfielder's head so that he has to turn and chase it, or (ii) **in the gap** between two out-fielders (meaning, hitting the ball into an unoccupied space in the outfield more or less equi-distant between the left fielder and center fielder, or between the right fielder and center fielder, so that it drops uncaught and rolls toward the fences), or (iii) **down the line** (meaning the ball is hit along either foul line, just inside fair territory) and **into the corner** (meaning, it rolls into the right-most or left-most corner of the outfield, so that the outfielder has a good deal of running to do before he retrieves it).

Before we go any further, allow me to pause for a moment and tell you about my most memorable experience with a ball hit "down the line." It might have gone "into the corner" as well but in most Little League fields, including our local field, there are no sidewalls, and no outfield fences, and therefore no "corner" where the two meet. There is just, well, grass and then more grass.

Our neighborhood field, about six blocks from my house in Astoria, is called simply "ICYP." The "CYP" means either Christian or Catholic Youth Program, but no one seems to know what the "I" means. International? Instructional? Invitational? At any rate, it is a large square field that contains four baseball diamonds, one in each corner, so that the furthest edges of the outfields overlap and it is not uncommon to see an outfielder from one game darting across the outfield of another game to retrieve a well-hit ball.

ICYP is a typical Queens Little League field. There is a little field house where hot dogs and various snacks are sold, including excellent bubble gum for only a nickel, and often by the entry gate there is a league official peddling tickets for a fund-raising raffle, with the prize invariably being tickets to a Yankees or Mets game. The crowd, meanwhile, is a lively mix of old "Astoria's Finest" standbys who have been in the neighborhood for generations, groovy "*Nouveau* Astorians" who found their way from Manhattan to more moderately priced Queens housing, and, of course (Queens being Queens), a healthy dose of new immigrants from all over the world bringing their kids to participate in **the national pastime**.

On the day in question, my son Phillip was about ten years old, and was at the end of his first year of Little League baseball. Unlike William, who, in the younger division, stepped up to the plate like he owned it, Phillip's first year in baseball proved to be a challenging one. In fact, the entire season went by without him collecting even one base hit. Every time his turn came to bat, he would gamely march up to the plate and, within minutes, he would trudge back to the bench and take his seat. March up; trudge back. This went on all season.

Eventually, mercifully, the last game of the season came upon us. Little Phillip marched up to the plate in the first inning; trudged back. Marched up in the fourth inning; trudged back. Then he marched up in the seventh, and, since the games in that age group were only seven innings long, he bravely took his position aside the plate in what would undoubtedly be his last at bat in this long season.

The pitcher wound up; Phillip swung. Inexplicably, bat met ball. CRACK!

Phillip's swing was a bit late, a bit slow. Had he hit the ball in mid-swing, it would have been propelled off into the middle of the field. Instead, he hit it more towards the beginning of his swing, so that the ball rose in a high arc almost directly over the right field foul line, high over first base. As the desperate right fielder sprinted toward the foul line and as Phillip raced towards first base, all eyes were on the ball. Would it land fair? Would it hook foul? His teammates left the bench and spilled onto the field, watching in silence as the ball descended from the heavens.

Finally, the ball dropped. It was fair by no more than six inches. The place erupted. His teammates threw their hats in the air; parents stood and cheered. "Way to go, Phillip!" his coach shouted. "Way to go!" On his last at bat in the last inning of the last game of the season, Little Phillip got his hit, and he now stood safely on second with a smile on his face that was too beautiful for this thankful father to ever forget.

And that's what I mean by a hit "down the line."

Where was I?

A runner's decision not to stop at first base, but, instead to **try for** or **take the extra base** (otherwise known as **stretching** a single into a double, or a double into a triple), is facilitated by signals from the first base coach and the third base coach. For example, if, with a runner on second, the batter gets a hit to right field, that runner on second would have to turn full around while advancing to third in order to keep track of the ball. This would slow him down considerably. Instead, he will run full speed, eyes straight ahead, to third base, and the third base coach will keep track of the hit ball for him. Depending on how quickly he thinks the outfielder will return the ball to the infield, the third base coach will signal that runner to either keep going to home plate or to stop at third. The third base coach, it is said, will decide to **send the runner** (signal to him that he should try for home, usually with a wind-mill motion of his arms), or **hold him up** (signal to him that he stop at third, usually by holding out the palm of his hands as if he were trying to stop a speeding train).

Some final notes on the base coaches:

- A first or third base coach's decision to send the runner will be based at least in part on pre-game studies of the opposing outfielder concerned. If the ball is hit into right field, for example, the coach's decision will be influenced by what he knows about the right fielder's fielding and throwing ability. If the right fielder is known to have a strong throwing arm, the coach will be more likely to play it safe and hold the runner up.
- If the third base coach, for example, holds the runner up at third, there is no guarantee the runner will follow his instructions. If he's feeling particularly ambitious and really thinks he can reach home safely, the runner may just decide to **run through the sign** and try for home anyway.
- If there is a danger that the runner coming to third base may get thrown out at third, the third base coach may signal the runner to slide or, if not, he may signal the runner to **come in standing up**, meaning, there is plenty of time and he doesn't have to slide to be safe.

That's basically all there is to know about hits. Single, double, triple, home run. Easy stuff.

But wait! There are two other hits, one a type of double and one a type of home run, that are rare but are good to know about. The first is called a **ground rule double**. It happens when the batter hits the ball into the outfield in fair territory, it bounces on the grass then promptly hops up over the outfield fence and into the crowd. In this case, the ball is dead and the batter automatically goes to second base, with any runners on base advancing two bases as well. (Remember, a home run, in contrast, is when the ball goes over the outfield fence in fair territory *on the fly*.)

The second rare hit is called an **inside the park home run**. It happens when the batter, and he has to be very lucky and very fast, hits the ball into a remote spot in the outfield that no outfielder is anywhere near. Then, for good measure, something unexpected happens— and this is where the "very lucky" part comes in—that makes the ball even more difficult to retrieve. For example, the outfielder, monitoring the flight of the ball, anticipates that it will bounce off the outfield fence and therefore situates himself to catch the anticipated ricochet, but instead of ricocheting towards him, the ball just dies where it drops and doesn't ricochet at all, sending the outfielder scrambling toward it to make up for lost time. Or, just the opposite: the outfielder charges towards the ball and it takes a funny bounce and ricochets right past him, making it necessary for him to turn around and take off in hot pursuit. Meanwhile, while all this is happening the runner—and this is where the "very fast" part comes in— races around all three bases and goes all the way home for a run. The inside the park home run is easily one of the most exciting plays in baseball.

By the way, earlier we discussed the defensive play called a fielder's choice: after fielding a ground ball, instead of throwing to first to get the batter out on a force, the fielder throws to another base to get a more advanced runner out instead. When the smoke clears on a fielder's choice, the batter will be safe at first, true, but he will not be credited with a single. After all, he's only safe at first because the fielder ignored him and tagged or forced out some poor, unfortunate runner ahead of him. Another of baseball's moral judgments? I'd say so.

Finally, some baseball terminology here:

- The area of the outfield closest to the infield is sometimes referred to as the **shallow** part of the outfield (as in "The Rays' Evan Longoria looped the ball just over the short-stop's head and out into shallow left field for a base hit") and the area of the outfield closest to the warning track is sometimes referred to as the **deep** part of the outfield (as in "Longoria blasted the ball into deep left field, over the left fielder's head, for an extra base hit").
- A hit in the bottom of the ninth, or in the bottom of an extra inning, that wins the game for the home team and brings the game to a sudden end, is called a **walk-off** hit, because afterwards, the game is over and the players walk off the field and no doubt go straight home to their loved ones. The A-Rod homer in the bottom of the fifteenth inning against the Red Sox was a walk-off homer. So was Bobby Thomson's "Shot Heard Round the World" and Kirk Gibson's heroic gimpy-legged homer against the A's.
- Only the home team can have a walk-off hit because, if the visiting team gets a hit in the top of the ninth or in the top half of an extra inning that puts them ahead, the home team still gets to hit in the bottom of that same inning. So, in effect, that hit,

though it might have been **go-ahead** hit because it put the visiting team ahead, did not result in anyone walking off the field and going home, so it can't be called a walk-off hit.

- When a batter hits a single, double, triple and a home run in the same game, it is said he **hit for the cycle**. It doesn't happen very often, because while a home run and even a double depend to a large part on a batter's power, a triple is more of a power-plus-speed based event, and not many players have both the power and the speed needed to hit for the cycle.

Walks

The rules of the game strongly encourage a batter to take advantage of every reasonable opportunity to hit the ball: if a pitcher throws a pitch into the strike zone and the batter doesn't swing at it, he is penalized with a called strike. But let's add another brush stroke to the picture we've been painting of the fundamental duel between batter and pitcher: the same rules strongly encourage the pitcher to *provide* that batter with reasonable opportunities to hit the ball, and if he doesn't, he too can be penalized.

Here's how: if a pitch is thrown outside the strike zone, and the batter does *not* swing at it, it's called a **ball**. If the pitcher throws four balls to a batter, the result is a **walk**, also called a **base on balls**, which means that the batter is awarded a free pass to first base and therefore can literally walk down to first and **take first** with impunity. (Most players actually trot down to first after being walked, but it's still called a walk, not, for example, a trot.) Again, play is dead on a walk, meaning the opposing team can't throw the runner out as he's walking to first, nor can they throw out any runner already on base who is forced to advance, who is bumper-carred ahead of the batter, because of the walk.

So now you have a fuller picture of the pitcher-batter duel. The pitcher doesn't want to walk the batter, but at the same time he doesn't want to give the batter a pitch that is easy to hit, so he is going to throw pitches that either (i) don't appear to be heading into the strike zone, but then are, so as to fool the batter into not swinging, therefore resulting in a called strike, or (ii) appear to be heading into the strike zone, but then aren't, so as to fool the batter into swinging at a difficult-to-hit pitch, therefore resulting in either a swinging strike or a poorly hit ball. The batter, on the other hand, knows that the pitcher doesn't want to walk him, and knows therefore that the pitcher will sooner or later have to throw him a pitch inside the strike zone, so he will want to be patient and either (i) swing only at pitches inside the strike zone, not only to avoid called strikes, but also because pitches inside the strike zone will give the batter a better opportunity of making solid contact and getting a hit, or (ii) not swing at pitches outside the strike zone, so as induce or, as the saying goes, **draw a walk**.

Terminology break:

- If a batter walks with the bases loaded, the runner on third will be forced to advance to home plate, and will score a run. The bases loaded walk, it is said, will have **forced in a run**.
- Baseball announcers will usually characterize a ball by its location, as in "Here's the pitch, and... it's **low**, ball one." Meaning, in that particular instance, that the pitch came in lower than or beneath the strike zone, resulting in the home plate umpire calling it

a ball. An extremely low ball that actually hits the ground in front of or on either side of home plate is referred to as **in the dirt**, as in "Here's the pitch, and... it's in the dirt for ball one." Other phrases used by announcers to describe the location of balls are: **high** or **upstairs** (pitch came in higher than the strike zone), **inside** or **in** (between the strike zone and the batter) and **outside** or **away** (outside the side of the strike zone furthest from the batter). A ball can be a combination of the above, for example "low and away" means the pitch was lower than the strike zone and outside the strike zone, on the side furthest from the batter, as well. Sometimes the announcers won't even tell you a pitch is a ball, they'll just assume that you can figure it out by their description of its location, as in "Here's the pitch... and it's high and inside."

- When a batter is at bat, announcers will invariably give what they call "the count" with each pitch. **The count** is simply the number of balls and strikes on the batter. Balls are mentioned first, strikes second, as in "The count on Roy Hobbs is 1 and 2. "That means there is one ball and two strikes on Hobbs, though the announcers would most likely shorten that to just "It's 1 and 2 on Hobbs." The count might just be included in or even substituted for a description of the pitch, as in "Here's the 1 and 2 pitch to Hobbs" or, more often, just "Here's the 1 and 2 to Hobbs."

- When the count on a batter is three balls and two strikes ("3 and 2"), it's called a **full count** because the batter cannot get any more balls without walking or any more strikes without striking out. On the next pitch, in other words, the batter could either walk or strike out. Of course, as we know, the batter could foul off the next pitch and an infinite amount of pitches thereafter and the count would **remain full**, but barring that, the next pitch would be decisive. In fact, the next pitch is often referred to as the **payoff pitch**.

OK, it's quiz time. What is the result in each of these situations? Roy Hobbs of the Knights is the batter.

"The count is 2 and 2 on Hobbs. Here's the pitch, Hobbs swings away and... it's fouled off back into the crowd."

Answer: the count stays at 2 and 2, as there are no third strikes on foul balls. It's as if the pitch never happened.

"Here's the 2 and 2 to Hobbs. And ... it's low and outside."

Answer: that's a third ball. So now Hobbs has a full count.

"Here's the 2 and 2 to Hobbs. And... he swings and misses!"

Answer: that's a third strike. Roy Hobbs has struck out swinging.

"Here's the 2 and 2 to Hobbs. And... Hobbs swings and hits the ball just over the shortstop's head and out into center field!"

Answer: this sounds like a standard single. Hobbs is now on first base and the next batter is coming up to bat. Again, when Hobbs comes to bat again, that 2 and 2 count will not count, as it were. It's erased from the books and he starts all over.

Pitcher vs. Batter: Casey, Continued

Throwing a ball can be simply a mistake. The pitcher might be trying to throw to a certain spot in the strike zone and he might just miss, and the ball might sail outside the strike zone for a ball instead. Some days, pitchers have more control over their pitches than others.

Even the best pitchers will have bad days, days where, it is said, they simply **can't find the strike zone**. Pitchers, after all, are not like, say, bankruptcy attorneys. A bankruptcy attorney doesn't come to work some days knowing more about the bankruptcy laws than other days. A pitcher, on the other hand, depends on the frail and fickle human body, a body made even more frail and fickle by the unique abuse a pitcher puts it through over the course of a year, and over the course of a career. Sometimes the body simply kicks back.

But sometimes throwing a ball is not a mistake. Sometimes throwing a ball is an important part of the duel between pitcher and batter. To illustrate, let's go back and reconsider Mighty Casey's ill-fated at bat.

To quickly review, we know that Casey did not swing at the first pitch because it just wasn't in what Ted Williams called his "happy zone." Strike one? No problem. Casey, like Wade Boggs, probably wasn't worried. But let's flesh out the second pitch a bit. As he watched the second pitch come toward him, it is safe to say that Casey thought it was headed outside the strike zone and therefore, we now know, would be called a ball. Therefore, Casey "ignored" it. To again paraphrase Lew Burdette, it most probably *was* a ball, then it *wasn't*.

Now we understand a little better why that second pitch make Casey so cranky.

Because he misinterpreted or misjudged that second pitch, the count was now 0 and 2 (pronounced "Oh" and 2, not "zero" and 2). The pitcher was now **ahead in the count**, meaning there were more strikes than balls on the batter, and had at a distinct tactical advantage over Casey. With his next pitch, he could really tease the barest of edges of the strike zone because even if he missed, it would only be ball one. He could throw *three* balls and still not walk Casey. But he needed only one more strike to get him out.

Suppose the situation were reversed. If, instead of 0 and 2, the count was 2 and 0, it would be Casey who was ahead in the count (more balls than strikes) and it would be Casey who would be at an advantage. Why? Because the pitcher, to avoid walking Casey, would be forced to now throw the ball more towards the center of the strike zone to make sure he got the called strike from the home plate umpire, and a ball thrown in the center of the strike zone, again, would easier for Casey to wallop. (By the way, when the pitcher is ahead in the count, you will often hear announcers say that it is a **pitcher's count**, and when the hitter is ahead, a **hitter's count**.)

But back to real life. Kind of. Ahead in the count 0 and 2, the pitcher might be tempted to purposely throw a ball (call **wasting a pitch**) to Casey to set up a killer fourth pitch strike. For example, the pitcher might want to purposely come way inside on Casey, almost to the point of hitting him with the pitch, just to put the fear of God in him, make him unconsciously shuffle back a few inches in the batter's box, then come back with the fourth pitch and bang the outside corner of the strike zone because, if the previous pitch, the inside pitch, backed Casey off a bit, the far end of the strike zone might now not be an area that he cannot reach as effectively.

Ahead in the count, with three pitches to waste on the corners, why did the pitcher decide instead to try to come right at Casey with another pitch in the strike zone? Two reasons. For the first, let's go back and look for the first time at the first five wonderful stanzas of the poem:

> *The Outlook wasn't brilliant for the Mudville nine that day:*
> *The score stood four to two, with but one inning more to play.*

And then when Cooney died at first, and Barrows did the same,
A sickly silence fell upon the patrons of the game.

A straggling few got up to go in deep despair. The rest
Clung to that hope which springs eternal in the human breast;
They thought, if only Casey could get but a whack at that-
We'd put up even money, now, with Casey at the bat.

But Flynn preceded Casey, as did also Jimmy Blake,
And the former was a lulu and the latter was a cake;
So upon that stricken multitude grim melancholy sat,
For there seemed but little chance of Casey's getting to the bat.

But Flynn let drive a single, to the wonderment of all,
And Blake, the much despis-ed, tore the cover off the ball;
And when the dust had lifted, and the men saw what had occurred,
There was Jimmy safe at second and Flynn a-hugging third.

Then from 5,000 throats and more there rose a lusty yell;
It rumbled through the valley, it rattled in the dell;
It knocked upon the mountain and recoiled upon the flat,
For Casey, mighty Casey, was advancing to the bat.

So it is clear: the pitcher is getting tired, or, as the saying goes, he's **running out of gas**. We know this because it was the ninth inning, and since in those days, relief pitchers were almost unheard of, this pitcher was now working the last inning of a long, tough game in an away stadium. After quickly getting the first two outs of the inning, he faltered, and gave up hits to two very weak batters (I'm assuming that, because although the specific meanings of "a lulu" and "a cake" as they relate to baseball, have been lost to us, the implications are clear), and he has gotten himself into trouble. When Casey stepped up, there is little doubt the tiring pitcher wanted to get this at bat over with as quickly as possible. Three pitches, three strikes: can't get any quicker than that.

The second reason the pitcher would elect to challenge Casey is that Casey lost his head. After the first two strikes, he was furious. He was ready to belt the ball out of the park. So, the pitcher figured, if he wants a ball that he can hit out of the park, that's what I'll give him. Or at least, I'll let him *think* that's what I'm giving him.

The pitcher's decision to go ahead and challenge Casey worked out well this time, but don't be surprised if, somewhere during the days after the game, his manager took him aside and chewed him out. After all, remember that there were runners on second and third. First base was empty, or **open**. If Casey walked, he would have taken first, but the runners on second and third wouldn't have moved up. Why challenge the mighty Casey when walking him wouldn't have cost them anything?

Well, that might not be entirely true. Mudville was down by two runs and had two runners on base. By walking Casey the pitcher would have **put the winning run on base**, meaning that if the next batter got an extra base hit and all three baserunners score, Mudville would have won. But unless the next batter was nicknamed "Mighty" as well, putting Casey on base might have been a chance worth taking.

Walking Casey would have taken the bat out of the hands of Mudville's strongest batter, true, but there would have been another advantage to it as well. When Casey came up, Mudville had runners on second and third. If Casey hit a ground ball, the fielders would have had to throw him out at first to get the third out. The runners on second and third, after all, wouldn't have had to run on Casey's hit and may have elected to just stay where they were. Or if they did choose to advance, the fielders would have had to execute the more difficult tag play to get either of them out. So there is a good chance that, on a ground ball, the play at first would have been the only one available.

But by walking Casey, the fielders would then have loaded the bases and created a **force at any base**, because with the bases loaded, if the batter after Casey hit a ground ball, all the runners would have been forced to advance, which meant that a force out would have been available at any base, including home plate. If a ground ball was hit to the third baseman, for example, instead of having to make the long throw to first to get Casey out, he could now just take the ball and step on third and force out the runner coming from second. A force out is much easier and much less risky than a tag out, and a force at any base is a fielder's dream.

Well, you might ask, if a walk to Casey would have been so beneficial, could the other team just walk him on purpose? Could they just throw him four balls that he couldn't possibly hit and get it over with? The answer is yes. The opponents decided on this particular day not to walk Casey, probably because they didn't want to put the winning runner on base, but had they decided that taking the bat out of his hands and creating a force at any base was the better option, they could have decided to walk him on purpose instead, called an **intentional walk**. The catcher simply stands up, steps to the side beyond the reach of Casey's bat—Casey, don't forget, has to stay in the batter's box—and the pitcher just soft-tosses him four pitches, all well outside the strike zone.

Oh, and by the way, Casey's at bat, we know, took place sometime in or before 1888. The previously mentioned spitball was not outlawed in baseball until 1920. Therefore, technically speaking, the movement on the ball that Casey faced that fateful day could have been caused by something more than the physics of the spinning stitches. Nevertheless, believing as I do (most of the time) in the nobleness of the human spirit, I prefer not to think that the opposing pitcher would have resorted to such duplicity, and I have accordingly left that factor out of my analysis.

Wild Pitch / Passed Ball

The crazy uncle of the ball is the wild pitch. A **wild pitch** is a ball accidentally thrown so far outside the strike zone that the catcher can't catch it. The ball sails beyond the catcher's reach, back towards the backstop, and the catcher must get up, turn around, and run back and retrieve it.

If there are no runners on base when a wild pitch is thrown, it's no problem, it's just a ball. But if there are runners on base, not only is the wild pitch a ball, but the ball is in play and, as the catcher races to retrieve it, the runners are free to advance as they see fit (unless the wild pitch goes directly into the stands or into a dugout, in which case the ball is dead and all runners advance one base only).

If there is a runner on first and the ball gets by the catcher, it's almost a given that the runner will advance to second, considering that a throw by the catcher from the backstop area to the second baseman is a long throw indeed and would in all probability not get to the second baseman in time for him to tag the runner out (and don't forget that it would be a tag out, not a force out, because the runner would have advanced to second by choice). A runner on second advancing to third on a wild pitch is less certain, as a throw by the catcher from the backstop area to the third baseman is much shorter, and more likely to result in the advancing runner being tagged out. A runner on third advancing home on a wild pitch is riskier still, because while the catcher is recovering the ball in the backstop area, the pitcher will come in and cover home plate, and the catcher would only have to throw it to the pitcher at home, who will then apply the tag on the runner.

Breaking pitches (again, those pitches with less speed but more movement) are much more likely to wind up as wild pitches than fastballs (more speed but less movement), because a breaking ball by design is intended to drop suddenly or veer from one side of the plate to the other as it gets near the plate. A slight miscalculation by the pitcher on his grip or his release of the ball and the result is a pitch that drops down more than intended or breaks to the left or the right more than intended, and there you have it: a wild pitch.

There are those, therefore, who would disagree with me that the second pitch to Casey was a slider and the third pitch was a curveball. There are those who would argue that throwing any breaking pitch with a runner on third would be too risky, especially given that the pitcher's team only had a two-run lead. If a wild pitch **brought home** the runner from third (meaning the wild pitch allowed the runner on third to score), the Mudville Nine would only be down by a run, with the tying runner now on third base (the runner on second would also have advanced on the wild pitch). All that is true, and because it is true, that is exactly why the pitcher might have thrown them after all: because Casey might not have been expecting them. If the pitcher had good command of his pitches, and if the catcher was familiar with the pitcher and familiar with the movement and the break on his breaking pitches, throwing them with a runner on third and a two-run lead would have been a risk well worth the taking.

Before moving on, we should briefly cover the **passed ball,** which is similar to a wild pitch in that both involve a pitched ball that gets past the catcher and goes back to the backstop while any runners on base are free to advance as they see fit. The only difference is that a wild pitch is the result of a pitcher's error, in that he threw a pitch so far out of the strike zone that the catcher couldn't be expected to catch it, while a passed ball is the result of a catcher's error, in that the ball is delivered properly by the pitcher, but the catcher for some reason fails to catch it. Usually it's because the pitcher and catcher have gotten **their signs crossed up,** and the catcher was expecting one type of pitch, while the pitcher thought he was supposed to deliver another. For example, the catcher might have been expecting the pitcher to throw a fastball, but the pitcher threw a curveball instead, the catcher wasn't prepared for the late drop, and, as a result, the ball skipped under his glove and past him.

Hit by Pitch

The third way a batter can get on base is to get **hit by a pitch**. The rule is simple: If the pitcher hits the batter with the pitch, the batter is automatically awarded first base and gets a free pass thereto. Like a walk, when a batter gets hit by a pitch, the play is dead. The opposing team can't throw the runner out as he's heading down to first, nor can they throw out any runner already on base who is bumper-carred to the next base because of the hit batter taking first.

Three important notes and one amusing side note about batters getting hit by a pitch:

First, if a pitch that hits the batter is in the strike zone, then it's considered a strike and not a hit batter. The logic is that the pitcher is entitled to throw a pitch in the strike zone, and if the batter is leaning so far forward that he's in the strike zone and thus almost trying to intentionally get hit by a pitch, he shouldn't be rewarded with a free base.

Second, a batter is considered hit by a pitch not only when his body is hit by the pitch, but any part of his clothing as well. If a pitched ball brushes the ripples on the shirt of the batter, he's considered hit and he takes his base. I'm reminded of the famous "shoe polish incident" in Game Five of the 1969 World Series between the Mets and the Orioles. A low pitch hit the dirt near Mets batter Cleon Jones' foot and bounced away toward the Mets dugout. Jones argued that the pitch hit his foot. The umpire disagreed, but when Mets manager Gil Hodges showed the umpire a smear of Jones' shoe polish on the ball, the umpire changed his mind and awarded Jones first base. Naturally, the next batter hit a home run and the Mets eventually won the game.

Third, a batter has a duty to avoid a pitched ball. If he sees it coming, he has to make an effort to get out of the way. However, seeing as how a pitch takes less than a second to get to the plate, it's not surprising that getting out of the way is not easy to do.

Here's the amusing side note. When you and I suffer some kind of injury, we reflexively grab that part of the body that has gotten injured. You bang your knee on the car door, you grab your knee and say, "Ouch!" Batters in baseball will almost never touch the spot on their body that got hit by the pitch. If they get hit on the leg, say, they might hop around a bit, but that's it. They will keep their mouth shut, they will limp down to first base and they will not touch or rub or examine their leg in any way. It's their way of saying to the pitcher: "I'm tougher than you. I can take the pain." It's crazy, because you know it must hurt like a son of a gun, but it's baseball tradition. I don't think I've ever seen it broken.

Keep that in mind when someone wonders aloud why soccer is having such a hard time catching on in this country. In soccer, if a player gets knocked down illegally then pops back up and keeps playing, his opponent will almost certainly not get penalized. But if that same player, instead of popping back up, writhes on the ground because he just ... can't ... stand ... the *pain!!!*—his opponent almost certainly *will* get penalized. As a result, in any given game, you will see soccer players making embarrassing spectacles of themselves with very poor acting performances, then, two minutes later, shamelessly popping back up to their feet and resuming play as if nothing ever happened. This is the polar opposite of the baseball mentality. Hit in the ribs with a rock hard object going 90 miles an hour? No problem. Didn't hurt a bit.

Pitchers hit batters with a pitch in one of three ways: completely by accident, sort of by accident, and intentionally. And here again we will add another very important brush stroke to our portrait of the pitcher-batter duel.

Like throwing a ball (meaning a ball as opposed to a strike), throwing a pitch that hits a batter can be *completely* by accident. We discussed above how the first pitch to Casey was an inside fastball. A tiny miscalculation by the pitcher could have brought that inside fastball a bit more inside than intended, and the result would have been that Casey got hit on the leg.

Or hitting a batter can be *sort of* by accident. The pitcher may have intended to throw the ball very close to the batter, may have intended to scare the heck out of the batter, even at the cost of the home plate umpire calling a ball on that pitch, but the pitch gets away from the pitcher that extra little bit and hits the batter anyway.

Why would a pitcher want to throw the ball that close to the batter? As discussed in terms of Casey's "style," batters generally don't like inside pitches, because they are too close for the batter to fully extend his arms and hit the ball with the sweet spot of the bat and therefore with maximum power. In response to a pitcher pitching inside, or to discourage a pitcher from pitching inside, the batter can do one or two things: he can move back in the batter's box and/or choke up on the bat, thus bringing the sweet spot of the bat closer into play. Or, just the opposite, the batter can move as far forward in the batter's box as possible, he can **crowd the plate**, almost daring the pitcher to pitch inside and risk hitting him.

In response to the batter crowding the plate, the pitcher now can do one of two things: he can be pressured into pitching outside to avoid hitting the batter, thus giving the batter a chance at full extension and maximum power, which is just what the batter wants, or, just the opposite, he can accept the challenge and pitch inside, even at the risk of hitting the batter. By pitching inside he can try to **brush back** the batter, meaning, come close to hitting him, scare the heck out of him, and hopefully push him back off the plate a bit. Sometimes brush back pitches get away and actually hit the batter. By accident. Sort of.

And that brings us to the third way the pitcher can hit the batter: intentionally. Not by accident, not sort of by accident, but absolutely and positively on purpose. It's rare, but when it's about to happen, when a pitcher is going to nail a batter on purpose, you'll know it. You might not know which batter is going to get hit, or in what inning, but when it's coming, it will be obvious.

First of all, who cares whether a pitcher hits a batter intentionally, as opposed to accidentally? The umpires care, that's who. The *Official Baseball Rules* state that "the pitcher shall not intentionally pitch at the batter," and "if, in the umpire's judgment, such a violation occurs" then the umpire, depending on the circumstances, can throw the pitcher out of the game, or he can throw the pitcher and his manager out of the game, or he can warn both teams that another such pitch delivered by either team will result in such an expulsion.

Since the umpires can't read the pitcher's mind (or the catcher's, who sends the signs to the pitcher, or the manager's, who consults with the pitcher and catcher between innings) they must weigh what basically amounts to circumstantial evidence when determining whether a batter was thrown at or hit intentionally. For example, if there was a preceding incident that might have provoked the pitcher to hit the batter intentionally, and if he has nothing to lose by hitting the batter intentionally (i.e., if first base is open and if the hit batsman does not represent the tying or winning run, for example) then the umpires, taking the totality of circumstances into consideration, may decide the pitcher intentionally hit the batter and throw him out of the game.

What "preceding incident" would make a pitcher want to intentionally hit a batter with a pitch, even at the risk of getting thrown out of the game? Baseball has an internally established and internally enforced unwritten code of conduct (called, simply the **Code**) by which the players, over the years, have decided that certain actions are impermissible because they needlessly threaten either the health of the players or the dignity of the game by which they all earn their living. Those who violate the Code and engage in these certain actions do so at the risk of getting smashed in their ribs, or legs, or arms with a rock-hard ball thrown at 95 mph. The Code is therefore not violated very often.

Here are some of the basic rules of the Code, and some of the most common causes of batters intentionally getting hit by a pitch.

First, showing up your opponent is a definite violation. Excessive celebrating on the field, especially if it's obviously not spontaneous, is not a healthy thing to do. A walk off home run where the batter is so happy he pumps his fist a few times as he circles the bases... OK, it's a walk off, he's genuinely happy, so within reason that would be permissible. But anything above and beyond that, anything intended to show up your opponent, will probably result in the batter, or someone on the batter's team getting hit.

For an example, let's go back to Babe Ruth's famous "called shot" in the 1932 World Series against the Cubs. Ruth, you'll recall, upset by heckling from the Chicago players and fans, pointed to the spot in the outfield stands where he would deposit the next pitch and, sure enough, that's exactly what he did. To finish the story, as he rounded the bases, Ruth made no effort to conceal his pleasure, loudly, and no doubt colorfully, deriding the Cubs pitcher and players as he ran. "By the time I reach home plate," the Eloquent One later recalled, "I'm almost fallin' down I'm laughin' so feckin' hard." The game ended shortly afterwards, and Ruth didn't come to bat again. But in the next game of the Series, in Ruth's first at bat, on the very first pitch he saw, guess what happened?

Second, running up the score on your opponent is also a problem. And it's not so much the amount of runs, as the manner, after a certain point, in which you get those runs. If a team is leading 10–0 and the pitcher throws a fat one right down the pipe, no one will expect the batter to miss it on purpose, or hold back on his swing on purpose, just because his team is already up by ten runs. If he smacks a home run and makes it 11–0, that's life. But if that same team were to get that eleventh run by employing certain other strategies (to be discussed later) that basically amount to intentionally kicking the opponent while he's down, someone is going to get hit.

Third, sliding hard into a fielder when there is no longer any need to may also be an infraction. Earlier, in relation to the Ground Ball Rules, we discussed how a runner can slide into a base cleat-first to try to reach the base safely, even when it is somewhat apparent his real intention is to knock the covering fielder down or force him to take evasive action so as to prevent him from completing a double play. No problem: this is just good, hard-nosed baseball. But if a runner slides hard into a fielder well after the he has thrown the ball and there is clearly no longer any need to, and if the fielder was injured or could have been injured by the late slide, or if the runner does so late in a one-sided game when there's clearly nothing to be gained by it, there's a good chance someone on the runner's team is going to get hit.

The greatest potential for Code-violating runner-fielder collisions occurs at home plate. Home-plate collisions can be very violent and can result in serious injuries to those involved. On May 25, 2011, for example, San Francisco Giants catcher Buster Posey suffered three torn ligaments and a broken bone in his ankle and was lost for the season after a brutal collision at home.

New rules enacted before the 2014 season have sought to limit the frequency and severity of home-plate collisions. Under the old rules, a fielder (usually the catcher) covering home who either had the ball or was preparing to receive a throw from another fielder, could block the path of an oncoming runner to prevent him from touching home plate and scoring. As a non-forced runner raced from third to home, the catcher would do his best to **block the plate** by crouching down or even kneeling in front of it, thus turning his body into a human barrier that prevented the runner from scoring before getting tagged out. The new rules modify this a bit by holding that the catcher can still block the plate if he actually has the ball in his possession, but he can no longer block the plate while he is still waiting for the throw. Violation of this rule may result in the umpire calling the runner safe at home regardless of the apparent outcome of the play.

On the other hand, under the old rules a runner trying to score, like a runner sliding into second or third, could veer slightly off to one side or the other to try to initiate contact with a catcher in the hopes of jarring the ball loose. The new rules, however, hold that a runner is now required to run in a direct line to home plate, and he may only initiate contact with the catcher if the catcher is in that direct line. Otherwise, the umpire may automatically call him out, again, regardless of the apparent outcome of the play.

Still, even within the new rules, as long as the fielder who is blocking the plate has already caught the ball and the runner runs directly towards the plate as he is trying to score, the potential for violent home-plate collisions remains.

Home-plate collisions, even Posey's, are usually considered good, hard-nosed baseball and accepted by both teams as just part of the game. Usually. Sometimes the catcher's team might take exception if, for example, the runner's team is so far ahead that running into the catcher was, in their opinion, uncalled for. If that's what they think, someone will get hit.

Finally, the most common reason a pitcher intentionally hits a batter with a pitch is because, well, someone on the pitcher's team was hit by a pitch. In other words: retaliation is the best revenge. But wait a minute, you're thinking: if a violation of the Code took place, and if as a result the pitcher on the opposing team took appropriate and warranted action by hitting the violator, or someone on the violator's team, then why would the violator's pitcher want to retaliate?

The problem is that violations of the Code are often in the eyes of the beholder. In each of the above four examples of Code violations, the word "intentionally" or some version of it was used. Whether or not an action was intentional is a matter of perception. If the opponent feels a violation of the Code was intentional, a batter gets hit. If the batter's team, on the other hand, does not think the original violation was intentional, retaliation for the hit batsman might follow.

Retaliation for a hit batsman, however, can be a complicated proposition. After all, who do you retaliate against? Seems easy: if your best player gets hit by a pitch, you retaliate against your opponent's best player. If they want to put your bread and butter in danger of injury, then it only stands to reason that you put theirs in danger of injury as well. Legendary Cardinals manager Tony La Russa described how in a game during the 2011 season the Brewers pitcher hit his star first baseman, Albert Pujols, so he ordered his pitcher to hit their star outfielder, Ryan Braun, the next time he came up. La Russa wrote that he viewed such retaliation "in biblical terms, an eye for an eye."

The eye-for-an-eye practice came into play in an interesting way in a May 15, 2012, game between the Mets and the Brewers when Brewers second baseman Rickie Weeks hit a seventh inning home run off Mets pitcher D. J. Carrasco that extended the Brewers already-formidable lead to 8–0. No doubt feeling a little cranky at his own ineffectiveness, Carrasco promptly plunked the next Brewers batter with a pitch. The umpire correctly judged that Carrasco hit the batter on purpose, and he was promptly ejected from the game.

The problem was, however, that the batter that Carrasco hit was the Brewers' best player, the very same Ryan Braun. As luck would have it, the Mets' best player, David Wright, was scheduled to bat the very next inning. Anyone who knew the difference between a ball and a strike knew that there was a darn good chance the Brewers would hit Wright in retaliation for the Mets having hit Braun, just as La Russa had hit Braun in retaliation for the Brewers having hit Pujols.

It never came to pass. And the reason it never came to pass, is that Wright's manager, Terry Collins, took the unusual step of taking Wright out of the game before he came up to bat. "I got news for you," he told the press afterwards. "In this game there are unwritten rules. And one of the unwritten rules is that if you hit my guy, I'm hitting your guy. They're not hitting my guy tonight. I'm not exposing him to getting hit."

Weighing in Collins' decision was no doubt the fact that in 2009, in a game against the Giants, the same David Wright was hit in the head with a pitch, knocking him out cold and causing him to spend nearly a month on the disabled list. Nevertheless, Wright was visibly upset at being taken out of the game. "If someone is going to be hit," he reportedly shouted at Collins, "let it be me!" The game ended without further incident, as apparently the Mets' loss of the services of their star for the final innings of the game was deemed payback enough for the Brewers. (In retaliation for Wright's 2009 beaning by the Giants, by the way, Mets pitcher Johan Santana threw at the head of the next Giants batter, missed, but plunked the following batter on the elbow.)

Suppose that David Wright wasn't scheduled to come to bat for the remainder of the game against the Brewers and the issue of retaliation was still on the table? Would the Brewers have been satisfied with hitting, instead, the best Mets player scheduled to come up in the next inning, whoever that happened to be? Or would they have elected to wait, instead, for the next game to exact justice on the Mets, and Wright? Suppose this was the last game of a home stand and the two teams didn't play each other again for two weeks? Three weeks? Four weeks?

By necessity, the wheels of justice sometimes grind slowly in baseball when the Code is broken. At the tail-end of the 2009 season, Prince Fielder, then of the Brewers, hit a walk off homer against the Giants and then took part in a bizarre, obviously rehearsed celebration at home plate where his teammates, once Fielder stepped on the plate, fell down around him like bowling pins. Needless to say, the Giants weren't too happy about it. The game ended, the two teams went their separate ways, the season ended, fall gave way to winter, winter gave way to spring and with spring came the preseason exhibition games of the brand new 2010 baseball season. In one of the preseason games, the Brewers played the Giants for the first time since Fielder's home plate celebration. Prince Fielder came up, and sure enough, more than six months after his "bowling pins" celebration, the Giants pitcher drilled him in the back with the first pitch he saw. Fielder, to his credit, didn't complain. "They have to do what they have to do," he said. He knew it was coming. That's baseball.

Sometimes, though, players are not as classy as Prince Fielder was. Sometimes, if a batter feels he was hit intentionally by a pitch, Code or no Code, a **bench clearing brawl** between the teams will ensue in which the aggrieved batter **charges the mound**, or runs out onto the field after the pitcher, looking to punch the heck out of him. Other players quickly join in, the dugouts empty onto the field, the bullpens empty onto the field, and chaos ensues. Usually the result is that players will be suspended and fined by the league. Sometimes, unfortunately, serious injuries can result.

The Code, as we now know, sometimes permits a pitcher to plunk a batter, but in almost every case the plunking will be delivered to the batter's arm, or leg, or back, or ribs, and, like Prince Feilder, in almost every case the batter will just take it and trot down to first base. But when a pitcher throws at or near a batter's head—sometimes called **high heat** or **chin music** or **head hunting**—serious physical injury can result and tensions on the field, therefore, can escalate very quickly.

Although normally the totality of circumstances is taken into account by umpires when deciding if a pitcher intentionally hit a batter, Major League pitchers are presumed to have the skill level necessary *not* to throw at a batter's head by accident. Pitches that hit or come close to hitting a batter in the head are therefore subject to a special level of scrutiny, regardless of surrounding circumstances.

The case of the Chicago Cubs' Adam Greenberg comes to mind. In July 2005, rookie Greenberg, playing in his very first game, was hit below his left ear by the very first Major League pitch that he saw. "I lost control of my eyes and thought my head was split open," he said later. "I kept saying 'Stay alive,' and just kept repeating that." Greenberg spent the next several years battling post-concussion syndrome and did not see his second major league pitch until seven years later, when, in September of 2012, the Marlins graciously signed him to a one-day contract to permit him to enjoy one official at bat in the Big Leagues. He struck out on three pitches.

I cannot go further without mentioning a rather amusing—to me, anyway—story involving Mike Piazza, widely considered one of the best catchers of the modern era and perhaps the best hitting catcher of all time. We know now that in retaliation for one of its players getting hit, a team will retaliate against an opposing player of similar stature. You hit my best; I hit your best. Like Manager La Russa said: an eye for an eye. But what happens when the opposing batter a manager chooses to hit in retaliation reveals that he didn't think as much of his own hit batter as, perhaps, that hit batter thought of himself?

Such a situation arose in 2005 when, while on the downside of his outstanding career, Piazza was hit by St. Louis pitcher Julian Tavarez. Piazza, who had been the Mets best player for years, expected that the Mets would respond by hitting the Cardinals' best player, Albert Pujols. Much to Piazza's disappointment, however, the Mets coaches decided that since Piazza, unlike Pujols, was past his prime, hitting Pujols in response wouldn't be fair. They elected therefore to hit the less stellar David Eckstein. Piazza was outraged. "A couple of years before, I'd have been an even exchange for Pujols," Piazza wrote. "Don't get me wrong, Eckstein was a tough dude and I admired the way he played; but he stood five foot six and muscled up for a home run about every other month or so. All of a sudden, the payback for me is *David Eckstein*? That was a big, fat humble pie in the face. It also let me know exactly what the Mets thought of me at that point."

Dock's Decision

I'll end this discussion with a short recap of one of the most bizarre instances of hit batsmen (note the plural) in the history of baseball. The date was May 1, 1974, the place was Pittsburgh, and the game featured the then mighty Cincinnati Reds, the so-called Big Red Machine, against the then not-so-mighty Pirates. Dock Ellis, one of the most, let's say, entertaining baseball players in memory, was pitching for the Pirates.

It's not that Dock Ellis didn't like the Reds. He was actually good friends with some of them. What Dock Ellis didn't like was the way his Pirates teammates showed too much deference to the Reds. Prior to games, his teammates, clearly in awe of stars like Pete Rose, Johnny Bench, Joe Morgan and Tony Perez, acted like doting fans instead of proud, self-respecting competitors. The Reds would obligingly chat it up with the Pirates before games, then go out and beat the hell out of them time after time, and, in Dock's eyes, laugh about it afterwards. Dock thought it was high time somebody took the Reds down a notch. So Dock Ellis, even before the 1974 season started, told everyone who would listen: The first time we face the Reds, I'm going to hit every batter I face.

No one paid much attention to Dock. He was a flake. A darn good pitcher, but a flake who, for example, wore hair curlers in the clubhouse and would sometimes go up to the children of heckling adult fans and tell the children that he would gladly go over their house for dinner, if only their parents would stop heckling him and extend an invitation. Three times, according to Ellis, he was invited to dinner in this manner and on all three occasions he made life-long friends.

On this particular night, Pete Rose led off for the Reds. On his first pitch, Dock Ellis threw a pitch at Rose's head. He missed, but his second pitch plunked Rose on the shoulder. Just before he jogged down to first base, tough guy Rose smiled, picked up the ball and tossed it back to Ellis, as if to say: "Is that all you got?"

It wasn't. The next batter up was Joe Morgan. Dock hit him in the back with his first pitch. Dan Driessen was the third batter. Dock's first pitch zoomed toward his head, but Driessen ducked out of the way. The second pitch hit him in the back. The bases were now loaded with hit batsmen.

The fourth batter, Tony Perez, ran away from four Dock Ellis pitches aimed for various parts of his body, walking on four pitches and forcing home Pete Rose from third. The next batter was Johnny Bench. He followed Perez's lead and ran away from two pitches aimed right at him. And that, finally, was where the madness ended. Pittsburgh coach Danny Murtaugh came out and yanked Dock from the game.

When word got back to them that Dock Ellis' performance was not only intentional, but planned months in advance, the Reds were not pleased. Two things happened as a result. First, the next time the Reds came to Pittsburgh, the two teams had a huge fight. Some baseball fights are more loosely choreographed dances than fights. Not this one. In this one, players punched, kicked, bit, and brawled for twenty minutes. This was serious.

Second, the Pirates, suddenly energized, suddenly the team everyone was afraid of, though probably for the wrong reasons, gained some swagger, some confidence, some pride. They won eight straight games after the brawl, then lost one game, then won nine out of the next eleven, and they began a climb that took them from last all the way to first place.

Four years later, in 1978, the rules of baseball were changed to allow umpires to be much more proactive in ejecting pitchers who have hit or even thrown at a batter intentionally. It is interesting, and perhaps amusing, to note that even after throwing at five straight batters, it was Dock Ellis' own manager, not the umpire, who removed Dock from the game. The new rule has changed things completely. As discussed, if going into a game there is reason to believe (because of past hostility, for example) that a pitcher may be throwing at batters, umpires are now allowed to warn teams even before the game starts that any hit batsman, any single hit batsman, will result in ejection of the pitcher and the pitcher's manager.

"The art of pitching," Sandy Koufax said, "is the art of instilling fear." The Dock Ellis story is atypical in many ways, but it does serve to illustrate how a pitcher will throw at a batter not only to correct a perceived injustice, but also, going forward, to instill in others a healthy fear of him and his team, a fear that just might, in the end, back a timid batter or two off the plate and win the far side of the strike zone for the pitcher. Like it or not, intentionally hitting a batter with a pitch is a tool in the pitcher's toolbox right along with his fastball and the curveball. It is a tool that will be used very sparingly, but when the situation demands it, it will be used. That hasn't changed since the days of Dock Ellis, and it probably never will.

Errors

The fourth and final of the basic ways a batter can get on base is when he reaches base safely as a result of a mistake by a fielder, which is called an **error**. There are two types of errors. A **fielding error** is an error where a fielder fails to catch a ball he should have caught and as a result the runner reaches base safely. For example: the fielder drops a routine fly ball or lets an easy ground ball go through his legs, or a fielder covering a base drops a throw from another fielder that he should have been able to catch. A **throwing error** occurs when a fielder catches a ball cleanly but then throws it so poorly to the fielder covering the pertinent base, that that the throw cannot be caught and the out cannot be registered.

I just said that an error occurs when a batter reaches base safely as a result of a fielding mistake. Let's break that down.

First, an error occurs when a batter *reaches base safely* as a result of a fielding mistake. If a ground ball is hit to the shortstop and the shortstop drops the ball but picks it up in time to throw the batter out, that's not an error. The batter in this case was not safe. He was thrown out. No matter how sloppy the fielder's play was, there was no error.

Second, an error occurs when a batter reaches base safely *as a result of a fielding mistake*. Here's where things get a little tricky.

Consider the following example: The batter, known to be a very fast runner, hits a slow ground ball down the left field line. The third baseman, knowing how fast the batter is, rushes in, quickly scoops up the ball with his bare hand, readies himself to make the long throw across the infield to the first baseman, but in his haste he bobbles the ball and nearly drops it to the ground. He quickly recovers, however, and throws on to first base, but not in time to get the runner. The speedy batter is safe at first. Did the batter reach first as a result of a fielding mistake by the third baseman? Or was he so fast that he would have been safe regardless?

Whether an error has been committed is a judgment call. Whose judgment? **The Official Scorer**, that's who. Official Scorers are appointed by the league, and there is one in attendance at each Major League game. They are the official in-game record keepers for Major League Baseball, and one of their duties is to decide, using the guidelines set forth in the *Official Baseball Rules*, whether an error has been committed on any given play. The term used is that the Official Scorer will **score,** or officially classify and record, the play as either a hit or an error.

As dictated by the *Official Baseball Rules*, the standard used to decide when an error has been committed is "ordinary effort." If a fielder, using ordinary effort, is able to either get a runner out or assist in getting a runner out, as appropriate, but fails to do so, then the fielder has committed an error. Ordinary effort is defined as "the effort that a fielder of average skill at a position... should exhibit on a play, with due consideration given to the condition of the field and weather conditions."

Getting back to our third baseman, and with the "ordinary effort" standard in mind, my guess is that he would not be charged with an error. Bobbled ball or no bobbled ball, it was a tough play to begin with, and, given the speed of the batter, maybe a darn near impossible play. Brooks Robinson of the Orioles teams of the 1960s and 1970s, the greatest fielding third baseman ever—sure, he could have made the play. But Brooks Robinson is not the standard here. The standard is "a fielder of average skill," and in my opinion, a fielder of average skill, using ordinary effort, would not have been able to make that play. Score it, therefore, as a single for the batter, not an error by the fielder.

An error, by the way, can be charged not only when a fielding mistake results in a batter reaching base safely, but also when a fielding mistake results in a batter who was already on base, advancing further on the bases (i.e., batter hits a clean single to center, the center-fielder fields it, throws it to second to hold the runner to a single, but accidentally throws it over the head of the second baseman, enabling the runner to advance) and when a fielding mistake results in a batter's at bat being prolonged (batter hits a foul pop down the right field line, first baseman gets under it, lines it up but then, inexplicably, drops it, so that instead of being put out, the batter is charged only with a foul ball, and his at bat continues).

Some terminology: errors that result in the runner getting safely to first base are usually just called errors, but when an error results in a runner going all the way to second or third, they are called, respectively, **two-base errors** and **three-base errors**.

To commit an error, by the way, is sometimes referred to as **booting the ball**. I imagine the origin of the term had to do with the fact that a careless fielder, when reaching down for a ground ball can, if he doesn't situate his feet properly, actually wind up kicking, or booting, the ball away from his own glove, thereby committing an error. The term is now used generally for all kinds of errors, regardless of whether the player's "boot" is involved or not.

Kramer's Dilemma

The ramifications of a hit ball being scored as an error as opposed to a hit was studied in depth by no less an authority than *Seinfeld*, the American comedy series that was very popular in the 1990s and early 2000s. Set in New York, the show often dealt with baseball related themes and featured cameo appearances by both Yankees and Mets players.

In an episode called "The Wink," George, one of the characters, who has a menial front office job for the Yankees, is tasked with getting all the Yankees players to sign a get well card for one of the club's executives, who has fallen ill. His friend, Kramer, coming across the card, realizes the value it might have to collectors of baseball memorabilia, takes it as a result of a misunderstanding and sells it to a collector, who, in turn, sells it to parents of a hospitalized child, a Yankees fan, in hopes it will lift his spirits.

George is outraged that Kramer took the card and demands that he get it back ASAP from the sick child. The sick child will only give it back to Kramer if Paul O'Neill, the Yankees right fielder, will promise to hit two home runs for him in that night's game. The scene is a tongue-in-cheek reference to a scene from the classic 1942 baseball movie *The Pride of the Yankees*, in which Yankees slugger Lou Gehrig, visiting a bed-ridden child in the hospital, promises to hit two home runs if the child will, in turn, promise to get up and walk one day. Gehrig delivers on his promise by hitting two home runs, and sure enough years later the boy shows up at a Yankees game to thank Gehrig personally, having made a full recovery. Kramer, in contrast, manages to get access to the Yankees clubhouse but is berated by a hilarious Paul O'Neill: "Home runs are hard!" O'Neill complains.

O'Neill hits one home run, all right, but in a subsequent at bat, a second long fly ball caroms off the top off the outfield fence, almost a home run, but stays in the park. Nevertheless, we can hear the announcer describing O'Neill hustling around the bases and it quickly becomes obvious that O'Neill may hit that second home run after all, albeit an inside-the-park home run. O'Neill rounds third and heads home and when the outfielder's throw sails over the catcher's head, he slides in safely and scores. When the announcer proclaims the inside-the-park home run, Kramer happily goes to retrieve the autographed birthday card.

Just as he is about to take it, however, the announcer reveals that the Official Scorer has ruled that it was not an inside-the-park homer after all, but a triple, with O'Neill scoring on a subsequent throwing error by the outfielder.

Kramer eventually gets the card, but only by promising the child that the next night O'Neill would catch a fly ball in his hat. Apparently, both Kramer and the child were ignorant of Official Baseball Rule 7.05(d), which holds that a batter is automatically awarded third base, with any and all runners scoring ahead of him, if a fielder deliberately touches a fair ball with his hat or with "any part of his uniform detached from its proper place on his person." Meaning, what... his shoe? But we'll leave that for another episode.

Which reminds me, for no particular reason, that on April 26, 1989, Giants outfielder Kevin Mitchell reached up and caught a long fly ball deep in left field with his bare hand, just for fun. Since neither his shoe nor his hat was in his bare hand when he caught the ball, the catch, and the out, counted.

Which in turns reminds me, also for no particular reason, that when Warren Spahn, hotshot prospect, first came up to the Big Leagues in 1942, he figured he'd impress veteran Braves catcher Ernie Lombardi during warm ups by unleashing what he thought was his deadly fastball. Lombardi caught young Spahn's deadly fastball with his bare hand, spat tobacco juice on it and disdainfully tossed it back. I guess I better work on my curve, Spahn said to himself.

A Pause

I remember that when I was, I guess, maybe twenty-two years old, we—meaning myself and my brothers and a bunch of friends—used to go to Mets games *all* the time. I was born and raised in Astoria, Queens. To say I could stand on my stoop and throw a rock and hit Shea Stadium in nearby Flushing was an exaggeration, but not much of one. We were young, we had a few bucks in our pockets—and in those days that's all you needed—and we had no responsibilities. What do you want to do tonight? I don't know, what do you want to do tonight? Let's go to the Mets game. Sure, why not?

Sometimes there were as many as fifteen of us. We used to pull into the parking lot about two hours beforehand and just hang out listening to music and drinking beer out of the trunk of my car. When game time rolled around, we used to stuff our coat pockets and pants pockets with cans of beer and waddle into the stadium with tickets in hand. I don't think we fooled anyone, but nobody cared. Those were different times.

When you're that age, and doing things like that—going to ballgames with your brothers and your pals and hanging around in the parking lot two hours before game time—you don't think that this is a phase of life that's actually relatively short and in the wink of an eye it will be behind you. You don't think that years later the memories of all those friends and all those loved ones together in one place will bring tears to your eyes. At the time, you just think: This is it. This is the way it is. It is, to paraphrase Lew Burdette again, but then it isn't. But, thankfully, you don't know that at the time.

Years later, I met my wife, Marya, on a city bus. She sat next to me—to this day, she denies that there were other seats available, but there were—and she opened a textbook, a biology book, and she started reading it. And I remember thinking, Man, this girl is beautiful, I have to try to talk to her. So I asked her why she was reading a biology textbook, and she said she was studying to be a nurse, so I said, Well, then you have to give me your phone number. She looked at me like I was crazy and said, Why should I give you my phone number? And I said, Because I'm a cop (which I was, for twenty-two years, but that's another story). She didn't know what to make of that, so I explained: Don't you know about nurses and cops? It's tradition. Cops and nurses always get together. So, like I said, you have to give me your phone number.

She didn't, but she let me give her mine. She didn't call, though, for about six weeks. I remember I was walking past the desk sergeant one afternoon and he said, Hey, Mahony, a girl named Marya called. She left her number.

I didn't remember exactly what she looked like, but I remember that she was good looking, so when I went to her house to pick her up on our first date, I was pretty excited. So I rang her bell and through the intercom she said she would be right down. And I remember turning my back on the door for a minute and looking out at the street and watching all the people going by, and then I heard the door open behind me and I turned and looked into her eyes and my life, at that exact moment, changed forever. That's all there was to it. I was crazy about her right from the start.

I remember I didn't win her over right away. In fact, it took a darn long time, and at the beginning it used to drive me nuts that it might not work out. One night we figured we'd have a bite to eat somewhere and then go to see the Mets. We were supposed to meet my brother Brendan outside the stadium and then we would buy tickets together. Anyway, while Marya and I were having dinner we had an argument, and it just didn't look good, and my heart was heavy. And to boot, we were late for the game. And the traffic was bad and we sat in the car without talking and man, I just wanted to reach out and grab her and not let go. But I couldn't do that.

So we got to the darn game about an hour late and Brendan was gone and for a while we weren't even going to bother going in at all, but I figured what the hell, we bought a couple of tickets and walked quietly into the stadium, took the escalator up to the mezzanine level, got off the escalator and bumped right into Brendan. It was a pretty amazing coincidence. Fifty thousand people and you just happen to bump into the one person you are looking for? In fact, you're not even really looking for him because you figure there is just no chance you'd ever find him? It was great to see him and our moods lightened a bit and I started to think of it as an omen, a sign. And I put my arm around Marya and pulled her close and she smiled—man, her smile used to kill me—and next thing you know we grabbed a few beers and we went in and we had a great time. Who can stay angry at a ballgame?

That night we were laying in bed in my apartment in Astoria and we were looking out the window and we saw a shooting star. I swear that's the truth. A shooting star in

Astoria, Queens. And that's when I knew everything would be OK, and I would win her heart, and we would spend the rest of our lives together. And we have. And her smile still kills me.

And I remember one night when my kids were still small, we were at a game at the old Yankee Stadium, where the upper deck was tucked in so close to the field that I often thought if I dropped a quarter from the front row, it would hit the third baseman on the head. I was there with my sons William and Phillip when William was maybe eight and Phillip was ten, and a bunch of their little friends to boot, and we just sat up there as happy as could be, the great stadium just unfolding around us in one of the most marvelous views this side of the Grand Canyon. There were only two problems. It was early in the season, so it was cold, and it started to rain. Not rain, really, as much as drizzle, but it was pretty rough. We didn't care, though. What's a little rain? Even if it is darn near freezing rain?

Eventually, the antifreeze started to hit the tanks in some of the teenage fans around us, and sure enough a group of about five or six of them, braving the cold and the rain, took off their shirts, gathered at the front row overlooking third base, and started flexing their muscles and posing and roaring, just having themselves a ball and letting off some steam and trying to get the players' attention down below on the field.

My kids loved it. As always, half the fun in going to a baseball stadium—especially when you sit in the cheap seats—is the other fans. I could see that little Phillip really got a kick out of them so finally I said, "Phillip, I'll give you five dollars if you take off your shirt and go over there and flex your muscles with those guys." I didn't get the sentence fully out of my mouth before Phillip had his shirt off and was racing to join them. But they didn't notice him at first. They were all looking down at the field still trying to get the player's attention and they didn't see him behind them. So finally, little Phillip lets out a yell: "Hey, guys!!!" and they turn around to see this little 70-pound, rail—and I mean *rail*—thin bare-chested tousle-haired kid behind them and as soon as they look at him, he strikes a pose, curling his arms and flexing his biceps—what there were of them—and the guys all roared their approval, "Come on over, little man!" one of them shouted and they pushed him in right to the front and with their new mascot in place, they flexed and roared with a renewed vigor.

And that's when Derek Jeter, playing shortstop for the Yankees way down there below us on the baseball field, looked up, laughed a little, shook his head as if to say, "You guys are crazy!" and gave them all a little wave.

And that's the truth. That really happened.

LEGALLY ADVANCING RUNNERS AROUND THE BASES

Where was I?

We know what the defense wants (three outs) and we know half of what the offense wants (putting runners on base). Now comes the other half: once it puts runners on base, the offense wants to legally advance them around the bases to score a run.

You'll be happy to know that you have already learned a great deal about runners advancing around the bases.

- You know that on a hit, an error, or a ground out, runners must advance ahead of the batter if they are forced to advance, and if they are not, they can choose to advance or not as they see fit.

- You also know that when a batter walks or gets hit by a pitch, the batter is awarded first base automatically, and any runner on base who is forced to advance as a result, does so with impunity.
- You also know that when a batter hits a home run, life is grand: the batter scores a run and everyone on base automatically advances and scores as well.

So, in summary, you already know that during the course of a game, opportunities will present themselves for runners to legally advance around the bases. But what you don't know yet is that a good manager is not just going to sit in his dugout and wait for those opportunities to arise. Instead, he is going to seize the initiative by employing certain time-proven strategies that will raise the odds that his runners will advance and, eventually, score.

This, dear reader, is where the real fun starts. Putting runners on base is one thing, but the strategies employed to advance them, and to prevent them from advancing, can be quite brilliant.

Scoring Position

Before we discuss the strategies employed to legally advance runners, let's discuss the goal. The long-term goal, of course, is to move the runners around the bases until they step on (or otherwise touch) home plate and score a run. But the short-term goal, and the best way to ensure that the long-term goal is met, is to first move the runner, to legally advance the runner, into something called scoring position.

Scoring position is simply second or third base. A runner on second or third base is in scoring position; a runner on first base is not. It is called scoring position because a reasonably fast runner on second, and certainly one on third, is expected to score, to run all the way home, on most routine singles hit into the outfield.

If a batter hits a double or a triple, fine, he's already in scoring position. But the vast majority of runners who reach base will only reach first. They will walk, they will hit a single, maybe they will even get hit by a pitch. Managers must be adept, therefore, in the various strategies involved in **moving a runner up** from first base to second base and, thus, into scoring position. In other words, managers must be adept at forcing or **manufacturing runs** even when—especially when—it is just one of those games where those runs just don't seem to be happening on their own.

Scoring position is a key offensive concept. Constantly, during a baseball broadcast, you will hear the announcers refer to the presence and the fate of runners in scoring position, as in "The Diamondbacks have a good opportunity here, as they have two runners in scoring position with only one man out," which is good for the Diamondbacks, because they have runners on second and third and a routine single could score two runs for them. Or, on the other hand, you might hear something like "One of the major reasons the Diamondbacks lost today is that they had nine runners in scoring position and were able to score only two runs," which is bad for the Diamondbacks, because it means they had plenty of opportunities to score runs during the course of that particular game, but failed to capitalize on most of them. When a team's turn at bat ends with runners still in scoring position, it is said that those runners were **left in scoring position** or were **stranded**, as in "The Diamondbacks stranded two runners in the first and one more in the second."

The Lead, the Pickoff and Rule 7.08(c)

In the context of studying the strategies employed to legally advance runners around the bases, a deceptively simple rule upon which much depends is Official Baseball Rule 7.08(c), which says: "Any runner is out when he is tagged, while the ball is alive, while off his base."

What exactly does that mean? Well, imagine that there is a runner on first. Here's the pitch. Imagine the catcher catches the ball, starts to return it to the pitcher, but notices, down on first, that the runner had strolled two or three steps off first base in the direction of second, perhaps to get a head start in case the batter had gotten a hit on the previous pitch. According to Rule 7.08(c), the catcher can throw to first base, and if the first baseman catches the ball and tags that runner before he takes those two or three steps back to first base, then that runner is out.

Fair enough, but before going any further, notice what the rule *doesn't* say. It doesn't say that any runner who is off his base is *automatically* out. He's only out if he's tagged out. Thus, the rule implies that a runner *can* leave his base if he so chooses, to, as in the above example, get a two or three step head start in anticipation of the batter putting the ball in play.

As a result of what Rule 7.08(c) says and what it implies, what you will see every time a runner gets on base is that the runner, just as the pitcher is preparing to deliver his pitch, will take a two or three step head start off his base in the direction of the next base and he will stand there, ready to either advance to the next base if the batter puts the ball in play, or return quickly to base in the event that the pitcher (before throwing the pitch) or the catcher (after receiving the pitch) suddenly throws it to the first baseman in an attempt to tag him out before he gets back to the base. The head start is called **a lead**, the process of taking a head start is called **taking a lead**, and the pitcher or the catcher trying to throw him out before he can get back to base is called **a pickoff attempt** with the throw itself called a **pickoff**.

To expand on the concept of leads and pickoffs, let's go back again to the wording of the rule: "Any runner is out when he is tagged, *while the ball is alive*, while off his base." When is the ball alive in baseball? Well, we already know a few times when it's not:

- Batter hits a home run: ball is dead, batter and any runners can score with impunity.
- Batter hits a ground rule double: ball is dead and batter goes to second and any runners move up two bases with impunity.
- Batter is hit by a pitch or batter walks: ball is dead, batter can walk to first and any runner forced to advance as a result can advance a base as well with impunity.
- Batter hits a ground ball foul ball: ball is dead and cannot be retrieved and put into play by a fielder.

In addition, the ball also becomes dead when an umpire, on his own, elects to call time out (when, for example, a player gets injured), and when an umpire calls time out at the request of a player or manager (when, for example, a manager requests time to make a substitution, or, after sliding into a base, a player requests time so that he can get up, dust himself off and get situated for the next play). The Rules list a few more times when the ball is dead, but outside of these exceptions, the ball is pretty much always alive in baseball.

This may come as a surprise because, let's face it, in baseball there seems to be a lot of standing around. After a pitcher pitches the ball, you will generally see the infielders and outfielders all relax for a few seconds until the pitcher is ready to pitch again. Even the runner will appear to relax. A runner may even be found chatting with the fielder covering the base while they wait together for the next pitch. You would think that there is some kind of time out going on, but there isn't, and if you watch the runner closely, you'll see that to avoid a surprise pickoff attempt, that runner will relax between pitches *while standing on the base*. And he will remain standing on the base right up until the moment the pitcher takes his position on the mound and prepares to throw the next pitch, at which point the fielders will assume ready positions and the runner will once again take his two or three step lead toward the next base.

That begs the question: Why does the runner feel free to take his lead when the pitcher is preparing his next pitch? What makes *that* moment so different? Well, to some extent it's common sense, because as the pitcher is preparing to pitch, he has a lot on his mind. He's looking into the catcher for the sign, he's arranging his grip on the ball according to whatever type of pitch is coming next, and he's worried about getting the batter out.

But there is another reason the runner feels free to take his lead when the pitcher is preparing to pitch, and that is that as the pitcher takes his position on the mound and gets set to pitch, certain rules that govern the manner of pitching converge to make it a more difficult for him to pick the runner off. We will turn to those rules now and add yet another few brushstrokes to our ongoing portrait of the duel between batter and pitcher.

The Stretch Position Rules

Pitchers in Major League baseball do not pitch underhanded. They do not "quick pitch" a batter before he is ready. They do not windmill their delivery in an attempt to hide the ball or distract the batter. Unlike their fellow pitchers in cricket, they do not take a running start before pitching or bounce the ball on its way to the plate. They do not pretend to pitch, hesitate, then pitch. They do not pitch with their back to the batter. They do not pitch from a seated position. They do not...

Why not? Why doesn't a pitcher in baseball do any of these things? Because there are several rules that say he cannot. There are also several rules that mandate the way a pitcher must stand, where he must stand, and how he must move while in the act of pitching. Sandwiched between what the rules say they cannot do and what the rules say they must do, pitchers all pretty much end up pitching the same odd, stepping, pivoting, kicking, lunging way.

The overarching purpose of the rules of pitching is to prevent trick throws, surprise throws, sneaky throws and gimmicky throws by the pitcher, either when pitching to the batter or when trying to pickoff a runner. Baseball does not see itself as a game based on unseemly now-you-see-it-now-you-don't trickery, but as a sophisticated game of strategy and tactics, of psychological diversion and deception. The rules, especially the rules of pitching, aim to keep it that way.

To set the stage, the rules state that a pitcher can only pitch from one of two positions. Pitchers can use either of the two positions, or even switch back and forth from one to the other, but each position has a distinct role. The first position, the **windup position**, aims to generate maximum power in each pitch, but because it involves a rather intricate progression

Above and opposite: A pitch from the windup position involves a high leg lift or leg kick, such as Juan Marichal's famous high kick. Mariano Rivera's more modest knee lift, in contrast, is typical of the set position. Marichal, by the way, is the guy with the high stirrups; Mariano, the guy without (National Baseball Hall of Fame Library, Cooperstown, New York).

of time-consuming movements, runners would be at liberty to take bigger and bigger leads while the pitch is being delivered. The windup position, therefore, is used almost exclusively when there are no runners on base.

In the windup position, the pitcher takes the sign while facing the catcher and with his **pivot foot** (throwing side foot) on the pitching rubber. The ensuing details may differ slightly

according to individual styles, but the rules keep differences to a minimum. Generally, in the windup position, a pitcher's hands are together in front of him and his pitching hand, with the ball in it, is in his baseball glove. At this point, inside his glove and out of the batter's view, the pitching hand is forming the grip on the ball that will define the next pitch.

The pitcher then gathers power into his throwing motion by simultaneously rotating his body to the side so that his throwing arm is away from the batter, raising his hands (still together so as to hide the tell-tale grip until the last possible second) and lifting high or kicking his non-throwing side leg. Then, in what Nolan Ryan called a "controlled fall toward home plate," he brings his raised leg down into a long, hard step towards home plate, drives forward with his pivot foot and fires the ball to the catcher.

The second pitching position, known mostly as **the stretch position** or, simply, **the stretch**, may sacrifice some power on the pitch, but it is much simpler and less time consuming than the windup position and therefore is most often used with runners on base. The pitcher begins already turned to the side so that his throwing arm is away from the batter. His pivot foot is on the pitcher's plate but his other foot is in front of it, closer to the batter. Thus, the whole pre-pitch pivot to the side is eliminated. This, and a much shorter arm raise and leg kick, make the stretch a much quicker delivery in total and, again, more ideal when there are runners on base.

Many of the rules that restrict pitcher movements when there is a runner on base apply to both the stretch and windup position. However, since, for reasons discussed above, the stretch is almost always resorted to when there is a runner on base, these rules are most often levied against a pitcher who is pitching from that position. Additionally, there are some restrictive rules that apply specifically to the stretch. We will refer to these restrictive rules collectively as the Stretch Position Rules.

I would venture to say that the Stretch Position Rules are second only to the Force Out/Tag Out Rules as far as being vital to an understanding and appreciation of the game of baseball. Every runner who gets on base knows the limitations placed on the pitcher by the Stretch Position Rules, and they will do their best to take advantage of them by taking their biggest leads at the exact moment when those limitations are the most restrictive. Pitchers, in response, will use speed and surprise to try to keep those limitations as narrow and as innocuous as possible. Since, again, runs will most often be generated not by home runs, but by a runner getting on base and then advancing, the Stretch Position Rules will be applied and tested and even disputed constantly during the course of the game.

Unfortunately, the authors of the *Official Baseball Rules* have opted for some reason not to present what I call the Stretch Position Rules in terms that might make them easy for anyone, never mind a beginner, to understand. Once again, therefore, it is left to me to humbly attempt to put together a clear set of guidelines in their stead. In the interests of full disclosure, I must tell you that out of necessity, other sources besides the obscure verbiage of the *Official Baseball Rules* had to be taken into consideration, such as instructional umpire videos, books written by pitchers, and, again, the game as I see it played on a day-to-day basis.

OK, ready? Here we go.

Stretch Position Rule #1: The pitcher's pivot foot must remain in contact with the pitcher's plate throughout the pitching motion, beginning with when he is taking the sign from the catcher.

- *You remember the pitcher's plate, that 2' by 6" white slab of rubber that sits on top of the pitcher's mound? The Official Baseball Rules say that as long as the pitcher is not in contact with the pitcher's plate, he is just like any other infielder and is no more constrained in his movements than they are.*
- *However, any hopes the pitcher has of staying a free-wheeling, devil-may-care infielder for long are dashed by Stretch Position Rule # 1. This rule forces the pitcher to come to the pitcher's plate and place his pivot foot on it before he takes the sign from the catcher— thereby forcing him to come under the rules governing pitching as opposed to the rules gov-*

erning infielders—and to keep one foot in contact with the pitcher's plate throughout his pitching motion. This is why pitchers in baseball don't take running starts, and this is what keeps them on the pitcher's mound while they pitch.

Stretch Position Rule #2: After taking the sign from the catcher, the pitcher may commence his own unique "natural preliminary motion" prior to pitching. The second rule is that during his preliminary motion, the pitcher must have one hand at his side.

- *The preliminary motion is the routine, the movement, a pitcher goes through before he gets into the actual pitching position. It is, you might say, the stretch that gave the stretch position its name. The preliminary motion is unique to each pitcher and is each pitcher's way of establishing his balance and getting comfortable on the mound. After each pitch, the momentum of the pitch will throw the pitcher off to the side of the pitcher's mound. The preliminary motion helps them regain and reestablish their position as they prepare for the next pitch.*
- *Once they've found a preliminary motion that works for them, pitchers will use it before pitch after pitch, year after year, and the preliminary motions of the better pitchers will be imitated and adopted all the way down the line from the Major Leagues to the Little Leagues.*
- *In his preliminary motion, for example, Craig Kimbrel of the Braves starts in the upright position, his non-throwing side turned towards the batter. Then, in one flowing movement, he turns his upper body so that it is square with the batter and he bends forward at the*

Craig Kimbrel takes the sign while pausing in his unique preliminary motion. By holding his empty right or pitching hand at his side, Kimbrel is actually fulfilling the requirements of one of the rules governing pitching motions (Jake Roth, USA TODAY Sports).

waist towards home plate until his chest is virtually parallel to the ground and he seems about to tip over. At the same time, he raises his throwing hand out to the side as if, as one announcer said, he were resting his arm on a table. From this position, Kimbrel will pause, peer into the catcher for the sign, then, having gotten the sign, he will swing back into the upright position while turning his side to the batter again. Does he have to bend over so extensively to get the sign from the catcher? Of course not. He could see the catcher just as clearly standing erect. But this routine, again, is his own personal way of re-establishing his balance and poise on the mound so that he can deliver the next pitch with maximum effectiveness.

- *The second Stretch Position Rule requires one hand to be at the pitcher's side during the preliminary motion so that the world knows that a pitch is not imminent. As long as one hand is at his side, he is still in the preliminary motion, and everyone, including runners, knows he is still in the preliminary position. There will be no sudden throw, surprising either batter or runner, as long as his hand is dangling by the pitcher's side. Kimbrel's raising his right hand to the side as if he were resting it on a table may look a bit odd, but essentially it is his own way of fulfilling this obligation.*

Stretch Position Rule #3: After his preliminary motion ends and before he throws his pitch, the pitcher must **set** or **come set** or **come to the set** or **come to the set position**, which means that he must hold the ball in both hands in front of his body and his hands must come to a complete stop.

- *The effect of the third rule is that everyone will now know that the pitcher is about to pitch. When the pitcher finishes his preliminary motion and comes to a full stop with the ball in front of his body, he is notifying the world that the preliminaries to the pitch are over. The pitch is imminent.*

Stretch Position Rule #4: There are two ways a pitcher can legally interrupt his pitching motion to attempt a pickoff. The first way is to step off the pitcher's plate *backwards* with his pivot foot before throwing to a base in a pickoff attempt.

- *Remember that the pitcher, before he pitched, had to place himself under the jurisdiction of the pitching rules by placing his pivot foot on the pitcher's plate. By now stepping off that pitcher's plate, he essentially disengages himself from those rules again and gains a great deal of flexibility in how he deals with runners on base. The catch, however is that he may only take his pivot foot off the pitcher's plate by stepping backwards off of the plate.*
- *The pitcher has to step backwards off the pitcher's plate because the lords of baseball want the runner to be given fair notice that a pickoff attempt may be coming. If the pitcher could step off the pitcher's plate to the far side of the plate, or in front, where a runner might not be able to see it, the runner could be fooled. Like I said, baseball does not fancy itself to be a game of deceit and trickery.*
- *But at the same time, be advised that a pitcher does not step backwards off the plate, then turn towards the runner, then throw a pickoff throw. And what I mean by this is, there is no "then" to it. Major League pitchers are very good at what they do: It all happens very, very quickly and in one smooth motion. Yes, the runner will have a clear view of that pivot foot stepping back off the rubber, but it will only give him a moment's notice that the pickoff is coming. The runner, therefore, has to pay close attention to the pitcher's position on the*

pitcher's plate. If he sees the pitcher begin to step backwards off the plate, it's a clear sign that a pickoff throw is coming, and coming very quickly.

Stretch Position Rule #5: The second way a pitcher can legally interrupt his pitching motion to attempt a pickoff is that he can make the pickoff throw while his pivot foot (back foot) is still in contact with the pitcher's plate, but he must first step in the direction of the targeted base with his non-pivot foot (front foot) before throwing.

- *A pitcher, therefore, has a choice. He can step back off the rubber to throw to a base, but, again, the runner will see his foot stepping back and he will therefore have notice—however brief—that the pickoff is coming. Or the pitcher can avoid giving this notice by staying on the rubber with his pivot foot while he throws to the base, but in that case he must step in the direction of that base with his other foot, his non-pivot foot, before throwing. This, in effect, also gives the runner notice that a pickoff is coming, the notice being the step toward the base. Again, the notice is extremely brief. The pitcher doesn't step toward the base, then wind up, then throw: Here too, there is no "then" involved. It all happens almost instantaneously. Tom Seaver wrote that pitchers need "quick, almost dancing feet" to carry out this move. The rules call it a "step and throw," but I have seen it called a "jump turn" and I think that captures the speed of it more accurately.*

Be advised, however, that it is only a "jump turn" for a right-handed pitcher, who naturally has his back to first base. He has to jump and turn towards first in order to throw. A lefty pitcher is already facing first and so it is infinitely easier for him to throw to first. He doesn't have to jump or turn at all. He just has to step toward first and throw.

Stretch Position Rule #6: Finally, once the pitcher begins to pitch, once "his natural pitching motion commits him to the pitch," he must go ahead with the pitch and may not at that point turn to pickoff a runner.

- *This rule prevents the pitcher from faking a pitch, then suddenly turning to make a pickoff attempt instead. At the moment the pitcher has physically committed to a pitch, the runner knows he is no longer in danger of a pickoff attempt. The runner can now increase his lead dramatically.*

And those, dear readers, are your six stretch position pitching rules, the rules that will come into play whenever a runner is on base. In summary: the pitcher must make contact with the plate before and while pitching, the pitcher must hold one hand at his side while in his preliminary motion, the pitcher must come to the set, or full stop, position after his preliminary motion and before he pitches, the pitcher can only throw a pickoff if he first either steps backwards off the pitchers plate or steps toward the base he is throwing to and, finally, once he has physically committed to the pitch, he must go through with it.

What if a pitcher breaks one of those rules? What if, for example, while he is in contact with the pitcher's plate, he snaps off a pickoff throw to first base without first stepping towards first or without stepping backwards off the pitcher's plate? If the pitcher breaks any one of these six rules, or any one of the several less common ones that we haven't even mentioned here, the home plate umpire will call time, step from behind the plate, wave his hands and announce that the pitcher has committed a **balk** (pronounced "bawk"), which means that he broke one of the rules of pitching. The penalty for a balk is that the ball will be dead,

Now that Tim Lincecum, the Giants pitcher, has committed to his pitch and the danger of a pickoff is over, behind him the runner for the Milwaukee Brewers, Prince Fielder, is at liberty to increase his lead from first. Notice the position of the Giants' first baseman. Apparently he was trying to keep the runner's lead to a minimum by positioning himself on first base and "holding the runner," which we will discuss shortly (Eric Broder Van Dyke\123rf).

and any runners on base will advance one base with impunity. A runner on third base will come home to score.

There are no less than thirteen ways to commit a balk, and most baseball fans don't know, and they don't need to know, more than one or two of them. I would say that the balk rule violation that most fans are familiar with and that comes up most often is the failure of a pitcher, when coming to the set position, to come to a full stop with the ball in front of his chest before pitching. Like cars coming to a stop sign, pitchers, in their haste to pitch the ball before the runner takes too big a lead, often confuse a rolling stop for a full stop and get called for a balk as a result.

I haven't discussed any windup position rules because, frankly, they are almost never at issue. Like the pitcher in the stretch, the pitcher in the windup position must keep his pivot foot on the pitcher's rubber when pitching, and there are some weird little rules that define the windup movements, but they are really not worth going into because, well, you just never hear anything about them. Again, the rules that we have been discussing, the rules regarding movements toward the runner, are the pitching rules that are most often contested and they are virtually never called against a pitcher in the windup position because, again, pitchers don't normally use the windup position when there are runners on base.

Rundowns and Rule 7.01

With these Stretch Position Rules in mind, let's explore a few pickoff scenarios:

Pickoff Example # 1. Runner on first takes a lead of a few steps. Pitcher comes to a set position. Runner didn't anticipate the pickoff, didn't **read the pickoff** correctly, and thought the pitcher was going to go ahead with the pitch and, as a result, has taken too big a lead. Pitcher (a righty) suddenly "jump turns" and throws to the first baseman. Runner tries to get back to first base and, at the last second, dives headfirst, his hand reaching out to first base in an effort to **beat the tag**. But, alas, the first baseman takes the throw and slaps down his glove on the runner's hand before it touches first base. Runner is tagged out on the pick-off.

When I say the runner didn't "read the pickoff," I mean that he detected nothing in the pitcher's movements that indicated the pickoff attempt was imminent. Like batters looking for certain mannerisms in a pitcher that might reveal, in advance, whether he is going to throw a breaking ball or a fastball, runners look for what are called **tells**—tell-tale signs— in a pitcher's stance or pre-pitch mannerisms that might reveal, in advance, whether he going to go ahead and pitch the ball to the catcher, or turn suddenly and attempt a pickoff. Coco Crisp of the Oakland A's, one of the game's most prolific baserunners (and the holder of one of the game's great names) listed the following tells:

- As a whole, said Coco, careless pitchers have a common tell: they dig their toes on their back foot into the ground when they are about to pitch, probably to get a better push off. But when they intend to turn and throw a pickoff, they don't.
- More specifically, there was one pitcher on the Twins who, when Coco was on first, would come to the set position and stare down Coco as Coco took his lead. Then the pitcher would quickly turn his head, look in at the catcher and pitch, all in one motion. Coco knew that once the pitcher turned his head towards the catcher, the pick-off threat was over. If the pitcher, once he turned his head toward the plate, had varied the

The first baseman is about to catch the pickoff throw, and the runner, to avoid the tag, has dived back to first base. It looks to me like he'll made it back in time (shutterstock.com/Jamie Roach).

amount of time he looked in at the catcher before pitching, or even, on occasion, had he looked in at the catcher and then looked back at Coco again, his movements would have been less predictable and Coco could not have been so sure what he was going to do next.

- A certain pitcher on the Orioles, says Coco, would take a slightly different stance on the mound when he was preparing his pitch as opposed to when he was preparing to throw a pickoff. As a left-hander, he would be facing Coco as he stood on first. If Coco could see the inside of his thighs, that meant he was preparing to pitch. When he was preparing to throw a pickoff, says Coco, his stance closed up.

Pickoff Example # 2. Again, runner, unable to spot a tell and believing the pitcher was about to pitch, has taken too big a lead. Pitcher suddenly "jump turns" and throws to the first baseman. Runner knows he'll never **beat the throw** back to first, so, instead, he takes his chances on running to and trying to safely reach second. First baseman catches the pitcher's pickoff throw and then throws it on to the second baseman, but the runner slides under the tag and is safe at second base.

Wait a minute. Hold everything. Let's get back to Rule 7.08(c), which says: "Any runner is out when he is tagged, while the ball is alive, while off *his* base." Doesn't "his base" in this situation mean "first base?" In which case, isn't this runner obligated to return to first, as opposed to trying to advance to second?

Again, let's look at what the rule doesn't say: it doesn't say a runner will be out if tagged while off his "*original* base" or his "*previous* base" or his "*preceding* base." Nor, on the other hand, does it say "his previous base or a *subsequent* base" and it doesn't say "*any* base." It only says "his base."

So what exactly does "*his* base" mean? For help, let's turn to another rule, Rule 7.01, which simply states: "A runner acquires the right to an unoccupied base when he touches it before he is out." The rule is pretty open-ended, putting no specific condition precedent on just how the runner has to "acquire the right to" an unoccupied base. In other words, the rule doesn't say that a runner acquires the right to an unoccupied base when he advances to that base because of a teammate's hit, or walk, or getting hit by a pitch, or because of a fielder's error. The runner *could* get to a base by any of those means, of course, but he doesn't *have to* get there by any of those means. He just has to, well, *get there*. And, apparently, he can get there by whatever means possible, like the runner in our second example, above, who advanced safely to second on his own when he realized he'd be thrown out if he tried to make it back to first.

"Any runner is out when he is tagged, while the ball is alive, while off *his* base." If we reconsider Rule 7.08(c) now in light of what we now know about Rule 7.01, it becomes clear that the words "*his* base" were not meant to be words of limitation that might keep a runner on one base or another. "His base" is, basically, whatever base he happens to be on or whatever base he is trying to get to at the time.

One more example might clear things up a bit:

Pickoff Example # 3. Again, the runner has taken too big a lead. As the pickoff throw comes to the first baseman, the runner realizes he'll never make it back safely to first. Instead,

The Dodgers runner, in grey, is caught in a rundown between two Cubs fielders. Note that the Cubs fielders are running toward him to limit his running room as the rundown unfolds (David Banks, USA TODAY Sports).

he chooses to try to advance to second. The first baseman takes the pickoff throw from the pitcher and throws it on to the second baseman. The runner, halfway to second base, sees that he will be tagged out at second if he continues to advance. Therefore he changes his mind and decides that maybe returning to first would be the better option after all. He stops in his tracks on his way to second, turns around and starts running back to first. The second baseman, seeing this, throws the ball back to the first baseman. The runner, seeing that he will be tagged out at first if he continues to advance, changes his mind yet again and decides that maybe the view from second base is better after all. He therefore stops in his tracks on his way to first, turns around yet again and starts running back to second. Once again, the first baseman throws to the second baseman in an effort to get him out.

When a runner, caught between two bases, runs back and forth like this between the bases in an effort to avoid a tag out, it is called a **rundown**. And the runner is said to have been **caught in a rundown**.

The runner in this rundown is free to either advance to second or to return to first if he gets the opportunity to. If, for example, while the runner is running towards second, the relay throw from the first baseman accidentally sails over the second baseman's head out into left field, the runner will no doubt take advantage of the mistake and run safely to second. If, on the other hand, while the runner is running back towards first, the first baseman accidentally drops the relay throw from the second baseman, the runner will no doubt take advantage of that mistake and run back safely to first base.

The rundown is therefore living proof that a runner's movements on the base paths do not have to be dictated by other events, such as the fortunes of a subsequent batter. His decision to try for second base in the first place, and his subsequent attempts to arrive safely at either second or first by running back and forth between them, is completely of his own volition, and this ability of a runner to act independently on the base paths will be very important to our next discussion.

But before moving on to our next discussion, let's finish up with a few observations about rundowns.

The fielders involved in the rundown, say for the sake of argument, the first baseman and the second baseman, while tossing the ball back and forth between them, will move progressively closer to the runner to cut down on his running room. Since the runner has to stay relatively close to the base line and cannot evade the fielders by straying too far from side to side, eventually most rundowns end with the runner being tagged out.

And that begs the question: if he is going to get tagged out anyway, why would a runner put himself through the embarrassing spectacle of scampering back and forth and back and forth between fielders in a rundown? There are two reasons.

First, the runner has nothing to lose. Knowing for certain that if he tries to return to first he will be tagged out on the pickoff, he might as well try for second instead. After all, why not? As long as he keeps changing directions and forces the fielders to keep throwing the ball back and forth to each other, there's a chance that one of them will mess up on either the throw or the catch and the runner will arrive safely at a base because of the error.

The second reason a runner might subject himself to a rundown is that if there is another runner on base ahead of him, while all the commotion is going on with the rundown, the lead runner just might be able to move up if the fielders get distracted by the rundown and forget he's there. Suppose, for example, there are runners on first and third. Suppose the runner on first gets caught in a rundown between first and second. Rules 7.01 and 7.08(c) apply to the runner on third as well as the runner on first in the sense that the runner on third is free to take a lead and run home if the fielders stop paying attention to him.

Stealing Bases

The Peak of the Mountain

While I was planning this book, the challenge I feared most was explaining stolen bases. It just seemed the penultimate oddity in a game that was full of oddities. Force outs, tag outs, walks, errors, ground rule doubles... I could get a handle on all of them after setting the stage with a few preliminaries. Stealing bases, however, was just another animal completely. The preliminaries needed to set the stage just seemed endless.

Earlier, when I was contemplating writing this book and trying to measure what I might be getting myself into, I approached a friend of mine, a big baseball fan, and asked him how he would explain stealing bases to me if I had absolutely no knowledge of baseball.

"That's easy," he said. "I would tell you that as long as the ball is alive, a runner is free to advance to the next base, and if he gets there safely, well, there he is!"

"What's a runner?" I asked.

"It's a batter who reaches base," he said.

"What's a batter?" I asked, "And what's a base?"

"A base is... The runner needs to run safely around three of them to score a run." he said.

"Fine, but what's a batter?" I asked, "And what's a run? And when is a ball alive and when is it not alive? And why did you say he has to run safely? What happens if he runs unsafely?"

"Leave me alone," my friend said.

You'll be happy to know that the perhaps dozens of preliminaries needed to approach the issue of stolen bases have all now been covered in this book. If you've come this far, and if you've been able to follow me so far, then, without knowing it, you've nearly reached the mountaintop of baseball logic and knowledge. You're almost there. Stolen bases, the peak of the mountain, is now within view.

Stealing a Base

The rundown and Rule 7.01 establish that a baserunner has a certain amount of independence as to how he advances from one base to the next. Nevertheless, every time we've discussed a runner, already on base, advancing legally to the next base, he has advanced at least initially because of something that someone else did. A runner on first, for example, advances when a teammate gets a hit, or walks, or gets hit by a pitch. Or, for that matter, a runner on first tries to advance to second because the pitcher has him picked off at first and forced him into a rundown.

But if we take Rule 7.01 literally, that there is no condition precedent necessary for a runner to "acquire the right to an unoccupied base," then doesn't that mean that the runner could advance to the next base whenever the heck he wants to? Doesn't that mean that as long as the ball is alive, he can just, well ... *go?*

Yes. That's what it means.

But wait a minute. If that's true, if within those very wide parameters, runners on base are free to advance to the next base on their own as they see fit, why isn't your average baseball game just a free-for-all of runners getting on base and dashing from one base to the next with the fielders falling all over themselves just trying to keep up with them? Why do runners stop on a base at all? Why don't they just keep running, advancing from one base to the next in rapid succession?

The answer is: they would if they could. In reality, however, the pitcher would just stand there, picking them off one after another like toy ducks at a shooting gallery. Therefore, if a runner decides to try to advance to the next base on his own, he has to be very careful and plan his attempt so that he initiates it at that moment when the fielders are least likely to throw him out as he is advancing. How does he do that?

You already know the answer.

But first, let's get the terms down: A runner who advances to the next base on his own, unaided by a hit, walk, error, out, hit by pitch, balk, passed ball or wild pitch, is said to **steal the base**, with the completed act being referred to as a **stolen base**, and the attempt being a **stolen base attempt**. If the catcher throws out the runner before he steals his base, it is said that the runner was **caught stealing** or **thrown out stealing**.

There are two components to successful base stealing.

First, prior to his stolen base attempt, the runner will shorten the distance between the base he is on and the base he intends to steal by taking as big a lead as possible. We already know what's involved here: on one hand, we know about the dangers of getting picked off, and, on the other hand, we know about the Stretch Position Rules and the balk rules that limit the pitcher's pickoff movements, and on the third hand, we know about the tells that enable the alert baserunner to take as big a lead as possible.

Second, after taking his lead, the runner will, when the moment is right, suddenly sprint to the next base in an attempt to steal it. When is the moment right? We know that once a pitcher physically commits to his pitching movement, the danger of a pickoff is over and he must go ahead and pitch the ball. That exact moment of physical commitment—followed as it is by a second or so when the ball will be flying through the air on its way to the catcher and under no fielder's control—is the moment that the runner will begin his steal attempt. If the runner has been successful in reading the tells and taking a good lead and then getting off to a good running start at exactly the proper time so as to maximize the possibility of success, it will be said that he **got a good jump** on the pitcher in his stolen base attempt.

This is how it will happen:

There is a runner on first base. He takes his lead. The pitcher comes to the set position, turns his head and peeks back over his shoulder at the runner. Suddenly, and very quickly, the pitcher "jump turns" toward first and fires the ball to the first baseman in a pickoff attempt. The runner dives safely back to first base. The first baseman tosses the ball back to the pitcher. The runner gets up again and stands on the base. The pitcher then steps back on the mound, places one foot on the rubber, and looks into the catcher for the sign. The runner again takes his lead. The pitcher comes to the set position, and again peeks back over his shoulder at the runner. The runner is crouched down, ready to either return quickly to first in the event of another pickoff attempt, or spring towards second once the time is right. The pitcher turns away from the runner, looks back at home plate then lifts up his front knee, cocks his pitching arm, drives forward and... Suddenly, just a fraction of a second before he releases the ball, the runner takes off in a mad sprint towards second base. The pitch flies through the air. The batter swings but misses. The catcher, seeing the steal attempt, catches the pitch, stands, and fires the ball to the second baseman, who is already running over to cover the base and receive the throw. The ball, the runner and the second baseman all converge on second at almost the exact same time. The runner slides, the second baseman catches the throw and slaps down the tag on the runner's spikes. Safe? Out? The second base umpire steps forward to make the call...

Any base can be stolen. A runner on first can steal second, a runner on second can steal third, and a runner on third can, believe it or not, steal home, but that's a very rare feat indeed, usually involving a very fast and very daring runner at third, a right-handed batter (who naturally obstructs the catcher's view of the runner on third) and a left-handed pitcher (who naturally stands on the mound with his back toward the runner on third) who has, for a fatal moment, stopped paying attention to that runner.

The vast majority of stolen bases, however, involve a runner on first stealing second. Why? Because once he's on second, he's in scoring position, and, especially if he's fast enough to steal second in the first place, he can most probably score on a routine hit to the outfield. But there is another benefit to stealing second, and that is that it **erases the possibility of a double play**. While that runner was on first, any routine ground ball hit to the right side of the infield had a good possibility of resulting in a force-at-second-force-at-first double play. Once that runner on first steals second, however, the only force play left is the batter being forced at first. Hence, the danger of a double play is removed.

Stealing third normally just isn't worth the risk. There are some advantages to having a runner on third instead of second, and we'll discuss those shortly, but for now suffice it to say that stealing second, and therefore putting a runner in scoring position, is the primary stolen base scenario and one of the primary tools in a manager's toolbox to legally advance runners around the bases.

Two Historical Stolen Bases

We're not quite done with stolen bases yet, but by way of taking a small break, allow me to talk a bit about how deceptively important a single stolen base can be.

When one thinks of dramatic game-changing offensive plays, home runs usually come to mind. Fair enough, but an experienced baseball fan knows that a well-timed stolen base has the potential to be just as pivotal, just as consequential. In fact, one could argue that two of the most important offensive plays in modern baseball history were stolen bases.

For the first, let's return, painful though it may be for me personally, to the year between 2003 and 2005. I've already told how that year the Red Sox rallied from a three game deficit to beat the Yankees in the AL Championship Series. I've also told how, in game four, they were even losing—by a score of 4–3—going into the bottom of the ninth. Only three outs separated the Red Sox from yet another embarrassing post-season elimination at the hands of the hated Yankees, and from yet another season without a championship.

When Red Sox outfielder batter Kevin Millar strode to the plate to lead off the bottom of the ninth, facing him on the mound was Mariano Rivera, the greatest relief pitcher in the history of baseball. Rivera was tough enough as it was, but in the postseason, hard as it is to believe, the Master of Control actually kicked it up a notch. The Yankees had made the playoffs every year since 1995, and since 1997 Mariano had won eight postseason games, lost only one, and walked a microscopic six batters in 84 postseason innings. If ever a game, and a series, seemed in the bag, this was that game, and this was that series.

Mariano walked Kevin Millar on five pitches.

As soon as they got over the shock, the Sox pulled Millar for pinch runner Dave Roberts, a gifted base stealer. If Roberts could steal second, the tying run would be in scoring position, still with no one out. As Roberts edged off first and took his lead, life began coming back to the Red Sox faithful packing Fenway Park. Down three games to none, losing in the ninth inning and facing Mariano on the mound, the buzz in the crowd no doubt represented the triumph of hope over experience, but such, for many, many years, had been the lot of the sturdy Red Sox fan.

Roberts took his lead, eyes staring at Mariano's back for a tell that he would be coming to first with a pickoff attempt instead of pitching. Suddenly, Mariano turned and rifled the ball to first baseman Tony Clark. Roberts dove safely back to the bag. Clark returned the ball to Mariano. Mariano set. Again Roberts took a lead. Again, Mariano threw over. Again, Roberts dove back to the bag. Three close pickoff attempts in a row; three times Roberts dove back, got up, dusted himself off, and the battle of wits continued.

Finally, Mariano turned and pitched to batter Bill Mueller. And when he did, Roberts took off like a shot and stole second, barely beating out catcher Jorge Posada's throw. Now the Red Sox had what they wanted: the tying runner in scoring position with nobody out. And the ever-resilient Red Sox fans were back in the game in a very vocal way.

The next batter, Bill Mueller, took ball one, then, on Mariano's second pitch, sliced a sharp grounder right up the middle, too far to Mariano's right and too far to shortstop Derek Jeter's left for either of them to make a play. As the ball sped untouched into centerfield, Dave Roberts flew around third and scored the tying run.

Ten days later, the Red Sox were the world champions for the first time in eighty-six years.

Boston is a great sports town. Considering its size, it is probably home to more great sports events per square foot than any other city in the country. And yet, in 2011, when the New England Sports Network took a poll for the greatest moment in Boston sports history, Dave Roberts' stolen base was voted in as one of the top four. Think about that. Dave Mueller's base hit that drove in Roberts to tie the game wasn't even mentioned in the polling. Nor was Roberts actually scoring the tying run. Nor, for that matter, was Big Papi's home run in the bottom of the twelfth that eventually won that game for the Sox. No, it was Roberts stealing second that advanced so far in the poll. Why? Because Boston fans were sophisticated enough to know that everything that happened after that, *everything*, would not have happened were it not for that single stolen base.

The second important historical stolen base I'd like to discuss is Brooklyn Dodger infielder Jackie Robinson's steal of home plate in the first game of the 1955 World Series against the Yankees.

Jackie Robinson was the first African American to play in Major League baseball. Prior to April 5, 1947, when he broke the color barrier by playing first base for the Brooklyn Dodgers in a game against the Braves, African Americans were excluded from the Majors and had no choice but to play either abroad, or in what were called the **Negro Leagues**, a succession of leagues dating back to 1885 that were comprised of professional teams made up of black and dark-skinned Latin players. Jackie Robinson broke in with the Kansas City

Monarchs of the Negro Leagues, but he played there only one season before enterprising Dodgers owner Branch Rickey shattered the institutionalized racism of the Majors by signing him up for Brooklyn.

The story of Jackie Robinson, grandson of a slave and son of a man who worked on a plantation for twelve dollars a month, is the subject of several books and is too sweeping and complex a topic to try to summarize here, but I will say that it is very important to keep in mind that when Jackie Robinson took the field for the first time for the Dodgers, the Civil Rights movement was still several years away. School busing, desegregation, the emergence of Civil Rights leaders and legislation, were all still far down the road. Jackie Robinson was not only a pioneer in desegregation and equal opportunity in baseball, but a pioneer in the very concepts themselves. Jackie Robinson, as one writer put it, was "Martin Luther King's warm-up act."

As I researched this book and delved further into Jackie's story than I ever had before, I found that what he went through, even after all these years, is embarrassing. That his teammates circulated a petition to not play with him, and other teams threatened to go on strike rather than play against him; that he was not allowed to stay in the same hotels with his white teammates, and his teammates went ahead and stayed in those hotels anyway; that one opposing team actually used bats to mimic machine guns and made motions from the dugout as if they were shooting at him; that his wife, in the stands, somehow hoped that her body would block the racist taunts shouted by fans behind her so that Jackie, on the field, wouldn't hear them... I'm wrong. Embarrassing is not a strong enough word.

In Brooklyn now, there is a Minor League team, an affiliate of the Mets, called the Brooklyn Cyclones. Outside there is a beautiful statue portraying Jackie and his teammate, Pee Wee Reese, standing side by side, their eyes focused off into the distance, with Pee Wee's arm draped tenderly around Jackie's shoulder. The statue depicts an incident in 1947, Jackie's first year in the Majors, when Pee Wee, during pre-game warm ups, became the subject of vicious verbal abuse by the opposing team because he was playing alongside a black man. "Pee Wee didn't answer them," Jackie later wrote in his autobiography, *I Never Had It Made*. "Without a glance in their direction, he left his position and walked over to me. He put his hand on my shoulder and began talking to me. His words weren't important. I don't even remember what he said. It was the gesture of comradeship and support that counted. As he stood talking with me with a friendly arm around my shoulder, he was saying loud and clear, 'Yell. Heckle. Do anything you want. We came here to play baseball.' "

Jackie Robinson was fast. As a base stealer, he added the element of speed and surprise and daring to the Dodgers and seemed a big step forward to bring a first world championship ever to Brooklyn fans who, like the fans of Dave Roberts' Red Sox, had gone through decades of frustration and disappointment. "Wait 'til next year!" was the motto of the perennially disappointed Brooklyn Dodgers fan.

Jackie was an exciting, unpredictable, unorthodox player, whose forte was stealing home, a rare and wonderful feat that seems to defy belief. A pitcher, after all, is throwing the ball to the catcher at speeds in excess of 90 mph. How can a runner, from third, beat that throw home and slide safely across the bag? Jackie would go on to do it 19 times in his relatively short career.

And yet, in 1947, the year Jackie came to the Majors, it was the Yankees, not the Dodgers, who won the World Series. In fact, the Yankees would go on to win World Series champi-

Pee Wee Reese and Jackie Robinson statue at MCU Park in Brooklyn (photograph by Mike Carey).

onships in 1949, 1950, 1951, 1952 and 1953. In four of those six World Series, they would beat these same Jackie Robinson-led Dodgers.

By the time the 1955 World Series rolled around, pitting, yet again, the Dodgers and the Yankees, Jackie Robinson had seen his best days. He was 36 years old, his legs were giving him trouble, he was arguing with his manager, his performance had leveled off, and he wasn't playing near as much as he used to. He knew going into the '55 World Series that it might be his last chance to win the World Championship he so coveted.

Jackie started the first game for the Dodgers, but with the Yankees winning 6–3 going into the top of the eighth in Game 1, it seemed like things were heading down an all-too-familiar path. Carl Furillo led off the top of the eighth for the Dodgers with a single, but Gil Hodges—who as manager of the 1969 Mets, would be involved in the famous "shoe polish incident" discussed earlier—flied out for the first out.

Then the Dodgers caught a break. Jackie, the next batter, hit a hot ground ball that was mishandled by Yankees shortstop Billy Martin (the same Billy Martin who, as manager of the Yankees, would later instigate the aforementioned Pine Tar Incident), and when the smoke cleared, Furillo was on third and Jackie was on second, still with only one man out. Then Dodgers second baseman Don Zimmer hit into a fly-ball out that allowed Furillo to score and moved Jackie to third.

The Dodgers had narrowed the Yankees' lead to 6–4, and they had Jackie on third base, but now the Yankees were just one out away from ending the inning. Jackie took his lead off third and watched pitcher Whitey Ford go into a windup. Pitching from the windup position, as opposed to the stretch position, was perhaps a curious choice on the part of Whitey. The high leg kick of a full windup, as discussed, meant it would take that much longer for the ball to get to the plate. Jackie was surprised. "Whitey Ford was winding up. With me on third? Any time they give me a run that way," he said after the game, "I take it."

"I just took off," he wrote in his autobiography, "I really didn't care whether I made it or not—I was just tired of waiting." And by waiting, he meant waiting for a championship, waiting to bring home a World Series flag for himself and for the ever-loyal fans in Brooklyn.

The play at the plate remains one of the most controversial plays in baseball history. Over fifty years later, it is still debated whether Jackie Robinson was safe at home. Yogi Berra, the Yankees catcher who applied the tag, insists to this day that he tagged Jackie out. Jackie, on the other hand, never relented in his belief that he was safe.

The facts are as follows: Berra, having caught the pitch, did not have time to come out and fully block the plate. All he could do, from behind the plate, was reach across it and place his hand on the ground between it and the sliding Jackie's right foot. Did Yogi's gloved hand get down before the tip of Jackie's foot touched the plate? The umpire called Jackie safe. Berra was outraged. He proceeded to argue long and loud with the umpire, gesturing wildly and jumping up and down. Sixty-three thousand Yankees home-town fans rained down their disapproval. But the result stood. The score was now 6–5, but there were two outs, and no one on base.

The Yankees got out of the inning without giving up another run, and they eventually won the game. But it didn't seem all that important. "Aging Robinson Sets Dodgers Afire!" headlined one newspaper. "His hair is grey," another newspaper proclaimed, "but he showed a nation... that the Dodgers can beat the Yankees." "Whether it was my stealing home or not," Robinson wrote modestly, "the team had new fire."

Seven days later, the Dodgers were the champions for the first time ever.

Yogi Berra, the poet laureate of baseball, summed up his feelings about the Robinson steal with a classic Yogi-sim: "It was a close play," he said, "but I had him easy."

Important Stolen Base Factoids

- Two bases can be stolen at once. If both a runner on first and a runner on second simultaneously attempt to steal the next base, it is called a **double steal**.
- If a runner attempts to steal and, while he is running, the batter hits a foul ball, the runner must return to his original base. You cannot steal on a foul ball.
- The batter can, of course, swing at a pitch while the runner is attempting to steal. If the batter hits the ball, then the ball is in play and the play proceeds normally. The would-be base stealer is now trying to advance around the bases just like any other runner.
- If the batter doesn't hit it, the pitch counts. Suppose the pitch is thrown, the batter doesn't swing at it and the ump calls the pitch a ball. The runner on first, meanwhile, has taken off on a steal attempt. The ball will count regardless of whether the catcher subsequently throws out the base stealer or not. (If the ball is the fourth ball, the batter will walk and the stolen base attempt will, in effect, be cancelled, as the runner will have been forced to second by the walk anyway.)
- If, a base stealer is thrown out for the third out of the inning, and if, as a result, the batter who was up at the time has not completed his at bat, he will lead off the next inning, starting all over with a count of 0 and 0. For example, suppose there are two outs, runner on first, and the batter has a count of 1 and 1. Here's the pitch: there goes the runner. The home plate umpire calls the pitch a strike. The catcher catches it, stands, and throws the runner out, ending the inning. The inning has ended with the batter still at the plate, with a 1 and 2 count. The batter did not get the chance to finish his at bat. He therefore will lead off the next inning with a clean slate. This will also be the case if a runner is picked off base for the third out.
- If the batter in a stolen base attempt has two strikes, and then swings and misses for the third strike, and if, after catching the third strike, the catcher is able to throw out the runner trying to steal a base, the result is a double play—the strikeout being one, the throwing out of the runner attempting to steal being the second. This type of double play is often referred to as a **strike 'em out, throw 'em out double play**.
- A base stealer (or any runner, even in a non-base stealing situation) can't get so wrapped up in reaching the next base safely that he doesn't pay attention to the ball. If a runner is hit with a batted ball before the ball is touched by a fielder, the runner is automatically out.
- A base stealer (or any runner, even in a non-base stealing situation) also can't get so wrapped up in reaching the next base safely that he forgets the basic rule that he has to actually step on or "touch" a base in order to be safe on it. If a runner accidentally does not step on or touch a base while advancing, the umpire can call him out for missing the base, but the umpire will only get involved if two conditions are met.

First, the runner must have advanced to a subsequent base and play must be dead. As long as play is alive, that runner, whether he realizes the mistake himself or is advised of his mistake by a base coach or by teammates screaming at him from the dugout, can correct his mistake by running back to the missed base and touching it. If he gets there before he's thrown out, outside of valuable time wasted, no harm done. Once play is dead, however, and that runner is standing on a subsequent base, the option of returning to the missed base and correcting his mistake is gone. This will be the case when the runner has no idea he missed the base, and therefore kept advancing.

Second, once play is dead, and before the next pitch is thrown, the manager of the fielding team must **appeal** the runner's safe arrival at the subsequent base by notifying the umpire that he believes the runner failed to touch a previous base. Only after the fielding team manager makes his appeal, but not before, will the umpire at the allegedly missed base make a ruling. Before the appeal is made, as a formality, the appealing team's pitcher will soft toss the ball over to the fielder covering the base in question, who will then step on the disputed base.

- Runners missing bases happens more than you would think. A runner on first who is advancing to third, say, on an extra base hit, will normally just step on a corner of the base or even kick its side as he is running past. If he's not paying attention (if, for example, he's looking into the outfield to see where the ball is, or looking over at the third base coach for instructions) he's liable to just miss. It happens.

Oh, and by the way, suppose a batter hits a triple, gets to third, and sees that his frantic third base coach is telling him he missed first base. He can go back and touch first base, but to get there he has to run the bases in reverse order: he would have to go back to second, then back to first. He can't just dart across the infield to first base to correct his error.

- A stolen base attempt can be ordered by the manager in the dugout and communicated to the runner through a series of hand signals delivered by the third base coach, or it can be something that the runner decides to do completely on his own. However, not all runners are given permission to steal on their own. Only the runners most adept and most accomplished at base stealing are **given the green light** to steal whenever they please. (The third base coach, also through hand signals, will communicate to the batter and runners when they should employ other offensive plays as well, such as the hit and run, the sacrifice bunt and the squeeze play, all to be discussed shortly.)
- Staying on the third base coach for a moment, I must tell you that watching him give his signs to the batter and runners is really a lot of fun. Since the third base coach is so plainly visible to the opposing team, standing out there as he is in his coach's box, his signs by necessity have to be thoroughly masked within a whole series of decoy signs. Thus, before every pitch, you will see him performing about nine or ten quick and rather ridiculous-looking movements with his hands, all in the space of about two or three seconds, as the batter and runners watch closely. For example, he might pull his chin, scratch his stomach, take off his hat, put it on again, pat his left arm, tap his left knee, pinch his nose, clap his hands and then stop. Somewhere in there was the sign to the batter and runners on what to do next. Maybe the only thing that really mattered was what part of his body he scratched. Maybe scratching his stomach meant the runner should steal. Maybe scratching his shoulder meant the runner should not steal.
- I just said the third base coach will send signs before every pitch. What if there are no runners on base? As ridiculous as it still sounds to me, before every pitch he will send

a signal to the batter telling the batter whether he is allowed to swing at the next pitch or not. The vast majority of times, the sign will be for the batter to **swing away** as he sees fit. But that won't always be the case. When the count on the batter is 3 and 0, for example, the manager will often order him not to swing at the next pitch, to **take all the way**, and hopefully draw a walk.

Defending Against the Steal: The Basics

The base stealer seems to have an advantage over the fielders trying to stop him. He has only to run from first to second, while the defense must perform no less than eight separate actions involving three different players, quickly and without mistake, in order to get him out: (i) the pitcher has to complete his pitching motion and (ii) throw the ball and (iii) the ball has to be caught by the catcher and (iv) the catcher has to get the ball cleanly out of his glove with his throwing hand and (v) stand up and (vi) throw the ball to the second baseman and (vii) the second baseman then has to catch it and (viii) tag the runner out. The excitement of the stolen base play is not just the sight of the runner, one moment standing still, the next moment bursting into a full speed sprint toward the next base, but it is also the sight of three fielders coordinating to perform those eight steps with breathtaking quickness and dexterity.

Still, the runner does have an advantage, because, for one thing, he knows in advance when he will try to steal a base and the defense doesn't. To compensate, the defense will have its own strategies for dealing with a potential base stealer.

Let's begin by taking another quick look at the pickoff.

The interesting thing about stolen bases is that the contest is often misunderstood as being between the catcher and the runner: does the catcher have a strong enough arm to throw out the runner? Is the runner fast enough to beat out the throw? But actually the contest is often won or lost before the ball is pitched. If the pitcher does not have a good **pickoff move**, meaning, if he can't disguise his tells and his point of commitment effectively enough, and/or if, once he commits to pitching, he takes too long to actually pitch the ball, and/or if he becomes too predictable in the timing and the pattern of his pickoff throws versus his actual pitch, and as a result, he gives the runner the opportunity to take a bigger lead and get a good jump, the runner is said to **steal off the pitcher**, meaning that by the time the ball actually got into the catcher's mitt, the contest was already decided. "I can't throw the ball to second base," Tigers catcher Bill Freehan once complained, "until I get it from the pitcher's mound."

Again, even if it is already decided, the catcher will make a good attempt to throw the runner out, and if the runner beats the throw, the unsophisticated fan will stand up and yell: "The catcher **has no arm**!" But, again, he may well have an arm after all. Maybe it's the pitcher who has no arm. Or at least he's lacking in that part of his arm, and head, that combine to create a good pickoff move and **keep the runner close**, as in, close to the base with a short lead. If you ever see (and you will) a catcher throw out runners stealing in one game, then fail to throw them out in the next game, there's a good chance that that inconsistency can be attributed not to the catcher, but to the varying quality of the pickoff moves of the different pitchers the catcher was working with in those two games.

Now let's look at the strategies the defense will put in place to lower the odds that the opponents will steal on them successfully.

First, and probably most importantly, a pitcher and a catcher will get together before a game and familiarize themselves with what players on the opposing team are most likely to attempt a steal once they are on base. It's won't be difficult to figure out. Although there is more to being a successful base stealer than just speed, generally, the fast runners steal, the slow runners don't. A quick review of their opponents' steal statistics should give them all the information they need.

Second, when he thinks a runner might attempt a steal, the pitcher will want to get the ball to the catcher as soon as possible so that the catcher will have a better chance of throwing the runner out. Therefore, while there is a threat to steal, the pitcher and catcher will favor fastballs over breaking balls. Fastballs get to the catcher quicker, and they get to the catcher in a straight line. Once that runner takes off, the catcher doesn't want to be waiting for and then chasing breaking pitches that veer to the left and to the right.

Defending Against the Steal: The Pitch Out

If a pitcher and catcher could somehow read minds and know for sure that a runner would be **going** (attempting to steal) on the next pitch, to save precious seconds and increase the odds of throwing the runner out, the catcher would stand up and step clear of the batter in advance of receiving the pitch, thus putting himself in a position to make his throw right away without having to first get out of his crouch and set himself to throw. The pitcher, in turn, would forego the planned pitch and throw the ball to the catcher in this new position at the side of the plate. Sure, it would be an intentional ball, but the tradeoff would be that they would have a much better chance of throwing the runner out.

The pitcher and catcher never know for sure, of course, when the runner might be trying to steal, but there are certain situations when the odds are increased dramatically and calling for such a maneuver, called a **pitch out**, might be worth the intentional ball. For example, let's suppose (i) you have a runner on first who has a history of base stealing and who is a darn good base stealer, (ii) second base is open, (iii) and the runner's team is badly in need of a run and, hence, badly in need of putting that runner on first in scoring position. Think that runner might try to steal second? Sure, he will.

But on which pitch will he try to steal? The first? The second? Base stealers, like batters and pitchers, have their habits, and those habits can be used against them. Some runners prefer to steal on the first pitch, others want to wait a few pitches to study the pitcher's pickoff move and increase their chances of success.

The disadvantage of a pitch out, of course, is that it's a ball, and as such its application is limited. If you call for a pitch out and, it turns out that the runner **isn't going**, well, you just gave the batter a free ball. Would you want to take that chance twice with the same batter? Probably not. Three times? Certainly not.

Defending Against the Steal: Positioning the First Baseman

Another defensive strategy against the steal involves positioning the first baseman in such a way as to suggest that a pickoff is imminent, thereby discouraging a runner from taking too big a lead.

The first baseman, as we know, doesn't usually position himself directly on first base. His normal position is behind the base and to his right, somewhat in the direction of second base, so that he can cover a greater percentage of the field to his left and to his right. If a runner, on first base, sees that the first baseman is in this usual position, he knows he does not have to fear a pickoff move because, frankly, there is no one on first for the pitcher to throw the pickoff to. The runner can therefore take a bigger lead than normal, shorten the distance to second, and increase the odds of a successful base steal should he attempt one.

But if, on the other hand, the first baseman positions himself directly on first base, so that at any second the pitcher can wheel and throw a pickoff throw to him, that alone will act as a strong deterrent to any runner from taking too big a lead. When the first baseman is thus stationed at first ready to receive a pickoff throw, it is said he is **holding the runner**, as in, holding him to a short lead.

The downside of holding the runner is that it **opens up a hole** on the right side of the infield, where the first baseman would be usually playing. A ground ball hit on the right side, between first and second, now has a much better chance of going through for a single, while before, the first baseman would have been there to field it.

The first baseman may opt for a middle ground between holding the runner and playing his usual position, in that he may elect **to play behind the runner**, which means he will instead position himself just behind the runner, just off the runner's left shoulder, close enough to first so that he can dash to the bag at a moment's notice to receive a pickoff throw from the pitcher. Playing behind a runner opens less of a hole on the right side of the infield, but, at the same time, allows the runner to take a bigger lead than if the first baseman were actually holding him on at first.

Thus, holding the runner, and even, to a lesser extent, playing behind the runner, both involve a tradeoff: the runner's chances of stealing are diminished, but the batter's chances of getting a hit on the right side of the infield are increased. This is especially true if the batter is a lefty, whose natural tendency is to hit the ball to the center-right side of the field.

Wait, what did he just say? Natural tendency to do what?

OK, this is important, so listen closely.

Batters have a tendency to hit the ball to one side of the field or the other, depending on which side of the plate they bat from. When a righty batter swings at a pitch, just the natural movement of his body and the way the bat comes around on a well-timed swing, makes him more likely to hit the ball to the left and left-center side of the field. A lefty batter, on the other hand, is more inclined to hit to right right-center side of the field. Batters such as these, who swing the bat in what might be called an instinctive attempt to hit the ball with as much power as possible, are called **pull hitters**, and it is said that they **pull the ball**.

Some batters have also perfected the art of **hitting the ball to the opposite field**, in other words, hesitating or delaying their swing or shortening their swing ever so slightly so that the bat comes around a tad bit later than usual and is thus more inclined to drive the ball to the *other* side of the field. Babe Ruth wrote that to hit the ball to the opposite field "required me to delay my swing until it (the pitch) was almost past me." You will therefore hear announcers refer to an **opposite field hit** or, for example, an **opposite field single**. (My son Phillip, in our earlier story, hit an opposite field double. I'm sure it was unintentional, but who cares?). Because of the shortened or delayed swing, opposite field hits are generally not hit with as much power as pulled ball hits.

The first baseman holds the runner, meaning he is standing at first, at the ready for a pickoff throw from the pitcher. This forces the runner to be more cautious in taking his lead (shutterstock.com/ alens).

Getting back to holding the runner, in the famous third playoff game between the Brooklyn Dodgers and the New York Giants in 1951, we know that Bobby Thomson hit a three-run homer in the bottom of the ninth to win the game. We can now add that that inning, and that miraculous comeback, started when Giants shortstop Alvin Dark hit a single and the Dodgers manager decided to have Gil Hodges, the Dodger first baseman, hold him at first to prevent him from stealing second.

With a 4–1 lead, and with Dark now on first, some think it would have been a better choice to have Hodges play his normal first base position or, at least, play behind Dark, thus increasing his chances of turning any ball hit to the right side into a ground ball out. Even if Dark was able to take a bigger lead and steal second as a result, the run he represented was of no great concern, as it would only have cut a 4–1 lead to a 4–2 lead.

As it happened, the next batter up, Don Mueller, a lefty batter, hit the ball to the right side of the infield, as lefties tend to do. In fact, he hit a ground ball right into the spot where Hodges *would* have been had he not been holding Dark on first. Instead of Hodges catching that ground ball and throwing Mueller out at first, or Dark out at second, or possibly even initiating a double play, the ball bounced past him out into the outfield for a base hit. When the smoke cleared, Dark was safe at second, Mueller was safe at first, and in the Giant dugout, Bobby Thomson was getting ready to come to the plate and make history.

And on that dramatic note, I am pleased to announce that that's it for stolen bases. You're done. You've reached the peak of the mountain. Congratulations!

The Hit and Run

Resuming our discussion of the strategies employed to legally advance runners around the bases, suppose you have a runner on first with no one out or one out. Suppose you need a run and you need to get that runner into scoring position. You also want to move him up because you want to remove the possibility of a double play. Normally, you'd consider having the runner steal second, but suppose conditions aren't ripe for a steal attempt, meaning either the pitcher is too hard to steal off of, and/or the catcher has a cannon for an arm, and/or the runner is just, well, not that good a base stealer.

There is another strategy that might be appropriate here. It is similar to a stolen base attempt, but unlike the stolen base, it relies less on the outright speed of the runner than on a coordination of efforts between the hitter and the runner, and it is therefore called, ingeniously, **the hit and run**.

Here's how it works. First, as soon as the pitcher physically commits to the pitch, the runner on first will dash to second in an apparent stolen base attempt.

But let's hit the pause button for one moment here and take a look around the infield. As you know, the second baseman is positioned to the right side of second base, looking out from home plate, and the shortstop is positioned to the left. Both are about equidistant from second base, and either one can therefore effectively come over to cover second and take the throw from the catcher in a steal situation. Which one will cover, depends on the batter. A lefty batter, as we've discussed, has a tendency to hit the ball to the right side of the field. In a steal situation involving a lefty batter, therefore, a defensive manager will want to play the odds and have his second baseman stay put to cover the right side of the field, and have his shortstop come over and cover second. Likewise, with a righty batter up, a manager will want his shortstop to stay put, and his second baseman come over and cover second.

The batter's manager, meanwhile, *knows* that the defensive manager will play the odds in which fielder he chooses to cover second base in the steal attempt, and he therefore also knows where in the infield there will be a nice big empty gap for his batter to try to poke through a ground ball, once his runner takes off in a steal attempt. By calling for the hit and run, the batter's manager will essentially be trying to lure either the second baseman or the shortstop out of position, and then, if everything goes according to plan, the batter will, in the immortal words of Wee Willie Keeler, "hit it where they ain't."

Let's suppose there is a righty batter up, and let's hit the play button again.

The pitcher completes his motion. Here's the pitch. The runner is dashing to second, the shortstop is staying put, and the second baseman is running over to cover second. The batter, knowing in advance that the second baseman will be covering, cracks an opposite field hit into the exact spot on the right side of the field that the second baseman has just left vacant. The batter is safe at first with an opposite-field single and the runner makes it all the way to third because of his early jump.

Of course, that's the best-case scenario.

Hit and runs are hard. You can't try them with every batter, because not every batter has the **bat control** to pull it off successfully, meaning not every batter can be depended on to hit to the opposite field into the vacated area. What makes the hit and run even more difficult is that once the manager calls for the hit and run, there is no turning back: the runner *will* be going, so the batter has no choice but to swing at and try to make contact with the next pitch. Even if the pitch is way outside, or way inside, or high, or low, and would be a pitch the batter would normally take as a ball, he is still obligated not only to try to make contact with it, but to try to drive it to the opposite field. If the batter doesn't swing at the pitch, or if he swings and misses, there's a very good chance the runner will get thrown out stealing.

Legendary Orioles manager Earl Weaver, a combative personality who was once ejected from a game for arguing with the umpire during the pre-game exchange of lineup cards, had serious reservations about the hit and run. He wrote: "You often give the opposition an out on the hit and run play. That's because you can't trust the pitcher to throw a strike, so the hitter is often waving weakly at a ball that's off the plate. That usually results in a weak grounder that gets the runner to second, but the batter is usually retired at first.... I'll take my chances with a normal swing anytime."

Keith Hernandez, in his tome *Pure Baseball*, penned an eight-page dissection of the hit and run play that reads like a physicist's dissection of the atom, and in it he discusses the valid concern about the batter being forced to wave weakly at a ball that's off the plate. His response is that the hit and run should only be executed when it is likely that the pitcher will throw a ball that's *on* the plate, and thus more likely to be a pitch that the batter can hit well. Thus, when the count on a batter is 2-and-1, or 2-and-0, that is the perfect time to call for the hit and run because there is a high likelihood that the pitcher, wary about falling too far behind in the count, will throw a strike.

A Pause

Whenever I think of Keith Hernandez, I think of the summer of 1987. Most fans think of Hernandez and his key role with the Mets in 1986, when they won the World Championship. I always think of the year after.

In the early morning hours of March 17, 1987, my best friend and my younger brother Patrick, 27 years old, died suddenly of heart disease. We knew that he had problems with his heart, we knew he was seeing a doctor and taking medication, we knew that sometimes, for no reason at all, beads of sweat would appear on his forehead. But we didn't really know how bad his condition was until it was too late. An autopsy showed that his heart was so badly diseased that only a heart transplant might have saved him. His name was Patrick, and he died on St. Patrick's Day.

I spent months after he died in a daze, hanging out with a friend in a little pub in the West Village, and I avoided coming to terms with the loss of my brother by drinking way too much beer and watching baseball, mostly the Mets, almost every night of the week. That year, the Mets were absolutely decimated by an uncanny string of injuries to almost every one of their starting pitchers. They struggled to stay in the race, and we rooted hard for them, but it was futile. There was nothing they could do.

One of the things I remember most about that summer was how hard Keith Hernandez fought in every at bat to try to keep his team afloat, even as the season fell apart around him. Massive at bats: eight-, nine-, ten-pitch at bats, where he would foul off pitch after pitch after pitch that were too close not to swing at, but too far off the center of the plate to hit meaningfully. And I remember how with his eagle eye he would take pitches a hair outside the strike zone, just praying that the ump had vision as good as he had. Many of these epic battles ended in a walk, or a basic single into the outfield, and though I knew that in the record books those results went down just as a walk, just as a single, the reality was that each one of them was the remarkable work product of a man who had no quit in him.

All through that dismal summer of 1987, I watched Hernandez fight and fight a battle his team was destined to lose. After a while he must have known that too, but there he was anyway, in every game, in every at bat, stepping up to the plate, glaring out at the pitcher with his sharp, dark eyes, ready to go at it again.

When the season ended, I walked out of the bar and said to myself: Enough. That's enough, now.

And that's all I have to say about that.

The Sacrifice Bunt

Moving on to our next runner-advancing strategy, suppose you're leading 2–1, and it's late in the game, and the opposing pitcher is being very, very stingy. Somehow you are fortunate enough to get your leadoff runner on first in, let's say, your half of the seventh. That

Shortstop Bud Harrelson, one of the key players for the 1969 World Champion Mets, lines up a bunt. When bunting, a batter doesn't swing the bat, but instead slides one hand up toward the middle of the bat, lines up the bat with the incoming pitch and allows the ball to hit it (National Baseball Hall of Fame Library, Cooperstown, New York).

runner is very valuable to you because you know there's a good chance that if you can bring him in to score, that run may lock up the win. A 3–1 lead, on this day, against this stingy opposing pitcher, is going to seem a heck of a lot safer going into the final innings than a 2–1 lead.

Furthermore, you know that if you leave this valuable runner at first, with every pitch that's thrown, you risk losing him to a double play. Just like that, you can go from a fairly promising no-outs-with-runner-on-first, to two-outs-with-nobody on. Moving that runner into scoring position would not only increase your chances of scoring, but it will also erase the possibility of a double play.

Suppose finally that, for whatever reason, conditions aren't ripe for either a steal attempt or a hit and run. Maybe the runner isn't fast enough for a straight steal; maybe the batter doesn't have the bat control for the hit and run. Still, you need to get that runner over...

Well, let me ask you this: Would you consider giving up an out to get that runner to second base? Would you intentionally have the next batter make out, if doing so would get that runner to second base, into scoring position, and out of double play danger? If you asked most Major League managers, they would probably say yes.

The concept of trading or sacrificing an out to get a runner from first into scoring position, is what the **sacrifice bunt** is all about: the batter purposely grounds out in such a way that the only play the fielders have is to throw *him* out at first base, thus enabling the runner previously at first to advance safely into scoring position.

The batting technique that will produce the type of ground ball out required get this done is called a **bunt**. A bunt involves the batter—the sacrificer, as it were—not swinging the bat at the ball, but, instead, as the pitcher releases the ball (but not before, so as not to tip his hand), turning his body so that he is facing the pitcher, called **squaring to bunt**, sliding his top hand about halfway up the length of bat and, simultaneously, bringing the top of the bat down so that the bat is now parallel to the ground and perpendicular to the incoming pitch, at about mid-chest height. The batter then does his best to line up his bat with the incoming pitch so that the ball hits the bat in such a way that the ball is driven downward at a sharp angle. The ball, ideally, hits the ground a few feet in front of the batter and then continues to roll forward, though not too quickly, until it is nearly equidistant between the catcher and either the pitcher, first baseman or third baseman. As the third baseman, for the sake of argument, charges towards the slowly rolling ball, the runner at first, having received the signal from the third base coach that the sacrifice is on, has already taken off towards second, so that by the time the third baseman catches up with the ball, the only play he has is to throw the runner out at first base. When that happens, the sacrificing bunter has accomplished his mission.

Bunting is as difficult as it sounds. Not many players can do it well, and a bad bunt can backfire quickly. A bunt that travels too far, too fast, will get scooped up by the pitcher or the first or third baseman and the runner at first will be in danger of getting thrown out at second; a bunt that travels too slowly and not far enough, will get scooped up by the catcher coming out from behind the plate with the same result. A bad bunt that's popped up can be caught on the fly like any other fly ball for the out.

Not only is the act of bunting difficult, but the sacrifice bunt is very limited in its application.

First of all, the sacrifice bunt is normally used with no one out. If there is one man already out, the sacrifice out would be the second out, leaving the offense with only one out to spare as it tries to bring in the runner from second.

Second, the sacrifice bunt is normally used when there is only a runner on first. Sometimes it is used with runners on first and second (in which case both runners would advance), but you don't see that as often, because with two runners on and no one out, the tendency would be to play for the big inning, rather than give up an out to move the runners up.

Third, the batter who executes the sacrifice bunt should not be as good a batter as the batter or batters scheduled up after him. A sacrifice is called a sacrifice, after all, because the batter is sacrificing his at bat in order to legally advance the runner so that the ensuing batters can drive him in. Suppose the batter coming up in a sacrifice situation is your best hitter? Would you **take the bat out of his hands** (the expression used) and have him purposely make an out so that ensuing batters, maybe not as good as him, can drive in the runner? That wouldn't make much sense. If your best batter, or one of your better hitters, is up in a sacrifice situation, you'd have to forego the sacrifice and let him swing away.

I just said, "The batter who executes the sacrifice bunt should generally not be as good a batter as the batters scheduled up after him." Put that in the context of the National League, where pitchers come up to bat. In the National League, pitchers will almost always bat ninth. They are followed in the batting order by the leadoff hitter, who is usually one of the better hitters on the team (that's why he's batting leadoff!) Pitchers, therefore, virtually always sacrifice bunt when they come to bat with a runner on first and nobody out (or even sometimes, because with a pitcher you have nothing to lose, with one out).

Fourth, the sacrifice bunt is most often used late in the game. Early in the game, with a runner on first and no one out, you would more likely play for the big inning. You might try the steal or the hit and run, if you could, but you would probably be less inclined to limit your offense by giving up an out early in the game. Remember the scenario we opened this section with: it was late in the game and the dominance of the opposing pitcher throughout the game made the sacrifice a valid option.

Finally, the sacrifice is best used with no strikes, or possibly one strike, on the batter, because it is very easy to fouls balls off on a bunt. Unless the batter squares the bat to the ball perfectly, the ball is going to glance off the bat and ricochet back behind the batter for a foul ball.

What's so bad about that, you might ask, since the batter can foul off as many pitches as he wants and still not get called for a third strike? Well, my friends, I hate to tell you this, but that's not the case. Long ago, when you were first learning how a foul ball can never be a third strike, I warned you that there was one more important rule regarding foul balls and third strikes that we would leave off discussing until later. Later is now, and here is that important rule: since it is so easy to foul off a pitch when bunting, the lords of baseball, not wanting bunters to stay up there all day fouling off pitches, hold that a bunted foul ball on two strikes counts as a third strike. As a result, once a batter has reached two strikes, he usually switches from bunting to swinging away.

Defending Against the Sacrifice Bunt

It's no big secret when a sacrifice bunt will be used: It's late in the game, the team at bat badly needs a run, they have a runner on first, he's not a threat to steal, there is nobody out, there are no strikes or one strike on the batter, and the batter is not as good a hitter as the batter or batters to follow. Because it's so easy to anticipate a sacrifice bunt, the defense will have a chance to employ a strategy to defeat it.

The defense will try to defeat the sacrifice bunt by positioning the first and third baseman much closer to home plate than usual, called **playing the infield in** or **up**. Normally, each are positioned off to the side of their respective bases, maybe halfway back on the infield dirt. From that position, there is no way either can run in, pick up a well-placed bunt, and throw either the batter or the lead runner out. If the defense suspects a bunt attempt is at hand, both the first and third baseman will play closer to home, possibly even **on the grass** or **on the edge of the grass**, meaning off the infield dirt completely and on the grass between the infield dirt and home. Then as soon as the pitch is thrown and the batter squares to bunt, but not before, they will both literally come charging in toward him, anticipating the slow, rolling bunt coming their way.

The reason that the first baseman or third baseman doesn't charge in sooner—even before the pitch is thrown—is because then the batter might take advantage by **bluffing bunt** and suddenly swinging away instead, with the goal of rapping a hit over the incoming first or third baseman's head.

Not buying it? Still think it's not worth trading an out to get a runner from first to second? Neither do a lot of people, including, of course, Earl Weaver. In *Weaver on Strategy* he has a chapter called "The Bunt: Rarely Worth the Trouble," in which he writes: "Its name, the sacrifice bunt, tells you something. Sacrifice means you are giving up something. In this instance, you're giving up an out to the opposition. There are only three an inning, and they should be treasured.... Give one away and you're making everything harder for yourself."

Weaver was a big believer in letting his players **swing for the fences**, or try to hit home runs: "The easiest way around the bases is with one swing of the bat," he wrote. Of course, Weaver could afford to say that, because in the late 1960s and early 70s, his teams featured a collection of "big boppers" that did not have much difficulty walloping home runs. Less fortunate teams are left trying to manufacture runs with stolen bases, hit and runs and, yes, sacrifice bunts.

Some final notes on bunts:

- First, a surprise sacrifice bunt is sometimes used with a runner on third base to try to bring him in for a run. This type of sacrifice is called either a **squeeze play**, if the runner on third waits for the batter to make contact with the ball to first make sure the bunt is conducive to running home, or a **suicide squeeze**, when the runner on third dashes home as soon as the pitcher has physically committed to pitching the ball, taking a chance that a proper bunt will be executed.
- Second, some batters are good at bunting, and they won't be happy just using their bunting abilities to sacrifice runners over to second. Suppose a batter comes up with first base open, looks around, and sees the infield is playing at its usual depth, expecting him to swing away. If the batter is very good at bunting and is also a fast runner, he may just decide to surprise everyone by **laying down a bunt** and then trying to **beat out the bunt for a hit.**

One of the techniques a batter might use to try to make this happen is that he will bunt the ball to his (the batter's) left when facing a righty pitcher and to his right when facing a lefty pitcher. The reason for this is that, after a pitch, the pitcher's follow-up tends to have them fall awkwardly off toward one side of the mound. If the batter can take advantage by bunting the ball toward the *other* side of the mound, then the pitcher will have to stop and turn completely around before running towards the bunted ball, losing valuable seconds in the process. These types of bunts are sometimes referred to as **push bunts**, in that the batter intentionally tries to push the ball towards a vacant part of the infield in order to get a base hit.

When it comes to bunting for a base hit, you'll also hear the term **drag bunt**, which describes a lefty-batting bunter who, instead of squaring to the pitcher, will actually be leaning towards first base, preparing to run, as he bunts. (Righty hitters can't drag bunt because if a righty hitter leaned towards first base as he bunted, he'd be leaning over the plate, and remember: if you get hit by a pitch while you are in the strike zone, you'll get a nice bruise, but you won't get awarded a free pass to first base.)

The batter, however, will only get one chance to surprise the fielders like this. If the batter unexpectedly squares to bunt but then fouls off the pitch, for example, the element of surprise will have been lost. The fielders will now cheat in a few steps to defend against another such attempt on the next pitch, so the batter will probably just elect to swing away after that.

Also, if a batter tries to beat out a bunt for a hit too often, the rest of the league will be alerted, the word will get around, and soon every team will take preventive measures, probably by having the first and third baseman cheat in a little as soon as the batter comes up. Baseball is a funny game that way: in the Major Leagues, everyone gets figured out in time. Fairly often you will see a rookie come up and tear up the league... for a few weeks, and then, suddenly, disappear again into obscurity. If a Major League ballplayer has a weakness, a pattern, a tendency, a tipoff, a tell, it will be found out and it will be exploited again and again until the player either adjusts and overcomes, or doesn't, and finds himself back on the bench, or gone.

Advancing on Fly Ball Outs

You've come far, pilgrim. You now have a good working knowledge of some of the strategies and counter-strategies applied in advancing a runner around the bases. We are now going to return to fly ball outs for a moment, and, specifically, we are going to address how runners can legally advance on the bases after a fly ball out. I've purposely put off this discussion until now because these rules can best be grasped by backing into them with the knowledge you now have about base-advancing strategies.

The Fly Ball Rules: Tagging Up

Advancing on fly ball outs is much less complex than ground ball outs. I only needed to draft two rules to make up for the cryptic verbiage of the framers of the *Official Baseball Rules*.

Fly Ball Rule # 1: Neither the batter nor any runners, no matter what base or combination of bases they are on, will be **forced** to advance on a fly ball out.

Fly Ball Rule # 2: A runner may **choose** to advance after a fly ball out is caught, but he can only advance if (i) when the fly ball out is caught, he is touching the base he was on when the fly ball was hit or (ii) having left that base and being off that base when the fly ball out is caught, he first returns to touch that base before advancing.

With a runner on first, if the batter hits a ground ball, we know he is forced to run to first base, and if there is a runner already on first, that runner is therefore forced to run on to second. Per Fly Ball Rule #1, however, on a fly ball out the batter is not forced to run to first base, and therefore if there is already a runner on first at the time, that runner is not forced to run to second. As he watches his fly ball's flight into the outfield, the batter will run down toward first base, but then, when the ball is caught, he'll stop, turn around and jog back to the dugout. The runner who was on first at the time, not having been forced to run to second, can just stay put.

A runner can choose to stay put, but he can also choose to advance. Let's now turn to Fly Ball Rule # 2 to examine how a runner can legally advance on a fly ball out.

First, let's look at an example of Fly Ball Rule #2(i) in action. Roy Hobbs on second. Bump Bailey, his teammates on the Knights, is at bat. Hobbs takes a lead. Here's the pitch. Bump belts a high fly ball to right. Hobbs watches it soar into the air. He sees the right fielder get underneath it, look up and raise his glove preparing to catch it. It looks at that point like it's going to be a fly ball out, so Hobbs returns to second base and stands on it until the fly ball is caught. At the exact moment the fly ball is caught for the out, but not before, Hobbs takes off running like a bat out of heck to third. Per Fly Ball Rule # 2(i), Hobbs was touching his base with his foot when the fly ball out was caught, and was therefore entitled to then legally advance to third.

Now let's look at an example of Fly Ball Rule # 2(ii): Roy Hobbs on second. Bump at the plate. Hobbs takes a lead. Here's the pitch. Bump belts a sharp fly ball to right. It looks like it might go over the right fielder's head. Hobbs takes a bigger lead. The right fielder, however, makes the catch. Hobbs, *after* the catch is made, quickly returns to second base, steps on it, and then runs like a bat out of heck to third. Hobbs, having left his base and being off his base when the catch was made, first returned to touch his base before advancing, and was therefore entitled to legally advance to third.

Question: In both these examples, if Hobbs is legally entitled to advance to third, and if the defense wishes to get Hobbs out before he safely arrives at third, will the play at third be a force or a tag? Hobbs was not forced to advance to third; he chose to advance. Therefore the defense will have to tag Hobbs before he touches third in order to get him out.

One more example for Fly Ball Rule # 2(ii):

Hobbs on first this time. Bump at the plate. Hobbs takes a lead. Here's the pitch. Hobbs takes off in a stolen base attempt. Bump belts a sharp fly ball to right. The right fielder makes the catch. Hobbs, who was attempting to steal, is almost all the way to second base when the catch is made. The right fielder quickly realizes that Hobbs, being off his base when the catch was made, did not first return to touch his base before advancing and was therefore not legally entitled to advance to second. Before Hobbs can return to first, the right fielder throws to the first baseman and Hobbs is out.

Question: Will the play at first be a force or a tag play? Hobbs was forced by the *Official Baseball Rules* to return to first base before advancing. He had no choice in the matter. Therefore it will be a force play, and all the first baseman has to do, when he receives the right fielder's throw, is to step on first before Hobbs gets back.

Now for some vocabulary: if a runner, before advancing on a fly ball out, correctly either (i) touches his base when the fly ball out is caught or (ii) if, having left his base and being off his base when the fly ball out is caught, he first returns to touch his base before advancing, it is said he **tagged up** before advancing. If he did not, it will be said he **left early** and as a result can be **doubled off**, or forced out at, his original base.

Fly Ball Rules vs. Ground Ball Rules: Endy's Catch as Case Study

Now that you know about the Fly Ball Rules, and now that you know about the Ground Ball Rules, the million dollar question is: how do you know when which one applies? The answer is: you don't know which one applies until... it does!

Sure, sometimes it's easy to see which one applies. If the batter hits a ball that bounces ten times on the way to the shortstop, it's obvious right from the start that the Ground Ball Rules apply. And what that means is that a runner who is forced to advance to the next base, has to, and a runner who is not forced to advance to the next base, is free to choose to. And sure, if the batter hits a fly ball to the outfield and the outfielder jogs a few feet, then looks up and settles under the ball and catches it, it's obvious right from the start that the Fly Ball Rules will apply, and what that means, again, is that no runners are forced to advance, but all are free to advance once they tag up.

But sometimes it won't always be so obvious which set of rules will apply. And this makes me happy because it gives me a chance to tell another story.

Allow me to tell you now about one of the great catches of my lifetime, that being a catch made by Endy Chavez of the Mets against the Cardinals in the decisive seventh game of the 2006 National League Championship Series. The score was tied 1–1 in the top of the sixth. With one man out, the Cardinals had a runner on first, Jim Edmonds, when Cardinal batter Scott Rolen belted a high, soaring fly ball to left field that seemed well on its way to being a home run. As the ball soared through the night sky, Edmonds immediately took off running from first to second.

In essence, having assessed the arc of the ball and the manner in which the Met left fielder, Endy Chavez, was desperately running full tilt back toward the fence, the runner Edmonds figured that either (i) the ball was going out of the park, so it didn't matter if he left his base early, because, like all runners when a home run is hit, he gets a free pass home, or (ii) the ball was going to stay in the park but land well beyond Endy's grasp and fall in for an extra base hit. In this latter case, the Ground Ball Rules would have taken effect and Edmonds would not only have been forced to advance to second by the batter, Rolen, but beyond that he would have been free to advance all the way to third, or maybe even, with a little luck (and especially since he had gotten an early jump), all the way home. With the score tied 1–1, Edmonds was being aggressive because he knew that the run he represented might eventually prove to be the game winner in this low-scoring seventh and decisive game.

Meanwhile, Endy, his eyes gazing upward at the arching ball, took off running back, back, back to the 8-foot tall left field fence, across which was splashed an advertisement that read, ironically, "The Strength to Be There." And just as the ball descended into home run territory, Endy jumped up so high that his entire right arm from the elbow up was literally over the fence. And with the absolute very tip-top of his glove, Endy snared that ball just as it was about to fall behind the fence for a homer. So barely had he caught the ball that as he fell back to earth and landed heavily in the warning track, most of the white of the ball was clearly visible protruding from the top his glove. Edmonds, meanwhile, had never stopped running.

To paraphrase Lew Burdette again, it was a home run, then it wasn't. As over 50,000 Mets fans roared with delight, Endy Chavez recovered and rifled a throw back to the infield. Edmonds, who never figured the ball would be caught on the fly and so who hadn't tagged up, made a valiant attempt to get back to first before he was doubled off the base, but he was thrown out by a mile.

This is a classic example of how, for the runners, sometimes the difficulty lies in assessing whether the Ground Ball Rules or the Fly Ball Rules are going to apply on any given play. Edmonds, seeing the ball head toward the fences, took an educated guess, figured that if it wasn't a home run, the Ground Ball Rules would apply, and he accordingly started advancing around the bases. When Endy made his incredible catch, though, in the wink of an eye, the Ground Ball Rules were put aside and the Fly Ball Rules were made applicable, and Edmonds therefore was required to return to first before advancing, which, by that time, was impossible. Therefore you not only had Endy's great catch on Scott Rolen, the batter, for the second out of the inning, but you had Jim Edmonds, the runner, being doubled off first for the third out of the inning. Double play.

Oh, and by the way, a catch like Endy's, where the ball looks like a scoop of white ice protruding from the top of the closed, cone-like glove, is called a **snow-cone catch**.

Some final notes on the Fly Ball Rules:

- Here's a good one for you. Runner on first, nobody out. Runner takes a lead. First baseman, holding the runner, is standing on first. Here's the pitch. Runner takes off in a steal attempt. The batter rifles a hot line drive down the right field line. The first baseman, because he was holding the runner, happens to be right in its path. He reaches out, catches the line drive on the fly and then steps on first before the runner can get back to tag up. How many outs are there now?

The answer is two outs. Having caught the line drive on the fly, the first baseman registered an out on the batter. Having then stepped on first before the runner could get back to tag up, he registered an out on the runner. This is called an **unassisted double play** because the first baseman registered both outs on his own, without assistance from another fielder. Let's kick it up a notch. Runners on first and second, nobody out. Both runners take a lead. Second baseman, playing behind the runner on second, is a few feet behind second base. Here's the pitch. Both runners take off on a double-steal attempt. Seeing this, the second baseman takes three quick steps towards second to cover in case there's a throw from the catcher. The batter rifles a hot line drive right up the middle. The second baseman, because he took those three quick steps, happens to be right in its path. He reaches out, catches the line drive on the fly, then steps on second before the runner who was on second can get back to tag up, then turns towards the runner coming from first who, because of the steal attempt, is now only a six or seven feet from second base. The runner puts on the breaks when he sees that the second baseman has caught the line drive, but there's no way he's going to make it back to first to tag up. He backs up a few steps, but the second baseman is on him quickly, tagging him on his chest. How many outs are there now? The answer is three outs. Having caught the line drive on the fly, the second baseman registered an out on the batter. Having then stepped on second before the runner on second could get back to tag up, he registered an out on that runner. Having then tagged the runner coming from first before he could back to first to tag up, he registered an out on that runner. This is called an **unassisted triple play** because the second baseman registered all three outs on his own, without assistance from another fielder.

Needless to say, unassisted triple plays are rare occurrences. As of this writing, there have been only 15 in the history of baseball, and only once in the entire history of baseball has a triple play ended a National League game. In other words, only once did a triple play register the last three outs of an NL game. It happened on August 29, 2009, at Citifield, and wouldn't you know it, I was there with my wife, Marya.

The triple-player, as it were, was Phillies second baseman Eric Bruntlett, and the situation was exactly as described above. Runners on first and second, double steal attempt, hot line drive that, as luck would have it, was hit directly at Bruntlett, and then Bruntlett, thinking quick, making the most of it. Catch-step-tag: how long it takes to say those three words? That's about how long it took for Eric to turn the triple play. Catch-step-tag. And now the other Phillies were high-fiving Eric and now they were all leaving the field. I remember thinking: where are they all going? It happened so fast, that it took me a moment to realize what I had just witnessed.

- In the case of Jim Edmonds on Endy's catch, or the Mets runners on Eric's triple play, it was easy to see that they hadn't tagged up, because Edmonds immediately took off running thinking the ball would either be a home run or would drop beyond Endy's grasp, and the Mets runners all left their bases early on steal attempts. Other times, it won't be as obvious. Sometimes, in his haste, a runner, intending to tag up, will leave base a split-second before the fly ball actually settles into the outfielder's glove. Who decides if a runner left a base before the catch was made or not? The umpires, of course, but, as is the case with whether a runner stepped on a base or not, the umpires will only make a judgment on whether a runner left early if they are formally requested or appealed to do so by the aggrieved manager.
- Just as with a fly ball in fair territory, when a fly ball is caught for an out in foul territory, any runners on base can tag up and try to advance. The difference is that an outfielder can, with impunity, choose not to catch a fly ball in foul territory if the risks of doing so outweigh the rewards. For example, suppose with a runner on third and either no outs or one out, the batter hits a fly ball towards foul territory deep in right field. The outfielder, running over to make the catch, has to think to himself: if I catch this ball, it will be an out, and that's good, but at the same time that runner on third will tag up and probably score, because once I catch this, I'm going to be close to the sidewall and out of position to make a throw to home plate that, even under the best circumstances, would be a long and difficult throw to make. And that's bad. On the other hand, if I don't catch this ball, it will drop foul, and I won't get the out, and that's bad, but as is the case with all foul balls that hit the ground, the runner will be unable to advance, and that's good. Furthermore, like all foul balls, it will be a strike on the batter (though, of course, not a third strike), and that's not bad either.
- When there are two outs, there is no need to tag up on a fly ball out. The baserunners can just take off running as soon as a fly ball is hit.

What did he just say?

Well, think of it. Hobbs is on second with two outs. Here's the pitch. Bump Bailey hits a fly ball to left field. As soon as Bump hits the ball, Hobbs takes off towards third base without tagging up. The left fielder comes in, makes the catch, and, seeing that Hobbs didn't tag up, rifles a throw to the second baseman... for the fourth out?

The point is, by not tagging up, by just running full speed on any fly ball hit to the outfield with two outs, a runner has nothing to lose, and everything to gain. If the ball is caught, it will be the third out anyway and the inning will be over. But if it is not caught, the runner will have gotten that extra early jump on the ball and he may be in a position to take an extra base he wouldn't have otherwise. With two outs, therefore, **the runner(s) will be going** on any fly ball hit to the outfield.

On a related note, (this is a mouthful, so take it slow) when there are two outs, a full count on the batter, and all the runners on base are in a "force" position—meaning there are runners on first, first and second, or first, second and third (bases loaded)—all the runners will be going *on the next pitch.*

What the offense likes about **sending the runners**—another expression used—in this situation is that, like a fly ball with two outs, there is nothing to lose and everything to gain. Consider all the possibilities: (i) if the next pitch to the batter is a strike, that's the third strike and thus the third out and the inning is over anyway, (ii) if it's a ball, the batter walks and the play is dead and the runners are forced to move up anyway, and (iii) if it's a fly ball, and if the ball is caught by the outfielder, that's the third out and the inning is over anyway

On the other hand (iv) if the batter hits a ground ball to an infielder, it will be harder for the infielder to get a force at any base other than first because the other runner(s) will have gotten an early jump or (v) if the batter does get a hit or if there is an error in the field, the runner(s) will already be hustling around the bases and they will thus have a better chance of advancing further than they might have otherwise.

A Pause

Shea Stadium, where Endy Chavez made his great catch, closed after the 2008 season and was torn down to make way for a new and beautiful replacement, Citifield.

But before we leave Shea Stadium, I have to pause here and tell you about the earliest memory I have of going to a baseball game. I couldn't have been more than 10 years old, and my father took me, just me, to a game at Shea. I say "just me" because I had five siblings, and there weren't too many things that I did, just me, with my father. There weren't too many things that *any* of us did alone with my father, for that matter, because he was always working. Two jobs. Three jobs. Weekends. Overtime. He was always working, just trying to make his way in the New World.

Speaking of which, years later, decades later, my mother would still talk about which people on the block had been nice to them when they first moved in. We would pass a senior citizen on the street and my mother would stop and chat with her and then, afterward, she would say to me: "When we first came from Ireland, that woman welcomed us with open arms." After hearing so many stories like this, it suddenly occurred to me to ask her: "Mom, you remember all the people who were nice to you. What about the people who weren't nice to you?" "I don't remember them," she said. And I never asked again.

Anyway, I remember that on that one magic afternoon, my Dad and I went alone to Shea Stadium to see a game. I remember my Dad brought peanut butter and jelly sandwiches. I remember he brought a jar full of milk for me to drink. And I remember to this day how thrilled I was, eating my peanut butter and jelly sandwiches, drinking my jar of milk, watching a ballgame, sitting next to my Dad.

I suppose heaven will be just like that. At least I hope so.

The Infield(er) Fly Rule

Suppose there are runners on first and second and nobody out. Suppose the batter hits a soaring pop fly high above the infield Suppose, the shortstop looking up, follows its flight and anticipates it will come down on the infield dirt, somewhere in the vicinity of second base. Suppose he settles under it, and, looking up, waits for the ball to come down into his glove for the fly ball out.

But as he is waiting, suppose a great idea dawns on him. Hey, wait a minute, he says to himself. If I catch this ball, the only out I will get is the fly out on the batter. But if I *don't* catch it, if I just step back and let this pop fly drop right in front of me, I think I just may be able to turn a double play.

The ball still is still descending, so the shortstop continues his analysis: Here's how I can do it. As this pop up falls toward me in what should be an easy fly out, both the runner on first and the runner on second will anticipate that the Fly Ball Rules will apply and they will therefore stay close to their bases so as not to be doubled off. But once I let it drop in front of me, the Ground Ball Rules will kick in, they will both be forced to advance, and I can pick the ball up and throw to the third baseman to force out the runner on second going to third (which should be easy because he hasn't even left second yet), and then the third baseman can throw to the second baseman to force out the runner on first going to second (which also should also be easy because he hasn't even left first yet).

The lords of baseball didn't like the idea of fielders purposely not catching fly balls. "It's just not cricket!" they said to themselves. Or words to that effect. The **Infield Fly Rule** was devised to prevent these kinds of shenanigans. The Infield Fly Rule holds that, with runners on first and second, or with bases loaded, and no outs or one out, any pop fly in fair territory which an infielder can catch with "ordinary effort" and which can be "easily handled" by him will be announced as an Infield Fly by the umpire, and the batter will automatically be called out regardless of whether any infielder catches the ball or not.

Despite the name of the rule, the ball doesn't have to be coming down in the infield for the rule to apply. It can be coming down in the outfield as well. The only requirement is that an infielder be able to easily handle it and catch it with ordinary effort. Thus, if an infielder drifts back onto the outfield grass to catch a pop up, the umpire could still decide that the Infield Fly Rule applies. It seems, therefore, that the more appropriate title to the rule would have been the Infield*er* Fly Rule.

The Infield Fly Rule caused a great deal of controversy, and a fairly serious fan disturbance, during a one-game playoff between the Cardinals and the Braves, in Atlanta, on October 4, 2012. The incident, which one writer dubbed "The Pop Up Heard 'Round the World," occurred when the Braves, trailing 6–3 in the bottom of the eighth inning, put runners on first and second with one out. Braves batter Andrelton Simmons then hit a high pop up into left field. Cardinals shortstop Pete Kozma, half-turned away from home plate, raced seventy feet into left field, stopped, raised his glove in the air as if to catch the ball but then, realizing he didn't have it lined up after all, dropped his glove and took a few steps back towards the infield, apparently to give Cardinals left fielder Matt Holliday, coming in behind him, room to make the catch. Unfortunately for the Cards, just as Kozma had not gone far enough *out*, Holliday had not come far enough *in*, and the ball fell between them for what appeared to be a base hit.

Braves fan were ecstatic. Simmons was safe at first, the other runners had moved up and now the Braves had bases loaded with only one out. Clearly, a big inning was in the offing.

But wait! The umpire signaled that the Infield Fly Rule was in effect, meaning that the batter was automatically out, and the Braves, instead of having bases loaded with one out, still had runners at first and second, but now with two out. Braves fans, sensing that the call may have ruined any chance they had of mounting a rally and catching the Cards, immediately began tossing whatever they could get their hands on onto the field of play. Beer bottles, soda cups, hot dogs, programs all flew onto the field, sending the Cardinal fielders scurrying into the dugout for cover. The game was delayed twenty minutes before calm could be restored and the game continued.

The umpire's call was suspect. That the shortstop had to turn, with his back nearly turned to home plate, and race seventy feet into the outfield in order to have a chance at catching the ball, suggests that it was not a ball that he could "easily handle" and that much more than "ordinary effort" would be involved. The typical infield fly rule application involves an infielder who needs to take only a few casual steps in any direction to make the catch, not a full sprint seventy feet into the outfield with, again, his back nearly turned to the plate.

But what I find most revealing about this incident is not that the umpire might have made a mistake—the calls by MLB umps are overwhelmingly remarkably accurate and supported by instant replays—or even that the infield fly rule could have such an important effect on a game of this magnitude. No, what I find most revealing is that as esoteric a rule as it is, over 52,000 fans in Atlanta knew the rule and knew it well enough to know that it had perhaps been improperly applied. And that, in itself, is pretty darn impressive.

The Dropped Third Strike, Continued

Many pages ago we discussed that when a catcher drops a third strike, he has to pick up the ball and either tag the runner or throw to first to get the runner out. If he fails to do so, and the runner is safe at first, the inning would continue.

That was only half the discussion. I've saved the second half for now because the potential for the same kind of intentionally-drop-the-ball-to-create-a-double-play shenanigans we discussed in relation to the Infield Fly Rule, exists with the dropped third strike as well. After all, suppose there was a runner on first with one man out. Couldn't the catcher intentionally drop a third strike, forcing the batter to run to first and therefore forcing the runner already on first to run to second, thus opening up the possibility of a force-at-second-force-at-first double play?

The answer is: No. Fortunately, the lords of baseball are always one step ahead of ne'er do wells who would attempt such chicanery. The Official Baseball Rules hold therefore that the dropped third strike rule only applies when there are two outs, or when there are less than two outs but with no one on first. Thus, it is impossible to intentionally generate a double play on a dropped third strike.

Productive Outs

Now that you have enough background knowledge to follow this concept, I'd like to interject a brief word on what are called **productive outs.** A productive out is an out that helps the offense by serving to move a runner up from first to second and into scoring position, or a runner from second to third. A sacrifice bunt is a productive out. Here are some other examples:

Runner on second base. No one out. Here's the pitch. Batter drives a ground ball to the right side of the infield, as the runner on second takes off for third. The fielder who fields the grounder, be it the first baseman or second baseman, has two choices: he can either make the long, risky throw across the infield to third to try to get the runner on second going to third on a tag play, or he can make the shorter, safer throw to first to get the batter out on the force. Most of the time, fielders will choose the latter. This strategy is called **hitting behind the runner**. The ground out in this case is a productive out because it served to advance the runner to third.

In contrast, if the batter had hit the ball to the left side of the infield, it would have been hit *ahead* of the runner on second, and he would have been unable to advance because either the shortstop or the third baseman, whoever fielded the ball and either of whom would be very physically close to our runner at second, would have no doubt **looked him back** to second. What that means is that after catching the ball, while holding it in his hand, the fielder would have taken a good long look at our runner on second, partially to see if he's going to try for third, partially to *discourage* him from trying for third, and partially to bluff a throw to the second baseman to catch him off base. Once the runner on second had been looked back to second, the danger of him advancing would have passed, and the fielder could then have thrown on to first for the easy force out on the batter.

OK, moving on, suppose the batter has correctly hit behind the runner, advancing him to third. Thanks to that productive out, we have a runner on third with only one out. The next batter steps to the plate. Here's the pitch. Batter hits a deep fly ball to center. The centerfielder catches it for the second out, but since it's deep enough, the runner on third tags up and runs in for the score. That fly ball out was also a productive out because it brought in the run.

And there you have it. The runner goes from second to third and then scores from third because his teammates put together two productive outs in a row. This is a perfect example of a team manufacturing a run using basic, non-dramatic essential tools of the trade. Another word for this style of baseball, this scratching-and-clawing-for-every-run type of baseball, is called **small ball**, meaning "small" in contrast to mighty home runs or dramatic extra base hits.

Runner on Third

In our discussion so far about advancing runners, we've concentrated on advancing runners from first to second and thus into scoring position. Once on second, we know, a runner with fair speed can score on most hits.

The techniques used to advance runners from first to second can also be used to advance runners from second to third. A runner on second can steal third, a batter can sacrifice bunt a runner over from second to third, a runner can advance from second to third after tagging up on a fly ball out, and so on. These techniques, however, are used less to move a runner over to third because, after all, there is not as much to be gained by doing so. If a runner is already in scoring position on second, why lose an out by sacrificing him over to third, or why take the risk of him being thrown out stealing third, or being thrown out after tagging up and advancing to third?

Truth be told, there are advantages to having a runner on third. Obviously, he's closer to home plate, for one thing, and thus that much more likely to score on a hit or an error. But there are other situations when having a runner on third, as opposed to second, comes in handy:

- A runner on third can tag up and score on a well-hit fly ball out to any outfield, especially one hit to deep center, which is the point in the outfield furthest away from home plate. If a fly ball out results in a runner tagging up and scoring from third, it is called a **sacrifice fly**.
- A runner on third, if he takes a big enough lead and is fast enough, can score on a well-placed ground ball hit deep in the hole, meaning, again, far back on the infield dirt in the area of second base.
- A runner on third can score on a wild pitch or passed ball. This possibility may affect the pitcher's choice of pitches. As discussed in our analysis of "Casey at the Bat," with a runner on third the pitcher is more inclined to stick with fastballs, as opposed to breaking pitches, to cut down on the possibility of a wild pitch or passed ball that will enable that runner to come home. If the pitcher's main weapon is a fastball, fine, nothing is lost, but if a pitcher's best pitch is one with a lot of movement—a curveball, say—a runner on third takes away his bread and butter. And as long as that runner is on third, the pitcher becomes a weaker pitcher.
- A runner will score from third if a pitcher commits a balk.

Defending Against the Runner on Third

To discourage a runner on third from trying to score on an infield ground ball, or to prevent him from scoring should he try, a defense may choose to play the infield in. This means that, much like fielding a bunt, the infielders will position themselves closer to home plate so that, in the event of a ground ball, they have a better chance of throwing the runner out at home should he try to score.

There are actually five different variations on playing the infield in. For example, you can play all the infielders in; you can play them all halfway in; you can play some infielders in but not others; you can have them play back and then charge in at the last second, and so on. The speed of the runner at third, the side the batter hits from, the bat control of the batter, and the possibility that the charging infielders may be able to distract the batter, will all be taken into account when deciding which infield-in method to use.

The trade off in all five, however, is that infielders playing closer to the batter have that much less time to react, and a sharply hit ground ball has a better chance of getting past them for a hit.

The defensive team will only play the infield up when there are less than two outs, because on a two-out ground ball, the fielder would just ignore the runner on third and throw on to first to get the easier force out at first.

Furthermore, the defensive team would only play the infield up in a game where they were either behind or narrowly ahead and every run was important. If the fielding team was comfortably ahead, they would probably **play the fielders deep**, meaning at their normal positions, and **trade a run for an out**, meaning they would allow the run to score in exchange for getting the batter on the force out at first, thus short-circuiting the chances of a big offensive inning.

A great example of the ramifications of playing the infield in occurred in the seventh and deciding game of the 2001 World Series between the Yankees and the Diamondbacks. With the scored tied in the bottom of the ninth, the home team Diamondbacks managed to load the bases with one man out. Remember: with the bases loaded, there is a force at any base. The Yankees now had to make a choice: do they play the infield in to try to get the force out of the runner on third coming home? Or do they play the infield deep and try for an inning-ending double play?

If the Yankee infield plays in, and if the next batter, Diamondbacks outfielder Luis Gonzalez, hits a ground ball, an infielder who successfully fields the ball has an improved chance of forcing the runner on third out at home because the infielder, playing in, is that much closer to home to begin with and has a shorter throw to the catcher. The tradeoff is that a sharply hit ground ball has a better chance of getting past that infielder because, playing closer to the batter, he will not have as much time to react to the batted ball. In summary, it will be harder to field the ball if he plays in, but if he manages to field it, he will have a better chance forcing the runner out at home.

If the infield plays deep, however, it will be easier to field the ball because, playing farther from the batter, the fielder will have more time to react to the batted ball. But that's the easy part. What happens next is where it gets tricky. If a Yankees infielder fields the ball while playing deep, he will most probably be too far from home plate to try to throw out the runner trying to score from third. That means that any out he gets will have to be on the bases. And what *that* means is that the Yankees, if they play deep, will have to turn a double play to get out of the inning. If they only manage one out, the runner on third, Jay Bell of the Diamondbacks, will have trotted home with the winning run in the meantime.

As do most things in baseball, the side the batter hits from was key in this situation. The batter, Luis Gonzalez, is a lefty. Mariano Rivera, the Yankees pitcher, as discussed, throws almost nothing but cutters that break in on left-handed batters, and away from right-handed batters. There was a good chance, therefore, that if Gonzalez did make contact, it would be with the part of the bat below the sweet spot. And what *that* means is that there's a good chance that if he hit a ground ball, it wouldn't be a very strong one. It might be a weak ground ball, a slow ground ball, and if the Yankees played deep, by the time it rolled into a fielder's glove, it might be too late to turn a double play.

Luis Gonzalez managed to get his bat on Mariano's pitch, all right, and, as expected, he hit the ball with the lower part, the thin part of the bat. In fact, it was so low on the thinner end of the bat that the pitch broke Gonzalez's bat as he made contact. The result, though, was not a weak ground ball, but a weak little half-fly-ball-half-pop-up out towards where the infield dirt meets the outfield grass just to the left of second base. It was the kind of easy fly ball that shortstop Derek Jeter could have caught with his eyes closed if he were playing where he usually plays.

But he didn't, because he wasn't.

And the reason he wasn't playing where he usually plays is because the Yankees, realizing the difficulties of trying to turn a double play in this situation, had elected to play the infield in. Jeter was situated, therefore, on the inside of the infield dirt, closest to the batter, about ten feet forward from where he usually plays. As a result, Gonzalez's weak little pop fly dropped in behind him for a base hit, Bell scored from third and the Diamondbacks were the world champions.

"I didn't lose any sleep over it, other than the result," Joe Torre, Yankees manager, said of his decision to play the infield in. "But I know one thing: I wouldn't have done anything different."

Other Defensive Strategies

COVERING BASES AND BACKING UP THROWS

You already know a great deal about defensive strategies. For example, you know about intentional walks, pickoffs, holding the runner, pitch outs, and you know about playing the infield in against a bunt and against a runner on third. But there are just a few more defensive measures that you need to know about to round out your rapidly growing knowledge of the game.

In regards to defending against the sacrifice bunt, we discussed how the first baseman and third baseman play up on the grass and then come charging in as soon as the batter squares to bunt. Let's back up and paint a fuller picture of what happens when, with a runner on first, the batter bunts the ball up the first base line. Simultaneously,

- the first baseman will charge in to field the bunt,
- the second baseman will run over to cover first, ready to take the first baseman's throw to get the batter out,
- and since the second baseman is covering first, the shortstop will shift over and cover second in case there is a play there, either on the runner coming from first, or the batter, should he advance past first,
- and the right fielder will run in and to his left so as to be in a position to catch the ball should the first baseman's throw get past the second baseman, who is covering first.

The minute the batter bunts the pitch up the first base line, if not moments before, these four fielders will all be in motion, moving with speed and precision exactly to the assigned areas that this discrete situation calls for, and they will arrive knowledgeable of what their duties are and they will be ready to perform them. Indeed, by the time they play their first Major League game, every fielder will be drilled and drilled and drilled in their assignments in every possible defensive situation so that, in their sleep, they know where to go and what to do on any given play.

For example, suppose with the bases loaded, the pitcher throws a wild pitch that goes past the catcher all the way to the backstop. As rare as that event is, every fielder will know exactly what to do when it happens. The catcher's assignment, of course, is to run back to the backstop and retrieve the ball. The pitcher, meanwhile, will run in and cover home and be in a position to receive the throw from the catcher should the runner on third try to come home. The second baseman would run toward the pitcher's mound to back up the throw from the catcher to the pitcher. The shortstop would shift over and cover second, the third baseman would stay where he is and cover third, and the outfielders would, again, sneak closer to the infield to back up any throws.

Does a fan, even an advanced fan, need to know all the pre-planned coverage and backup assignments for, say, a single to left with no runners on, or a double down the right-field line with runners on first and second? Of course not. Not even close. But does an awareness of the efficiency and comprehensiveness of these well-oiled coverage and backup assignments help us better appreciate (and enjoy) the game itself? Absolutely.

Hitting the Cutoff Man and Relay Throws

In the story I told about the great catch by Met outfielder Endy Chavez, I said that, after his catch, Endy threw the ball to the infield and baserunner Jim Edmonds was doubled up at first. I didn't say, however, that Endy *himself* threw the ball all the way to first. Picture Endy Chavez, his back to the left field fence. Picture how far away first base is. If Endy had made that throw all by himself, as strong as his arm may be, there's a good chance the ball would have bounced once or twice as it reached the infield and lost a good deal of speed.

So what did Endy do instead? He **hit the cutoff man**, which in this case meant that shortstop Jose Reyes, acting as a **cutoff man**, left his position, came out towards Endy on the outfield grass, intercepted Endy's throw, then turned and fired the ball the rest of the way to the first baseman for the out. Think of runners in a relay race passing the baton. The throw from Endy to Reyes is called a **relay throw**.

Relay throws, and hitting the cutoff man, are together one of the basic defensive strategies employed by a team to minimize the damage done when an opponent gets a hit with runners on base. Here's how it works:

On plays to left field, either the third baseman or the shortstop acts as the cutoff man. On plays to right field, it will be either the first baseman or second baseman. The cutoff man, like Jose Reyes in the example above, will go out to the edge of the outfield grass and await the throw from the outfielder. At that point, he will be facing the outfielder, and he will have his back half-turned to both the infield and the runner(s) advancing around the bases. He will therefore need the assistance of one of the other infielders as to where to throw the ball once he catches the relay throw.

Behind him, therefore, one of the other infielders, most probably the catcher, will act as his assistant. The assistant will assess the progress and speed of the runners and decide which runner, if any, the cutoff man should try to throw out. If throwing a runner out is not possible, the cutoff man will instead direct the cutoff man to throw to that base which might keep the progress of the runners to a minimum.

For example: runners on first and second. Here's the pitch. The batter belts a liner over the head of the right fielder. The right fielder gives chase, the second baseman comes out to act as the cutoff man, and the shortstop moves over to cover second. By the time the outfielder comes up with the ball, the runner on second is already rounding third and heading home, and the runner on first is already rounding second and heading to third. The catcher may quickly realize that there is nothing they can do about either of those runners, and the best they can do now is try to keep the batter from advancing from first to second. Instead of wasting a throw on either of the first two runners, therefore, the catcher may direct the cutoff man to throw to second to hold the batter at first.

The beauty of an effective cutoff man is that his mere presence can deter aggressive base running. When baserunners see that a throw from the outfield is going to second base, for example, then only the runner going to second is affected. But when baserunners see that a throw from the outfield is going to a cutoff man, they all have to be cautious, because no one knows where the cutoff man will direct his relay once he has the ball.

POSITIONING THE OUTFIELDERS

Part of a team's preparation for a game involves detailed analysis of the strengths and weaknesses of opposing batters. Teams, for one thing, will study the spray charts on opposing batters, showing where and how deep they have tended to hit the ball in the past. Armed with this information, a team will know in advance where to position its outfielders, thereby increasing their chances of having a fielder in position to catch a fly ball out, or at least to cut down on the batter's chances of getting an extra base hit.

When a righty pull hitter steps to the plate, for example, the outfielders might take a few steps over towards the left side of the outfield. If that righty pull hitter also has a history of occasionally dropping an opposite field single down the right field line, the right fielder might stay where he is, with only the center fielder and left fielder shifting over to the left side of the outfield. This is why it is said that when you watch a ballgame, if you want to see where in the outfield any particular batter has a tendency to hit the ball, just look at the outfielders. Where they are positioned is where the batter will most likely hit it.

When a lefty batter's spray chart shows that he exclusively pulls the ball to right field and has virtually no history of opposite field hitting, the defense may employ **the shift**, meaning that the left side of the infield—the third baseman and shortstop—will be shifted completely over to the right side of the infield. The third baseman will move to what is normally the shortstop's position, the shortstop will move over to cover second, and the second baseman will become, basically, a fourth outfielder, positioning himself on the outfield grass halfway between the infield and the right fielder.

CALLING IT

We know now that a defense can maximize its performance by following prearranged plans of covering bases, backing up throws, and positioning outfielders to reflect a batter's hitting history. Often, however, despite these extensive preparations, unplanned things occur in the heat of battle and decisions must be made on the run. In these cases, players communicate those decisions the old fashioned way: they yell at each other.

We know that a fly ball hit squarely to right, center, or leftfield will be caught by the fielder at those positions. But when a ball is lofted between two outfielders, they will both race towards it at full speed and there will be a danger that they will either *both* pull back, expecting the other to catch it, and allowing the ball to fall safely between them, or, worse, *neither* will pull back and they will race headlong into a collision. To minimize the chances of either happening, one of the outfielders will take charge and yell loudly, "I got it!" and the other outfielder will peel off and allow his partner to make the catch.

Likewise, when a fly ball is hit between an infielder and an outfielder, the shortstop, for example, will race out toward it and the left fielder will race in. Again, to avoid collision and maximize the chances of getting the out, one of them will take charge and yell, "I got it!" This is known as **calling it**, as in, calling who will catch the ball.

Fielders work out in advance which of them will take priority on balls hit between them. If there is a runner on base, for example, an outfielder running in, who will be facing the infield when he catches the ball, should take priority on a short fly ball over an infielder running out, whose back will be to the infield and who would have to turn to throw. Likewise, between two outfielders, the outfielder with more experience and a better arm (if there are runners on base) will take priority. Still, "I got it!" will be yelled to remove any doubt.

TAKE YOURSELF OUT TO THE BALLGAME ... ALMOST!

In every Major League ballgame, between the top half and the bottom half of the seventh inning, fans will be asked to participate in one of baseball's oldest, oddest and most enjoyable traditions: a sing-along of the 1908 classic, "Take Me Out to the Ballgame":

> *"Take me out to the ballgame,*
> *Take me out with the crowd.*
> *Buy me some peanuts and cracker jacks,*
> *I don't care if I never get back,*
> *Let me root, root, root for the home team,*
> *If they don't win it's a shame.*
> *For it's one, two, three strikes, you're out,*
> *At the old ballgame."*

Now that you are an expert in the game of baseball, I'm sure you think you are ready to grab a friend, buy a couple of tickets and take yourself out to an old ballgame. And you are... almost. Hold off for just a little while longer and allow me to now fill you in on the fascinating worlds of baseball statistics and of Major League Baseball. This way, when you do take yourself out to the ballgame, you'll not only know about signs, steals and sacrifices, but you'll also know about such other essentials as saves, slugging percentages and sabermetrics.

THREE

Statistics

Consider this broadcast of a 1963 World Series game between the Dodgers and Yankees:

"Koufax ... Koufax kicks, he delivers, it's up the middle! it's a base hit! Richardson is rounding first, he's going for second, the ball's into deep right center, Davis coming over to cut the ball off, here comes the throw, Richardson is going around first, he goes into second, he slides, he's in there! He's safe! It's a double! Look at Richardson, he's on second base! Koufax is in big trouble! Big trouble, baby!"

Having read this far, you know exactly what's going on in that game. Sandy Koufax, the great Dodgers pitcher, of whom it was said that he could throw a ball through a car wash without getting it wet, is in trouble. In fact, he is in big trouble, baby. Bobby Richardson, Yankees second baseman, has just hit a double and put himself in scoring position, setting the table for the powerful Yankees lineup to follow.

The problem is, had that really been an actual broadcast, it probably would have sounded something more like this:

"Southpaw Koufax had remarkable success against right-handed batters this season. Well, he had remarkable success against *everyone* this past season, compiling an amazing 25-and-5 record, with a microscopic ERA of only 1.88. I mean, those numbers are downright *scary*! But he's been particularly stingy against righties. Opposing righties hit a measly .179 against Sandy all year, so the platoon advantage falls on deaf ears when it comes to Mr. Koufax. However, it should be noted that when righties do hit Koufax, they hit him hard. Of 18 homers given up by Koufax this year, righties have hit 17 of them. Bobby Richardson, stepping to the plate for the Yankees, is not a power hitter, he has hit only three out all year, but he did hit 20 doubles, eight of them against lefties, so if Bobby catches one, he can do some damage. Koufax looks in for the sign now. Here we go... Koufax... Koufax kicks, he delivers, it's up the middle! it's a base hit!"

You cannot listen to, watch, or talk about baseball without a working knowledge and meaning of at least the basic statistics that are maintained at practically every level of baseball, even by some Little Leagues. The importance of statistics in understanding, discussing and analyzing baseball is so profound that a section on statistics could have easily been the first topic of discussion in this book, instead of nearly the last, but for the fact that the section would have meant absolutely nothing to a reader not familiar—as you are now—with the vocabulary of the game.

One reason statistics are so disproportionately important to baseball as opposed to other sports is just because they *can* be, because of the nature of the game. If you, like me, are a fan of Stoke City F.C. in the English Premier League and a fan of their captain, Ryan Shawcross, in particular, if you miss a game and if Shawcross didn't score, there is no way to know what he did for 90 minutes. Did he play well? Didn't he? What can you do? Ask your friends? Hope that a local sportswriter may have mentioned it?

In contrast, everything that happens on a baseball field can be counted and categorized and added up and preserved for analysis. If, for example, you are a Blue Jays fan and a fan of the renowned right fielder Jose Bautista in particular, and if you miss a game, not to worry: Every move Bautista made in that game will be preserved in a statistic and will be available for your review in the newspaper the next day (or on the Internet that same night): how many times he came to bat, how many walks, singles, extra base hits and RBIs he had, how many runs he scored and extra bases he racked up, how many times he struck out, grounded out (and to whom), flied out (and to whom), how many chances he had in the field, how many outs and assists on outs he made, and how many errors, if any.

As in every sport, baseball managers play the percentages, but unlike in every other sport, in baseball there just seems to be an infinite number of percentages to play. The announcer's analysis of a fairly routine game situation noted above reflects a manager's own, but a manager will have access to additional stats and scouting reports and on-field experience that the announcer won't.

Take them out to the ballgame? In this scene from *One Flew Over the Cuckoo's Nest* (1975), Jack Nicholson as McMurphy (center) and his fellow asylum inmates enjoy "watching" the World Series on television (Photofest).

As a final word before we begin, I will suggest that normally love, and a deep, piercing, obsessive and repeated dissection and analysis of the thing loved, a constant experimentation with the components of the thing loved, don't mix very well. But they do in baseball. Love fuels the analysis, the analysis fuels the statistics, and the statistics fuel the love. There's no explaining it. That's just the way baseball is.

By the way, did you recognize the World Series broadcast that I started off this section with? It is probably the most widely heard baseball broadcast of all time.

Need a clue? Here it is: "Ahhhhh, Juicy Fruit!"

The announcer for that game was none other than Jack Nicholson, in the role of Randle Patrick McMurphy, a petty criminal confined to a mental institution in the Academy Award winning 1975 classic, *One Flew Over the Cuckoo's Nest.* For those of you who haven't seen the movie, when he is not permitted to watch the World Series on the ward TV because most of his fellow inmates are too withdrawn from reality or too anxiety-ridden to vote for this dramatic change to their tightly controlled daily regimen, a dejected McMurphy can only sit alone and sulk in front of the darkened TV. Suddenly, however, as he looks up at that blank screen, his face brightens, and he begins to announce a fictitious game, making it up as he goes along. His rendition of the game is so enthusiastic, so convincing, that within minutes, as the drama of the "game" builds, he is surrounded by a crowd of inmates, staring, half in confusion, half in sheer joy, at the blank TV. When McMurphy announces a final thunderous home run by the Mickey Mantle, they all erupt in a clapping, jumping, hugging, display of utter happiness.

Speaking of statistics, *One Flew Over the Cuckoo's Nest* is one of only three films ever to win all of the five major Oscars: Best Film, Best Director, Best Actor, Best Actress and Best Screenplay. Talk about scary numbers!

Basic Statistics

THE OFFICIAL SCORER

We've already discussed the Official Scorer, the MLB-appointed eye-in-the-sky in attendance at every game who decides whether a batter reaches safely because of a hit or an error, and whether a ball that scoots past the catcher is a wild pitch or a passed ball. To flesh things out a bit, we can now add that these judgment calls are only a part of the Official Scorer's main job at a game, which is to keep a written record of every pitch and every play that happens in a game, and then, after the game is over, forward that record to MLB headquarters, where all the records from all the Official Scorers from all the games are boiled down to create the statistics you will read about now.

HITTING STATISTICS

Batting Average

A **batting average** (abbreviated as **BA** or **Avg** on statistics tables and in box scores, which we'll talk about later) is the percentage of hits a player gets in the times he's been at bat. A batting average is calculated by dividing the number of a player's hits by the number of his at bats. If Roy Hobbs, for the season so far, has 33 hits in 100 at bats, his batting average will be .333. (Batting averages, like all hitting statistics, are recorded to the third decimal).

Batting averages, by the way, are never calculated on a game basis. You'll never hear an announcer say: "Roy Hobbs is 1-for-2 so far today, so he has a batting average of .500 in this game." Instead, batting averages are always spoken of on a long-term basis, usually over the course of the season to date, though a variation might be used to illustrate some other long-term event, like a slump or a hot streak. Thus, you might hear the announcer say: "Roy Hobbs has a batting average of .310 for the year, but lately he's gone into a real slump and he has a batting average of only .225 over the last 15 games."

Actually, the terms "hitting" or "batting" would most probably be used to describe a batting average, as in "Roy Hobbs is *hitting* .310 for the year, but lately he's gone on into a real slump and he is *batting* only .225 over the last fifteen games."

All statistics are, of course, relative. If you're the principal of a school where 25 percent of the kids drop out, you'll probably get fired if the average drop out rate for the entire city is 10 percent, but you'll probably get a raise if the average drop out rate for the entire city is 50 percent.

Likewise, Roy Hobbs' .333 batting average, mentioned above, might not seem so remarkable to an outside observer—after all, a .333 batting average means the batter made out twice as often as he got hits—but a .333 batting average would certainly rank among the best in baseball at the end of a season. In fact, to bat .300 or over is universally recognized as a very special achievement. Over a century ago, Philadelphia outfielder Gavvy Cravath (who hit .341 in 1913) put it this way: "There is a certain charm about .300. If a man hits it he is a star, if he doesn't hit it he isn't a star." Only once in the past eighty years has a batter finished the season with a batting average of over .400, and that was Ted Williams, who hit .406 in 1941.

To familiarize you with the range of batting averages you might expect to see among the top players, as well as to give you a glimpse at some of the important names in today's MLB, here are the best batting averages in Major League baseball (based on an MLB-required minimum of 502 plate appearances in a season) over the last five seasons:

2013: Miguel Cabrera, Detroit Tigers, .348
2012: Buster Posey, San Francisco Giants, .336
2011: Miguel Cabrera, Detroit Tigers, .344
2010: Josh Hamilton, Texas Rangers. .359
2009: Joe Mauer, Minnesota Twins .365

The standard year-to-date batting average may be the most common one referred to by announcers and water cooler debaters, but it may be among the least useful to managers planning a game. Instead, there are several of what might be called subdivision batting averages that are calculated and studied earnestly by each team as part of its pre-game analysis of opposing batters and, indeed, its own batters as well.

As illustrated by our fictitious Sandy Koufax vs. Bobby Richardson faceoff earlier, the most critical batting average will be a batter's batting average against lefty pitchers as opposed to righties. This is where platooning comes in. As discussed, almost without fail, a righty hitter will have a higher batting average against lefty pitchers, and a lefty hitter will have a higher batting average against righty pitchers. Sure, a fan like myself might moan and groan through all the delays caused by platoon-based substitutions, but at the same time, if it were late in the game and my team was down by a run and the opponents had a lefty on the mound, if my manager did NOT pull a left-handed hitter who has a career batting average of .225 against lefties and send up a right-handed pinch hitter who had a career batting average of .295 against lefties, I'd be darn unhappy.

Other subdivision batting averages that managers will consider when deciding on a team's lineup for the day and on substitutions as the game progresses are the batter's batting average over the past couple of weeks (is he hot? Is he in a slump?), and then his lifetime and/or season-to-date batting average (i) against the opposing pitcher, (ii) against the opposing team, (iii) in that particular ballpark, (iv) in day games versus night games, (v) with runners on base, (vi) with runners in scoring position, and (vii) when he bats in certain spots in the lineup as opposed to others (some players feel more comfortable leading off, while others feel more comfortable batting second and so on).

OK, let's step back for a second. We said that a batting average is the percentage of hits to at bats. You know that a hit (abbreviated as **H**) is a single, double, triple or home run. And you can probably figure out what an at bat is: an at bat is a turn that the batter takes at the plate. If a batter is up four times during the game, well, he's had four at bats.

You would be right, but the catch is that when calculating a player's batting average, not all his turns at the plate, not all his **plate appearances**, count as a *statistical* at bat (**AB**). If the batter walks or gets hit by a pitch, these plate appearances do not count as statistical at bats, probably because when he is walked or gets hit by a pitch, through no fault of his own, he does not really have a proper chance to get a hit.

A batter is also not charged with a statistical at bat when he hits into a sacrifice bunt or a sacrifice fly. I would guess the reasoning behind this is that when a batter makes an out for the good of the team he's rewarded by, again, not being charged with an at bat. Just keep in mind the important difference between a sacrifice fly and a sacrifice bunt. A sacrifice fly is a fly ball out which allows a runner to score from third. A fly ball out which allows a runner to advance from first to second, or from second to third, is not scored as a sacrifice fly, and the batter will be charged with an at bat. In contrast, a batter will be credited with a sacrifice bunt and not charged with an at bat when his bunt moves up any runner to any base.

In short, a statistical at bat is a turn that the batter takes at the plate in which he's either made an out (but not a sacrifice bunt or a sacrifice fly), reached base on an error or gotten a hit. If, over the course of a season, a player has made 400 plate appearances, walked 70 times, gotten hit by a pitch 15 times, made sacrifice outs 15 times, and gotten 60 hits, his batting average will be .200. The reason is that when you subtract the walks, hit by pitches, and sacrifice outs from the batter's 400 plate appearances, the batter will end up being charged with 300 statistical at bats. 60 hits in 300 statistical at bats equals a .200 batting average.

An aside about terminology: During a game, the television or radio announcers will precede each batter's at bat with a shorthand summary of the batter's performance so far in the game. As Roy Hobbs steps up to the plate in the sixth inning, for example, you might hear the announcer say, "Hobbs is 1-for-2 so far today." The announcer is telling you, in abbreviated form, how many hits Hobbs has had so far that game, and how many statistical at bats (not plate appearances). The first number represents the amount of hits; the second number represents the amount of statistical at bats. Hobbs, in this example, has one hit in two statistical at bats, meaning he made a non-sacrifice out or reached on an error in his other at bat. If the announcer said Hobbs was "0-for-2 today" it would have meant that Hobbs had no hits in two statistical at bats. (Again, the announcers will never say "zero for two," they will say "Oh" as in the letter "O" for two.)

Now suppose Hobbs was up at bat three times, and in those three times he walked, singled and grounded out. Statistically, we know now, Hobbs has only two at bats, since he is not charged with an at bat for his walk, so to keep you fully informed, the announcer will supplement his summary of Hobbs' performance so far that day by adding that information to the end of it. Thus, he might say something like "So far today, Hobbs is 1-for-2, with a walk."

Again, the MLB requires a minimum of 502 plate appearances for a player's batting average to be considered for the batting average title. Keep in mind that every time a player steps up to the plate it counts as a plate appearance, but a player's statistical at bats, not his plate appearances, are used to calculate his batting average. In other words, plate appearances will get him into the race, but statistical at bats will win him the title.

Runs Batted In

A batter gets credit for a **Run Batted In** (**RBI** or **BI**) when, as a result of his actions at the plate, a runner on base scores a run. For example, the batter hits a single, and, as a result of that single, a runner on second is able to come around and score a run, or the batter draws a walk (abbreviated as **BB**, as in "base on balls") with the bases loaded, and, as a result, the runner on third is forced home and scores. In short, an RBI can be credited to a batter when a runner scores because of the batter's hit, sacrifice bunt, sacrifice fly, or walking or getting hit by a pitch (**HBP**) with the bases loaded. A batter can also get credit for an RBI if a runner scores as a result of his ground out or his hitting into a fielder's choice, but not as a result of his hitting into a double play.

A hit that results in an RBI is often called an **RBI single**, for example, or an **RBI double**, or, sounding out "RBI" as if it were a word, a **Ribby single** or a **Ribby double**. If more than one RBI results from a hit, you might hear the expression that the batter hit a **two-run single** or **three-run double** or **two-run triple** as the case may be. The batter who stroked an RBI hit will be said to have **driven in** a run or **scored** the runner or, depending on the circumstances, **singled in** a runner, **doubled in** a runner or **tripled in** a runner. As in "Yeonis Cespedes of the A's doubled in Josh Donaldson in the third inning, his single scored Jed Lowrie in the fifth, and his triple drove in Brandon Moss in the seventh—a good day for Cespedes!" When there is more than one runner on base, and a hit scores them all, it might be said that the hit **cleared the bases**.

Again, for the sake of completeness, I must add that a new and rather annoying term for an RBI is that a player **plated a run**, where the plate, I guess, is home plate, as in "Cespedes plated two in the third."

A batter who hits a home run (**HR**) automatically gets credit for an RBI just for hitting the home run. After all, he *did* drive in a run… himself! A batter who hits a home run with one man on gets credit for two RBIs, because he batted in himself along with the baserunner, and so on. Not surprisingly, the players who have the most home runs usually have the most RBIs as well.

The top RBI leaders in the Major Leagues over the last five years were:

2013: Chris Davis, Baltimore Orioles, 138
2012: Miguel Cabrera, Detroit Tigers, 139
2011: Matt Kemp, Los Angeles Dodgers, 126
2010: Miguel Cabrera, Detroit Tigers, 126
2009: Prince Fielder, Milwaukee Brewers, and Ryan Howard, Philadelphia Phillies, both with 141

The top Home Run hitters in the Major Leagues over the last five years were:

2013: Chris Davis, Baltimore Orioles, 53
2012: Miguel Cabrera, Detroit Tigers, 44
2011: Jose Bautista, Toronto Blue Jays, 43
2010: Jose Bautista, Toronto Blue Jays, 54
2009: Albert Pujols, St. Louis Cardinals, 47

Note: a batter does not usually get credit for an RBI when he hits the ball, a fielder makes an error, and a runner scores as a result of the error. However, if the Official Scorer decides that with less than two outs, the error is made on a play in which a runner on third would have scored anyway, an RBI can be credited.

On Base and Slugging Percentages

A player's **on base percentage** (**OBP**) is a variation of his batting average. Instead of the percentage of a player's hits to his total at bats, the on base percentage is the percentage of the total times he gets on base to his total at bats. On Base Percentage is important because it is a good measure of a batter's overall offensive productivity. As discussed, extra base hits and home runs are lovely but they are relatively rare. Most of the time, managers will be left trying to manufacture runs by trying to advance runners from first into scoring position. The more runners a team gets to first base, the better off it is, and how they got there— whether by hit, walk, or getting hit by a pitch—isn't really that important.

For the sake of figuring out a player's OBP, walks, hits and hit by pitches count as an "on base" for a player, but reaching a base on an error does not. Also, as is the case with batting averages, a minimum of 502 plate appearances are needed to qualify.

The OBP leaders over the last five years were:

2013: Miguel Cabrera, Detroit Tigers, .442
2012: Joe Mauer, Minnesota Twins, .416
2011: Miguel Cabrera, Detroit Tigers, .448
2010: Joey Votto, Cincinnati Reds, .424
2009: Joe Mauer, Minnesota Twins, .439

A player's **slugging percentage** (**SLG**) is another variation on his batting average. Instead of the percentage of a player's hits to his at bats, the slugging percentage is the percentage of his total bases (**TB**) (one base for a single (**S**), two for a double (**D**), three for a triple (**T**), four for a home run), to his at bats. It's a quick way to judge the player's power, his ability to get extra base hits, and is useful when compared to his batting average. If a player is batting .250 with a slugging percentage of .275, it means he's basically a singles hitter with an occasional extra base hit. If, on the other hand, a player is batting .250 with a slugging percentage of .450, it means that when he does get a hit, there's a good chance it will be for extra bases. Needless to say, your home run leaders will usually be somewhere near the top of your slugging percentage leaders as well.

The slugging percentage leaders for the last five years were:

2013: Miguel Cabrera, Detroit Tigers, .636
2012: Miguel Cabrera, Detroit Tigers, .606
2011: Jose Bautista, Toronto Blue Jays, .608
2010: Josh Hamilton, Texas Rangers, .633
2009: Albert Pujols, St. Louis Cardinals, .658

Again, 502 plate appearances are needed to qualify, but statistical at bats are used to calculate slugging percentage.

Other Batting Stats

Left on base (**LOB**) means the amount of runners a batter leaves on base at the end of an inning by making the third out of an inning. If a batter comes up with runners on first and second with two men out, and then makes the third and final out without driving them in, he is charged with leaving two runners on base. On the other hand, if a batter comes up with runners on first and second with nobody out, and then makes the first out without driving any of them in, he is not charged with leaving runners on base because the inning is not over and the next batter has a shot at driving them in.

Strikeouts (generally **SO** but alternatively **K** for a swinging strikeout and a backwards "K" for a strikeout looking) and walks are self-explanatory. Just a word of caution: strikeouts are one of those statistics that can be deceiving. On its face, a strikeout appears to be the least productive result that a batter can obtain. You don't get on base, you don't move runners up, and therefore you don't appear to contribute at all. But that might not be entirely true. To strike a batter out, the pitcher has to throw at least three pitches, after all, and he usually throws more than that, as a strikeout on three pitches is fairly rare. Often there will be a few balls and foul balls in the mix. Some strikeouts can be real battles between the pitchers and hitters, in which the pitcher will have to throw nine or ten pitches before getting the out. Forcing a pitcher to throw this many pitches is called **working the count** or **going deep in the count**. In these days of strict pitch counts, where most starting pitchers are limited to, say, a hundred pitches or so, a few long at bats like that can tire out the pitcher and force the manager to go to the bullpen quicker than he might have planned to.

A batter gets credit for a run scored (**R**) when he, you guessed it, steps on home plate and scores a run. Thus, when a batter hits a home run, he not only gets credit for a hit, a home run and at least one RBI, but he also gets credit for a run scored.

Stolen bases (**SB**) are important because, as discussed, they can not only move a player from first into scoring position, but effective base stealers can chew up a lot of a pitcher's time and energy and derail a pitcher's concentration as he throws pickoff after pickoff to try to keep his lead to a minimum. The top base stealers for the past five years were:

2013: Jacoby Ellsbury, Boston Red Sox, 52
2012: Mike Trout, Los Angeles Angels, 49
2011: Michael Bourn, Atlanta Braves, 61
2010: Juan Pierre, Chicago White Sox, 68
2009: Jacoby Ellsbury, Boston Red Sox, 70

Another stolen base stat is Caught Stealing (**CS**), when a baserunner is thrown out while attempting to steal.

Occasionally, in regards to stolen bases, you will hear of something called **Defensive Indifference**. That occurs when the defense is indifferent to a runner stealing a base and makes no effort to stop him. For example, suppose it's the bottom of the ninth, there are two outs and you're winning 10–2 and your opponent has a runner on first. He's taking a lead, it looks like he's going to steal second, but your pitcher, rather than throw over in a pickoff attempt, ignores him and concentrates on his next pitch to the batter as he tries to get the out, end the inning and win the game. Suppose the runner, emboldened, takes an even bigger lead, then there he goes! But your catcher, rather than risk an errant throw or an error by the fielder covering second, doesn't even try to throw him out. When this happens, the Official Scorer might rule this a case of defensive indifference, and the runner will not be awarded a stolen base.

Rounding out the list of most common batting statistics is the number of games in which a player has appeared (**G**), either as a starter or a substitute. If nothing else, the more games a player has appeared in is an indication of how valuable he is considered by the team.

Some rare, high-value players straddle both the power and speed columns of baseball statistics, and these players are often said to be members of the imaginary "**20–20 club**" or the "**30–30 club**," meaning they have hit 20 home runs and stolen 20 bases in a season, or hit 30 home runs and stolen 30 bases in a season. Only four players in the history of the game are members of the "**40–40 club**": Jose Canseco of the Oakland Athletics in 1988 (42 homers, 40 stolen bases), Barry Bonds of the San Francisco Giants in 1996 (42/40), Alex Rodriguez, then with the Mariners, in 1998 (42/46), and Alfonso Soriano, then with the Nationals, in 2006 (46/41).

The ultimate in all-around offensive productivity is for a player to win the **Triple Crown**, which means that at the end of the season, he leads his league in batting average, home runs and RBIs. In 2012, Miguel Cabrera of the Tigers became the first player in forty-five years to win the Triple Crown when he led the American League with 44 homers, 139 RBIs, and a .330 batting average. Including Cabrera, only 14 players have won a triple crown since 1900.

PITCHING STATISTICS

Earned Run Average

One of the most important statistics for pitchers is their **Earned Run Average** (**ERA**), which figures the average number of earned runs (**ER**) a pitcher gives up in a nine-inning game. To some extent, it's intuitive. Leaving aside for a moment just what an earned run is, as opposed to any old run, if a pitcher pitches three nine-inning games and gives up twelve earned runs total, the average number of earned runs he gave up over the three games—his earned run average for those three games—is four per game.

You arrive at a pitcher's ERA by taking the number of earned runs he's given up, multiplying it by nine, and dividing the total by innings pitched. For example, if a pitcher has given up 14 runs over the course of 63 innings, you multiply 14 by 9 (126) and divide that number by his 63 innings pitched. The pitcher's ERA is 2.00. OK, that was an easy one.

Let's suppose he's given up 14 runs over the course of 23 and 2/3 innings, because he was once pulled during an inning for a relief pitcher. You multiply 14 by 9 (126) and divide 126 by the number of innings pitched, with partial innings being recorded as a fraction of either .33 for one-third of an inning or .66 for two-thirds of an inning. Thus, in this case, you would divide 126 by 23.66. His ERA is 5.32. (ERAs are recorded to the second decimal).

Like batting averages, ERAs are only spoken of over a long period of time. You might hear an announcer say something like "This pitcher's ERA so far this year against righty batters is 4.50, while against lefties, it's 5.25." Or, he might note, "This pitcher is a notoriously slow starter. Over the course of his career, his lifetime ERA for the months of April and May is 5.25, while his lifetime ERA after June 1 is 3.25."

If a pitcher, in a game, holds the other team to three earned runs or less, you would have to say that he has kept his team in the game and put them in a position to win. Likewise, over the course of an entire season, an ERA of the mid–3s and below is considered solid. The ERA leaders in MLB over the past five years were:

2013: Clayton Kershaw, Los Angeles Dodgers, 1.83
2012: Clayton Kershaw, Los Angeles Dodgers, 2.53
2011: Clayton Kershaw, Los Angeles Dodgers, 2.28
2010: Felix ("King Felix") Hernandez, Seattle Mariners, 2.27
2009: Zack Greinke, Kansas City Royals, 2.16

For a pitcher to qualify for the ERA crown, he has to have pitched 162 innings in the season.

Let's back up a bit. We've been using the term "earned run" in this section, and it's time now to explain exactly what that means. A run, as you know, is a point scored by a team. An "earned run" is a term of art used solely for calculating a pitcher's ERA. The idea behind the term "earned run" is that some runs are the pitcher's fault, and some aren't, and it wouldn't be fair to judge a pitcher by using runs that aren't his fault.

The *Official Baseball Rules* hold that whenever an error is committed in an inning and a run or runs are subsequently scored in that inning, the Official Scorer, to determine how many of those runs were earned, will recreate the inning without the error. If a run would not have scored but for the error, it will be unearned. The example given is that after the first two batters in an inning ground out, the third batter reaches first base on an error, and then the fourth batter hits a home run. If you reconstruct the inning without the error, that third batter would have been the third out, and the fourth batter wouldn't have been able to hit his two-run homer. Thus, neither of those runs would be earned and neither would be charged to the pitcher's ERA.

Please remember that, like errors, unearned runs are statistical animals that only exist in the statistical world. On the field, unearned runs count the same as earned runs do; they just don't count toward the ERA statistics of the pitcher.

A pitcher is charged with an earned run if the runner gets on base while he is pitching, even if the runner eventually comes around and scores after that pitcher has been removed from the game. For example, your starting pitcher walks a batter and then gives up a base hit to the next batter. The manager pulls the starting pitcher and calls in a relief pitcher. The relief pitcher promptly gives up a double to the next batter and both those runners come around to score. Even though the starting pitcher didn't give up the RBI double, both those runners were his responsibility, he put them on base, so those two runs are charged to him and to his ERA, not the relief pitcher's. If that third batter hit a three-run homer instead of a double, the first two runs would still be charged to the starting pitcher, and the third run, the home run run, so to speak, would be charged to the relief pitcher, who actually gave it up.

Finally, earned runs are an important statistic for pitchers, to be sure, but they also can reflect the performance of a team's fielders in a particular game. You'll sometimes hear exasperated announcers, dismayed by an especially sloppy fielding day by their team, say something like "The Braves are already down 7–0 in the fourth inning, and only three of those runs are earned!" What that means is that four runs have scored because of errors. Not a good day for Braves fielders.

Wins and Losses

The next important pitcher statistic is **wins** and **losses** (**W** and **L**). Every game that is played has a pitcher who gets credit for the win, and a pitcher who gets charged with the loss. With the widespread use of relief pitchers, nowadays, each team might send four or five pitchers to the mound in the course of a game, but, again, there will only be one official winner and one official loser, and these two pitchers will sometimes be referred to as the **pitchers of record**. (A starting pitcher who gets credit for neither a win nor the loss is said to have had a **no decision** in that game.)

You will always hear of a pitcher spoken of in terms of his wins and losses, with wins given first and losses second. Every morning in the paper you'll have a list of that day's starting pitchers with their won-loss record listed right after their names, possibly with their ERA as well, and on the radio the morning before a game, you'll here something like "And tonight at Yankee Stadium, C.C. Sabathia, 12 and 6, goes against the Indians' Justin Masterson, 10 and 4."

A pitcher's won-loss record, though highly regarded, may not be the best barometer of his pitching ability. There are too many intangibles involved in a game that are completely out of the pitcher's control and that affect whether he will be credited with a win or charged with a loss. For one thing, pitchers on better teams will have better won-loss records because they have a strong hitting team behind them so that, if they give up four or five runs in a game, they'll still have a good chance of winning because their team may well score six or seven. On the other hand, pitchers on the lower ranked teams will not enjoy this kind of **run support** and so will have less impressive won-loss records in the end, even if their ERA is superb. After all, if a pitcher pitches a complete game and loses 3–2, did he pitch well? He sure did. Will he have a good ERA? Certainly. But he'll also have a loss.

Other observers, however, disagree and argue that wins are all that count. Low ERAs, after all, don't take a team to the playoffs. Wins do. "A pitcher's job is to bring home the bacon," Joe Morgan wrote, "not to hold down his ERA."

Winning 20 games in a year is a badge of honor for pitchers and is often a gateway to a lucrative, long-term contract. The shortcomings of the win-loss statistic notwithstanding, **20-game winners** are in the elite of their position. On September 27, 2012, after his pitcher R.A. Dickey became only the sixth pitcher in Mets history to win 20 games, coach Terry Collins said, "If there's a greatness in pitching, it's winning 20." In the last eight seasons, from the 2006 through 2013, only sixteen pitchers have won 20 games or more. Winning 30 games in a year is an incredible accomplishment, but one so rare that it has only happened twice in the last 80 years. The last 30-game winner was Denny McLain of the Tigers in 1968, and before him it was Dizzy Dean of the Cardinals in 1934.

Losing a game is simple, so we'll start with that statistic: the pitcher who surrenders what proves to be the opposing team's winning run will get charged with the loss. For example, if the starting pitcher gives up a run in the first inning, and his team goes on to lose 1–0, then that starting pitcher will take the loss. It doesn't matter that the starting pitcher was replaced eventually by a reliever, who in turn was replaced eventually by another reliever, and then another. The starting pitcher gave up the single run that proved to be the opposing team's winning run, so he takes the loss, no one else.

The rules regarding winning a game, however, are a tad more complicated, and, if I don't mind saying so, a tad bit odd. If you think the rainout rules were intricate, you're going to love these.

Before we begin, when crediting a win or a loss, the amount of runs scored by a pitcher's own team will naturally be as instrumental as the amount of runs he gives up. If a pitcher gives up three runs but, while he is pitching, his own team scores four, he can obviously wind up with the win. The key is that runs scored "while he is pitching" may include those runs scored by his team immediately after he leaves the game. To determine whether a pitcher will be credited with runs scored by his team "while he is pitching," keep these two rules in mind:

- First, when a starting pitcher's final inning is a *complete inning*, any runs scored by his team in their subsequent half inning are credited to that starting pitcher. For example, if the home team starting pitcher pitches seven complete innings and then gets taken out after pitching the top of the seventh, the runs scored by his team in the bottom of the seventh are credited to him for the purpose of determining whether he will win or lose the game.
- Second, when a starting pitcher's final inning is *not a complete inning*, and he gets replaced during his final inning by a relief pitcher who then finishes the inning, any runs scored by his team in their subsequent half inning are credited to that relief pitcher, or, if there was more than one relief pitcher, to the relief pitcher who eventually finished the inning.

With all that in mind, here are the rules regarding which pitcher will get credited with a win:

1. The starting pitcher will only get credit for the win if he pitches at least five full innings and if his team takes the lead while he is pitching and holds the lead for the rest of the game.
2. If the starting pitcher does not pitch at least five full innings, then, regardless of whether his team scored what proved to be the winning run while he was pitching or afterwards, the win will be awarded to one of the subsequent relief pitchers,
3. ... and if only one relief pitcher pitches the rest of the game, that relief pitcher will get credit for the win,
4. ... and if, more than one relief pitcher pitches the rest of the game, the Official Scorer will determine which of those relief pitches will be awarded the win based on which

of them was "most effective." However, only a relief pitcher who was pitching when the winning run was scored or subsequent to the winning run being scored, can be awarded the win.

5. Relief pitchers can get credit for a win regardless of how many innings, or fractions of an inning, they pitch. Unlike starting pitchers, there is no minimum innings requirement for a relief pitcher to be credited with a win.

As far as telling you what "most effective" means, I'm not even going to try, because the rule is just way too complicated and, more importantly, you just don't need to know it. Just be aware that if the starting pitcher does not complete five innings, and he is followed by more than one relief pitcher, the Official Scorer may have the last word as to whether the relief pitcher who was pitching when the winning run was scored or a subsequent relief pitcher will get credit for the win.

The rule that holds that a pitcher must pitch five complete innings to get credit for a win will actually come up fairly often, so it is a good rule to know. And the way it will come up, many times, is that a starting pitcher will not be happy if his manager wants to pull him for a relief pitcher before five innings are up and with that starting pitcher ahead in the game. Starting pitchers are judged by wins; their salaries are often determined at least in part by their wins. If they have the lead, even if they are in the process of losing it, they'll want to pitch five full innings. That's all there is to it. The MLB leaders in wins for the last five years are:

2013: Max Scherzer, Detroit Tigers, 21
2012: Gio Gonzalez, Washington Nationals, 21
2011: Justin Verlander, Detroit Tigers, 24
2010: Roy Halladay, Philadelphia Phillies & C.C. Sabathia, New York Yankees, 21
2009: Four pitchers tied with 19

Other important pitching statistics are, of course, walks, strikeouts, innings pitched (**IP**), complete games (**CG**) and **shutouts** (**SHO**) which is a complete game in which the pitcher does not give up a run, earned or otherwise.

And, finally, two other terms you should be familiar with in regards to pitching:

First, when a pitcher goes through an entire complete game without giving up a single, double, triple or home run, it is said he pitched a **no-hitter**. There are usually only one or two a year, and they are a big deal. (Games where pitchers give up very few hits in a complete game are also big deals, and can be referred to, as appropriate, as a **one-hitter**, **two-hitter** or **three-hitter**.)

There have been many memorable no-hitters over the years, but one worthy of special mention is the no-hitter thrown by New York Yankees lefty Jim Abbott in 1993. What made it so special is that Abbott was born without a right hand. As he pitched with his left hand, he would cradle his glove in his right arm then, immediately after he pitched, he would slip it onto his left hand. When he fielded the ball, he would catch it in his glove, slip the glove, with the ball, completely off his hand and cradle it between his body and his right arm, remove the ball with his left hand and throw it to the base. To say he did this smoothly and effortlessly is an understatement.

Abbott played no less than ten years in the Majors. He played most of them in the American League, where the Designated Hitter rule made it unnecessary for him to bat. But in his final year he played for the Brewers in the National League, had 20 at bats and, believe it or not, had two base hits and three RBIs.

Second, when a pitcher goes through an entire complete game and gets out every batter he faces, and thus not only gives up no hits, but also no walks, no hit batsmen, and no one reaches base on an error—in other words, when literally no one reaches base so that, in a nine-inning game, he faces the minimum of 27 batters and they all make outs—it is said he pitched a **perfect game**. No-hitters are a big deal, but perfect games are very rare (there have been only twenty three as of this writing) and an even bigger deal. President Barack Obama, a White Sox fan, actually called White Sox pitcher Mark Buehrle to congratulate him after he pitched a perfect game against the Rays in 2009.

As a spinoff, if a pitcher puts together, say, three or four innings in which every batter makes an out, it might be said that the pitcher was **perfect** for those innings, as in "Clayton Kershaw of the Dodgers was perfect for the first three innings before walking Seattle's Kyle Seager to lead off the fourth."

As a final note on no-hitters, be advised that if you are attending a game that enters the late innings and your home team pitcher still hasn't given up a hit, you can think "no-hitter" all you want, but don't say those two words out loud. One of baseball's strangest traditions is that a pitcher who is throwing a no-hitter just doesn't talk about it. His catcher, his teammates and his coach won't talk about it either. In fact, as the game and his no-hitter progresses, you may find that between innings the pitcher is increasingly isolated by his teammates, often left sitting by himself, all alone, at the edge of the bench.

Of course, there are those mavericks who insist on tempting the fates. The irrepressible Warren Spahn, after seven innings of no-hit ball in a 1960 game against the Phillies, entered the dugout and loudly announced to the bench, "All right, just nobody say I've got a no-hitter going!" His teammates were shocked. Hard to believe, but he got the no-hitter anyway. And Dock Ellis (who else?) said he never *stopped* talking about it during his 1970 no-hitter against the Padres. His loquaciousness, however, may not have been entirely due to enthusiasm over his unfolding accomplishment. Years later, he told a biographer he was high on LSD and amphetamines the entire game.

By the way, both a no-hitter and a perfect game are only awarded for a complete game, even if the game goes into extra innings. If, for example, a pitcher has a no-hitter going through nine, but gives up a hit in the tenth, then that is not considered a no-hitter.

Saves

A **Save** ("**SV**") is a statistic for relief pitchers. The basic premise is that if a relief pitcher comes into the game with his team leading, and if that relief pitcher preserves that lead and ends the game with that lead intact, he is awarded with a save for having preserved, or saved, the win.

Delving into the specifics, only one save will be awarded per game, and only then if the following criteria are met:

1. The pitcher cannot be the winning pitcher in the game,
2. he must be the final pitcher in the game and
3. he must pitch at least the last three innings of the game to be credited with a save, unless either

4. his team is winning by three runs or less when he enters the game, in which case he need only pitch the last inning of the game to be credited with a save, or

5. the potential tying run is either on base, at bat, or on deck when he enters the game, in which case he need only pitch the last out of the last inning to be credited with a save.

Just one quick example: Your starter is leading 2–1 going into the top of the ninth inning. After getting the first batter out, he suddenly gets tired, loses his edge, walks two batters, gives up an infield hit and suddenly the bases are loaded with only one out. The manager pulls him and, because it's the ninth inning and the game is on the line, he puts in his closer. The closer manages to get the next two outs without a run scoring, thus maintaining the lead and the win. In this situation, the starting pitcher gets credit for the win (because he pitched more than five innings and left with the lead which was not subsequently relinquished), and the closer will get credit for a save, because he was not the winning pitcher in the game, he was the final pitcher in the game and when he entered the game the potential tying run was on base.

A **Blown Save**. A blown save is charged to a relief pitcher who comes in the game in a save situation, but loses the lead he was sent in to preserve. A relief pitcher cannot get credit with a save and a win—it's either one or the other—but, ironically, a relief pitcher *can* get charged with both a blown save and a loss if it's appropriate. Life is unfair, even, sometimes, in baseball.

FIELDING STATISTICS

There are relatively few fielding statistics. We've already discussed errors (**E**), and that just leaves two others: Putouts (**PO**) and assists (**A**).

A fielder registers a **putout** when he actually makes the out. An outfielder who catches the fly ball on the fly gets credit for a putout. An infielder who, with the ball in his possession, either steps on the base to get the force out or tags the runner to get a tag out, gets credit for a putout.

A fielder registers an **assist** when his actions "contribute" to a runner being put out. The typical assist involves a fielder throwing the ball to another fielder, enabling that second fielder to make the putout. For example, a shortstop who fields a ground ball then throws it to the first baseman for the force out, gets credit for an assist. More than one assist can be given out on a play. When Endy Chavez threw to the cutoff man, Jose Reyes, who then threw on to the first baseman to nail Jim Edmonds, both Endy and Reyes were given assists on the play.

Fielding percentage, is, purportedly, the measure of a fielder's proficiency. It is the percentage of a fielder's putouts and assists over his putouts, assists and errors (the three taken together are often referred to as **chances**). Thus, if a player has 100 chances and ten of those chances are errors, he will have a fielding percentage of .900. (Fielding percentages of regular players tend to be up around the high .900s.)

Fielding percentages are flawed for a number of reasons. If an outfielder fields a sharply hit single and holds the batter at second by hustling over to the hit ball, catching it on a bounce or two and returning it quickly to the infield before the runner can advance to second, that does not figure into his fielding percentage, since it was neither an assist or a putout. Likewise, if that outfielder makes a catch deep in the outfield, he will get credit for a putout, but if he then makes a good strong throw to the cutoff man, preventing runners on base from tagging up and advancing, that does not figure into his fielding percentage since, again, it was neither an assist or a putout.

Furthermore, errors, as we have discussed, are judgment calls on the part of the Official Scorer. A quick-footed shortstop who gets to a ball quicker than most people but somehow, despite his heroic efforts, doesn't make the catch, can possibly be charged with an error, while a slow-footed shortstop who comes nowhere near the ball might not be.

Honestly, the only fielding statistic I ever found remotely interesting is outfielder assists. For an outfielder to get a lot of assists, means he probably throws out a lot of baserunners, and that means that that outfielder has cannon for an arm. An outfielder throwing out a runner is one of the most exciting plays in baseball, especially when that runner is thrown out at home plate.

The problem is that the glory of outfielders who get a lot of assists is usually short-lived, because as soon as runners pick up on the fact that an outfielder has a cannon for an arm, they just stop running on him. Instead of trying to take an extra base on hits to that particular outfielder, or instead of trying to tag up and advance on fly balls hit to that outfielder, they just play it safe, and as a result, the amount of assists that particular outfielder gets, quickly declines. And that deterrent effect is another intangible that is not picked up in any fielding statistic.

The Quest for Better Statistics

Over the years, an analysis of a player's performance has centered on the basic statistics discussed above. Batters are judged mainly on their batting averages, home runs and RBIs; pitchers are judged mainly on their won-loss records and their ERAs; fielders are judged on their fielding percentages. The shortcomings of at least some of these statistics are well known and have been well known for probably as long as they've been in existence.

The search for either new statistics or a better way of interpreting old statistics has been going on for many years. In 1951, innovative statistical analysis played an important part the previously discussed three-game playoff series between the Dodgers and Giants. In his spare time, a statistician at Standard Oil named Jack Carter compiled voluminous statistics on his favorite team, the Giants, and reworked known statistics into a brand new statistic called Equivalent Batting Average, which, unlike the traditional batting average, gave more weight to a hit which advanced a runner than to a hit with no one on base. Carter sent off samples of his findings to the Giants' front office, who promptly hired him as the team statistician. Manager Leo Durocher recognized the value of Carter's new approach and teamed with Carter to his advantage.

The Brooklyn Dodgers, meanwhile, employed their own analyst, named Allan Roth, who, like Carter, caught the front office's eye when he wrote them a letter about his statistical analysis of *his* favorite team, the Dodgers. Unlike Carter, Roth found no favor with Dodgers manager, Charlie Dressen. In the fateful third playoff game against the Giants, Roth, touting the statistics he had compiled from their previous matchups, urged Dressen to intentionally walk Bobby Thomson and have Ralph Branca pitch instead to the next batter, Willie Mays. Dressen ignored Roth's advice, and the rest is history.

Beginning in the early 1970s, a renaissance of new baseball statistical analysis blossomed in America. Much like that other Renaissance, the one with the painters and all that stuff, the renaissance of new baseball statistical analysis was borne along by several very bright people working independently of each other, at least initially, toward a common goal: to address the shortcomings of traditional baseball statistics in accurately reflecting player performances. And just as there were some specific facilitators for that other Renaissance—the invention of the printing press, for one—there was also a specific facilitator for this one: the invention of and subsequent dramatic technological advances in the desktop computer.

Here are some of the landmark events of the baseball statistics renaissance:

- In August of 1971, a sports writer named L. Robert Davids invited some forty hand-picked people whom he knew to be interested in baseball history and statistical research (he called them "statistorians") to a meeting in Cooperstown, New York, home of the Baseball Hall of Fame. Sixteen people accepted his invitation, and they established an organization called the Society of American Baseball Research (**SABR**).

Among SABR's initial objectives was the establishment of "an accurate historical account of baseball through the years." One vehicle to accomplish this goal was the semi-annual *Baseball Research Journal*, whose first volume, in 1972, contained an article called "Clarifying an Early Home Run Record" by John. C. Tattersall. The article is typical of the journal's approach in that instead of taking a given player's traditional statistical measurements at face value, it looked behind those statistics for previously ignored intangibles and variables that, once revealed, cast those traditional statistics in a brand new, and, in this case, significantly less flattering, light.

Tattersall's article focused on the then-record 27 homers hit by a player named Ed Williamson for the Chicago White Stockings in 1884, a record not broken until Babe Ruth hit 29 in 1919. The article revealed that much of Williamson's home run prowess could be credited to the "strangely shaped park with strangely regulated ground rules" that Williamson's team played in: Lake Park in Chicago. Although Lake Park is long gone and its measurements are no longer available, Tattersall was able to ascertain that not only was the right field fence probably no further than 230 feet from home plate, but it was so short that for years a special rule held that a ball hit over that fence was scored only as a double, not as a home run. The rule was abandoned before the 1884 season, and, sure enough, Williamson then went on to blast McHomer after McHomer over that Little League-ish right field fence.

In the magazine's second edition, in an article called "On Base Average for Players," mathematician Pete Palmer argued that one of a batter's main objectives is to simply not make an out. With that in mind, he championed a statistic called On Base Average (now called On Base Percentage) which combined hits, walks and hit by pitches into a measurement of how good a batter was at simply getting on base (which is the same as not making an out). On Base Percentage is one of the most influential and important statistics to come out of the baseball statistics renaissance.

SABR, by the way, now has 6,000 members (myself included) and dozens of chapters across the country.

- At about the same time that SABR first met in Cooperstown, a young baseball fan named Bill James, having drifted through college and some graduate school with the intention of being a writer someday, found a job as a night watchman in a pork and beans factory in his home town in Kansas. It was there, poring over baseball statistics and game results long into the night, that he found inspiration to self-publish a series of books which critiqued the way statistics are kept in baseball and proposed new statistics in their place.

Bill James' first self-published book, called the *1977 Baseball Abstract*, targeted fielding statistics most of all: "If [the batter] hits a smash down the third base line and the third baseman makes a diving stop and throws the runner out, then we notice and applaud the third baseman. But until the smash is hit, who is watching the third baseman? If he anticipates, if he adjusts for the hitter and moves over just two steps, then the same smash is a routine backhand stop—and nobody applauds." The first edition of *Baseball Abstract* sold 75 copies. James persisted, self-publishing a new *Baseball Abstract* every year and, in the process, developing a growing and very loyal following of like-minded baseball statistical nerds. In his books, James attempted to reframe the foundation of baseball statistics by asking a simple question: what is the main job of batters in baseball? To hit for a high batting average? To hit a lot of doubles, or triples, or even home runs? No. Baseball games are won when a team scores more runs than their opponent. The real job of a batter, therefore, was to create runs. James produced and championed several new statistics that measured a player's ability to do just that, including **Runs Created**, a complex formula which purports to show how many runs a player "created" or how many runs resulted from his actions, in a broader sense than mere RBIs or runs scored, and **Win Shares**, an even more complex formula which took Runs Created a step further by using it to identify how many times a player's actions contributed to his team's winning a game.
In the 1980 edition of his *Baseball Abstract*, James in effect joined forces with SABR and coined the phrase **Sabermetrics** to describe "the search for objective knowledge about baseball." that both he, the members of SABR, and an increasing number of other very bright baseball fans were engaged in. In 1988, James published the last of the annual *Baseball Abstracts*, but continued writing on the subject and in 2002 he was hired by the Red Sox to be their senior advisor on baseball operations, helping to shape the team that was to end the Curse in 2004.

- In 1980, some of those very bright fans, including Dan Okrent, writer for *Sports Illustrated*, began to meet regularly for dinner, exchanging ideas and debating baseball statistics. As an aside, they created and played a game in which they each drafted an imaginary team of MLB ballplayers and then, monitoring their performances every day in newspaper accounts of the previous night's games, awarded themselves points based on their players' performances in those games. The person with the most points at the end of the season, won. The game, called Rotisserie Baseball (named after the restaurant where they met) is now known as **fantasy baseball**, and along with its offspring, fantasy football, fantasy hockey, fantasy soccer, to name a few, is played by millions of fans across the globe. A 1982 *Sports Illustrated* article by Okrent on Bill James and sabermetrics introduced James to a wider audience and helped turn James' books into best sellers.

- In 1984, two other very bright fans, Jim Thorne and the aforementioned Pete Palmer, published a book called *The Hidden Game of Baseball*, an astounding book that continued to plumb the depths of the inadequacies of traditional baseball statistics. Among the statistics that the authors went on the attack against were:
  - the batting average, because it gives equal weight to a single as to a home run and to all hits regardless of the value or timeliness;
  - RBIs, because they make no distinction between a game-winning, walk-off RBI and an RBI that drives in the fourteenth run in a 14–1 game, and also because they give no credit to an earlier batter who may have moved a runner into scoring position and so made the subsequent RBI possible;
  - ERA, because, as discussed, once an error that would have been the third out occurs, everything after that is considered an unearned run, and a pitcher could give up five home runs after the third-out-error, and not one of them would be charged against him; and
  - slugging percentage, because a player who hits a home run in four at bats and a player who hits four singles in four at bats would have the same slugging percentage of 1.000, but clearly the player who hit four singles is more valuable to the team "in part because the run potential of four singles is greater, in part because the man who hit the four singles did not also make three outs."

The authors proposed their own alternative baseball statistic, called **Linear Weights**, an intricate formula different in the details from Bill James' Runs Created and Wins Shared, but similar in the goal of devising a statistic that would best reflect a ballplayer's value and productivity.

- In 2004, author Michael Lewis published *Moneyball*, an insider's view of how sabermetricians, working with the management of the Oakland A's in 2001 and 2002, used their unconventional new statistics and their new ways of measuring talent to help assemble a low-budget, no-name team that achieved stunning success for many years against teams flush with big stars and big money. *Moneyball* became a smash-hit bestseller, and in 2011 was turned into a movie starring Brad Pitt.

The success of *Moneyball*, however, had an unintended consequence. The cat—sabermetrics—was now out of the bag. Any team still stuck in the old ways of measuring talent quickly discarded them, jumped on the new sabermetrics train and soon the bargain basement of undervalued baseball talent was frequented not just by two or three pioneering team owners, but by *all* the team owners. The result? The teams flush with money outbid the other teams for the players valued under the new system just as they had outbid them for players valued under the old system. To cite just one example, outfielder Nick Swisher, highly prized by the early Oakland A's sabermetricians, was eventually scooped up by the Yankees and helped them win the World Championship in 2009.

The Lineup Revisited

Earlier, we spoke of the lineup card that the manager gave to the umpire at the beginning of the game. Now that you are familiar with basic baseball statistics and strategies, let's go back with those statistics in mind and flesh out the factors behind how a manager chooses which players to put in which spot in the lineup.

First of all, you want your leadoff batter to immediately get on base and start things happening. How he gets on base is not important. The leadoff hitter will therefore generally have one of the highest, if not the highest, On Base Percentage on the team. Leadoff batters also tend to have a high amount of stolen bases so that, once they are on base, they can put themselves into scoring position.

The second batter ideally has good bat control to avoid hitting double play ground balls should the leadoff runner get on base. He should also have a high batting average to either move the leadoff runner around the bases or drive him home if he is in scoring position.

Because the first two batters are the guys who hopefully start things on the right foot, they are sometimes called the **table setters**.

The third batter ideally has a high batting average, power, and a low strikeout percentage. If we have the leadoff runner on, and the second batter has either gotten a hit also and is on base himself or has moved the leadoff runner into scoring position, the third batter should be an RBI threat.

The cleanup hitter traditionally has the most power on the team, probably reflected in a high slugging percentage and a lot of home runs. The cleanup hitter, if everything works out, can come up with one or two men on base, or maybe even the bases loaded, and he should be a threat to get an extra base hit and drive in at least some of them.

The fifth batter ideally would also be a power hitter, with a slugging percentage as impressive as the cleanup hitter's. This is especially true in the American League, where, because of the Designated Hitter rule, teams are able to retain and find the room in the lineup for another big bat.

It is important to have the cleanup hitter followed by a fifth batter who is nearly as capable of hitting extra base hits and home runs. Often, when a strong cleanup hitter is followed by a weak fifth batter, the pitcher will either intentionally walk the cleanup hitter and take his chances with the weaker batter, or he will **pitch around** the cleanup hitter, which means he doesn't exactly intentionally walk him, but he **gives him nothing to hit**. He works the corners of the strike zone, and if he misses and walks him, well, that's better than having him slam an extra-base hit. If, however, the cleanup hitter is followed by another strong batter, the pitcher can't pitch around him because putting him on base would just mean that the next batter, also strong, will come up with a runner on and the potential to do double damage. Arranging your lineup so that your cleanup hitter is followed by a very good fifth batter is called **protecting** your cleanup hitter.

A perfect example is the case of Roger Maris and Mickey Mantle, two premier sluggers who played together on the Yankees from 1960 to 1966. In 1961, as discussed, Maris broke Babe Ruth's long time single-season record by clubbing 61 home runs. With power like that, one would think opposing pitchers would have intentionally walked him a fair number of times just to limit the damage he might do. The problem was, however, that Mickey Mantle batted behind him in the lineup, and Mantle was nearly as lethal, hitting 54 home runs that same year. Pitch around Maris to pitch to Mantle? That didn't make sense! As a result, pitchers had no choice but to deal with Maris and not once was he intentionally walked, not even once, the entire year.

In contrast, in 2001, when Barry Bonds hit his single-season record-breaking 73 home runs, he was intentionally walked 35 times. How many more home runs would he have hit that year if he also had the good fortune of having a Mickey Mantle behind him in the lineup? But it gets better. The next three season, Bonds hit "only" 46, 45 and 45 homers, but he was intentionally walked, respectively, 68, 61 and finally no less than 120 times in 2004! That year, Bonds made 617 plate appearances. That means that in 2004 he was intentionally walked nearly every fifth time he came to the plate! Barry Bonds led baseball in intentional walks ten times and was second three times in the 16 years from 1992 and 2007. His career intentional walks total, 688, dwarfs the runner up, Hank Aaron, at 293. One can only shudder to think of what kind of numbers Bonds might have put up if he had been better protected in the lineup.

Because the third, fourth and fifth batters are your best power and RBI guys, because they are the most likely to drive in any runners on base and to create runs with some extra base hits, they are often referred to collectively as **the heart of the lineup**, or **the heart of the order**, as in "The Nationals' Gio Gonzalez will be facing the heart of the Astros' lineup in the bottom of the ninth!"

Generally, there's a drop off in batting ability after the fifth hitter. In the National League, the sixth through eighth hitters are normally your weakest hitters, then, of course, the ninth batter will be your pitcher. In the American League, the sixth batter would have been the fifth batter if he weren't bounced back a spot by the Designated Hitter, so in the American League the sixth batter might have decent statistics, with the drop off coming from the seventh through the ninth batters.

If a manager is able to use nearly the same lineup day in and day out, it's a sure sign that not only does he like the results he's getting and sees no reason to mess with success, but also that he is blessed with an injury-free team. Many managers, of course, are not that fortunate. Dodgers manager Don Mattingly was forced to use 74 different lineups in 78 games when his team was plagued with injuries and slumps to start off the 2013 season. The irrepressible Billy Martin was known to pull names out of a hat to form his lineup when his team slumped. Still other managers like to mix things up once in a while just to keep things fresh. "It's kind of fun at times to try different things and see how it goes," said Twins manager Ron Gardenhire, "but it's so much easier when you can at least set six or seven guys in one spot and kind of play with the other guys and make sure everybody gets at-bats."

The Box Score, the Scorecard and the Scoreboard

Previously I wrote that if you were a fan of Jose Bautista of the Blue Jays and you missed a game, you could find out everything he did in that game in the newspaper the next day. I also wrote that sabermetricians playing fantasy baseball could also look in the newspapers the next day to find out all the statistics they needed on their fantasy team players' performances the previous night. What both the Jose Bautista fan and the sabermetrician would be looking at in the newspaper are called the **box scores**, which are tables published in newspapers that summarize, statistically, what each team did, and what each player on each team did, in their particular games the night before. Typically, newspapers will run an entire page or two of box scores, containing all the box scores from all the games the night before, or at least those games that had ended when the newspaper went to print.

Now that you know the meanings of such abbreviations as AB, R, H, HR, RBI (or BI), TB, IP, R, H, ER, E, and the rest, you will have no problem reading a box score, like this top portion of a box score, taken from the *New York Daily News* on October 2, 2013, for the one-game National League Wild Card elimination game between the Pirates and the Reds that took place the night before.

Box scores are generally divided into five sections. The lineups for both teams and their batting performances, including substitutions, are at the top of the box score. At first glance the partial box score shown here, which gives the Reds' lineup for the Wild Card game, might seem a bit confusing. Seventeen players are listed, many with just a string of zeroes to the right of their names. By way of an explanation, immediately next to each player's name is an abbreviation showing the position they played. All the players with the zeroes next to their names are pitchers. If you take a count, you will see that the Reds used a total of seven pitchers over the course of the game to try to gain every advantage they could as far as pinch hitters and platoon matchups. Most of the seven pitchers pitched an inning or even just part of an inning and were replaced by another pitcher before they came to bat, hence the zeroes next to their names.

If you're looking for reasons that the Reds lost this game, look at the heart of their lineup—their third, fourth and fifth batters. They had only one hit among them, going a combined 1-for-12 and striking out four times. The only player on the Reds who had a decent day offensively was left fielder Ryan Ludwick, who, batting second, went 3-for-4. Sounds good but look again: he neither scored nor drove in any runs.

By the way, once the postseason starts, a new set of statistics are maintained to show playoff performances. In the Reds' box score, therefore, the "Avg." column, the last column on the right, shows each player's batting average for the playoffs only, not for the season. Since this wild card game is the first game of the playoffs, all these averages start fresh as of this game. For the Reds, the playoffs ended with this loss, but the victorious Pirates went on to the next round, with their playoff batting averages being recalculated throughout.

Beneath the lineups you will find an inning-by-inning line score of the game. For this game, the line score looked like this:

```
Cincinnatti    0 0 0 1 0 0 0 1 0—2  6  1
Pittsburgh     0 2 1 2 0 0 1 0 x—6  13 0
```

The numbers to the left of the dashes represent the runs scored by each team in each of the nine innings of the game. The "x" in the bottom of the ninth shows that the Pirates didn't come to bat then because, as previously discussed, when the home team is ahead going into the bottom of the last inning, their at bat is cancelled because the game has essentially already been won.

The three numbers to the right of the dash are runs, hits and errors. The Reds had a total of two runs off six hits and committed one error; the Pirates scored six runs on 13 hits with no errors. It is tradition, at the end of each half inning, for announcers to sum up the team's performance so far in the game with those three numbers. For example, after the Pirates made their third out in the bottom of the second inning, you might have heard the announcer say: "And after two innings here in beautiful PNC Park, it's the Pirates two runs, three hits and no errors, and the Reds no runs, no hits and no errors."

Additional hitting details and pitching performances round out the rest of the box score.

Box scores hearken back to simpler times before television when fans listened to their local team on radios and got their information about other teams from the box scores in the morning papers. In the old days, fans would lay out the paper every morning, pore over the box scores and argue about what they proved, or didn't prove, about their favorite players and favorite teams.

The internet, of course, has changed everything. Newspapers still publish box scores, but, in a way, they don't really need to anymore. Now we can just click on a website or two and find out what's going on, in real time, in every ballgame across the country and view instantly updated box scores while we're at it. And, of course, we don't need to do that either if we have satellite TV and have paid a few extra dollars for the baseball channels, in which case we can use our remotes to switch back and forth between live broadcasts of every game. And, of course, we don't even have to switch back and forth all that much if we just use our DVRs or TiVos to tape one game while we are watching the other.

Something is gained, of course, but something is lost. In the excellent television special *The Ghosts of Flatbush*, about the Brooklyn Dodgers in the 1950s, a Dodger fan looks back fondly and remembers how, in those days before television and air conditioning, people sat out on their stoops socializing and listening to the ballgame on the radio. There were so many people out on their stoops listening to the Dodgers, he said, that you could walk an entire city block and not miss a pitch.

A box score is a statistical summary of a game, but it is not a chronological record of a game. A box score will show that a batter, like Russell Martin, went 3 for 4 with two RBIs, but it won't show when he hit those homers, and whether they gave the Pirates the lead or just padded a lead that they already had.

Pirates 6, Reds 2

Cincinnati	AB	R	H	RBI	BB	SO	Avg.
Choo cf	3	2	1	1	0	1	.333
Ludwick lf	4	0	3	0	0	0	.750
Votto 1b	4	0	0	0	0	2	.000
B.Phillips 2b	4	0	0	0	0	0	.000
Bruce rf	4	0	1	1	0	2	.250
Frazier 3b	4	0	1	0	0	1	.250
Cozart ss	3	0	0	0	1	0	.000
Hanigan c	3	0	0	0	0	0	.000
Ondrusek p	0	0	0	0	0	0	---
LeCure p	0	0	0	0	0	0	---
Cueto p	1	0	0	0	0	0	.000
S.Marshall p	0	0	0	0	0	0	---
Hoover p	0	0	0	0	0	0	---
a-Heisey ph	1	0	0	0	0	0	.000
Simon p	0	0	0	0	0	0	---
M.Parra p	0	0	0	0	0	0	---
Mesoraco c	1	0	0	0	0	0	.000
Totals	32	2	6	2	1	6	—
Pittsburgh	**AB**	**R**	**H**	**RBI**	**BB**	**SO**	**Avg.**
S.Marte lf	5	1	2	0	0	0	.400
N.Walker 2b	5	1	2	1	0	0	.400
McCutchen cf	3	1	2	0	2	0	.667
Morneau 1b	4	0	1	0	1	0	.250
Byrd rf	4	1	1	2	0	0	.250
P.Alvarez 3b	3	0	0	1	0	1	.000
R.Martin c	4	2	3	2	0	0	.750
Barmes ss	4	0	1	0	0	0	.250
Liriano p	2	0	1	0	0	0	.500
b-Snider ph	1	0	0	0	0	1	.000
Watson p	0	0	0	0	0	0	---
Grilli p	0	0	0	0	0	0	---
Totals	35	6	13	6	3	2	—

Cincinnati	000 100 010 —	2	6 1
Pittsburgh	021 200 10x —	6	13 0

a–grounded into a double play for Hoover in the 5th. b–struck out for Liriano in the 7th. **E**—Cozart (1). **LOB**—Cincinnati 5, Pittsburgh 10. **2B**—Ludwick 2 (2), Frazier (1), S.Marte (1), N.Walker (1). **HR**—Choo (1), off Watson;Byrd (1), off Cueto;R.Martin (1), off Cueto;R.Martin (2), off Ondrusek. **RBI**—Choo (1), Bruce (1), N.Walker (1), Byrd 2 (2), P.Alvarez (1), R.Martin 2 (2). **S**—Liriano. **SF**—P.Alvarez. **RLISP**—Cincinnati 4 (Frazier, B.Phillips 2, Hanigan); Pittsburgh 5 (N.Walker, Barmes, P.Alvarez 2, S.Marte). **RISP**—Cincinnati 1 for 10;Pittsburgh 1 for 8. **RMU**—Votto. **GIDP**—Heisey, Morneau. **DP**—Cincinnati 1 (Frazier, Cozart, Votto); Pittsburgh 1 (P.Alvarez, N.Walker, Morneau).

Cincinnati	IP	H	R	ER	BB	SO	NP	ERA
Cueto L, 0-1	3⅓	7	4	3	1	0	60	8.10
S.Marshall	0	1	1	1	2	0	20	-
Hoover	⅔	0	0	0	0	0	4	0.00
Simon	1⅓	2	0	0	0	0	22	0.00
M.Parra	⅔	1	0	0	0	1	9	0.00
Ondrusek	1	1	1	1	0	1	25	9.00
LeCure	1	1	0	0	0	0	9	0.00
Pittsburgh	**IP**	**H**	**R**	**ER**	**BB**	**SO**	**NP**	**ERA**
Liriano W, 1-0	7	4	1	1	1	5	90	1.29
Watson	1	2	1	1	0	0	23	9.00
Grilli	1	0	0	0	0	1	7	0.00

S.Marshall pitched to 3 batters in the 4th. **IRS**—S.Marshall 1-1, Hoover 3-1, M.Parra 1-0. **IBB**—off S.Marshall (McCutchen). **HBP**—by Liriano (Choo). **Umpires**—Home, Joe West;First, Dale Scott;Second, Dan Iassogna;Third, Rob Drake;Right, Lance Barksdale;Left, Tim Timmons. **T**—3:14. **A**—40,487 (38,362).

©*Daily News*, L.P. (New York). Used with permission.

If you go to a game, or even if you listen to or watch a game at home, you can keep your own chronological record of a game by following a tradition that has probably been around for as long as baseball itself. The tradition is called **keeping score**. To keep score you need two things: a scorecard and a sharp pencil.

A **scorecard** is a fill-in-the-blanks form that is split in two, either left-right or top-bottom. On each of the two parts of a scorecard is an identical grid. The left side or top grid is used for the visiting team; the right side or bottom grid is used for the home team. On each grid, inning numbers run across the top, left to right, and on the left-most column there are spaces designated for the team name and, under it, the players names and their positions, which are entered in the order they appear in the day's lineup. As the players in the lineup come to bat, a fan keeps score, or keeps a record of the game, by entering a symbol, denoting the result of his at bat, in the box next to batter's name, under the appropriate inning.

There is no one official or correct set of symbols for recording results. Paul Dickson, in his definitive book *The Joy of Keeping Score*, shows that the methods used to keep score are as idiosyncratic as the scorekeepers themselves. To record a single, a simple "S" has been used, or a single horizontal bar, or, in some cases, a small line from the bottom center of the box to the midpoint of the right side of the box, as if showing the path that the runner took from home to first. There is a corresponding wide variety of ways to show how the runner who hit that single either subsequently advanced around the bases or, perhaps, was thrown out stealing, or forced out in a double play. As many things as might happen in a game, there is a symbol for each, and as many fans keep score, the symbols they decide to use, and the ways in which they tweak those symbols, is completely up to them.

There is, however, one universal set of symbols used in scorekeeping, and that is the identification of fielders by assigned numbers, as follows:

Pitcher—1
Catcher—2
First Baseman—3
Second Baseman—4
Third Baseman—5
Shortstop—6
Left Fielder—7
Center Fielder—8
Right Fielder—9

These numbers are used to track the fielders involved in making an out. One number alone on a scorecard will indicate an unassisted putout; two or more numbers will indicate assists as well as the putout. A fly out to the center fielder, for example, will simply be recorded as an "8" on the score card, while a grounder that is fielded by the shortstop and thrown on to the first baseman to nail the batter, will be recorded as "6–3."

It might behoove you to be aware of this number system even if you don't intend to keep score, because it will occasionally be used by radio and television announcers. During the course of a game, you might hear an announcer describe a double play as a 6-4-3 double play, for example, or a 5-4-3 double play.

In an April 12, 2013, game against the Orioles, the Yankees turned what at least one press account called the first 4-6-5-6-5-3-4 triple play in Major League history. How they would know that, I have no idea, but here's how the triple play went. The Orioles had runners on first and second with no one out. O's batter Adam Jones hit a sharp ground ball to second baseman Robinson Cano (4) who scooped it up and threw it to shortstop Jayson Nix (6) to get the runner coming from first on the force. One out. Nix then threw it on to the third baseman, Kevin Youkilis (5), to get the runner on second going to third, but since the force behind him had been removed, the runner was able to stop on his way to third and try to retreat to second, prompting Youkilis to throw back to the Nix (6) and when the runner changed direction again, heading back to third, Nix threw on back to Youkilis (5) who promptly tagged the runner out. Two outs. Meanwhile, while all the attention was focused elsewhere, the batter who had safely reached first base decided to try to sneak into second. However, Youkilis, after he tagged out the runner at third, spotted him, threw on to first baseman Lyle Overbay (3) who then fired the ball to second baseman Robbie Cano (4) who tagged out the batter as he slid into second. Three outs.

Did you get all that? If you have a to take a second to read that again, go right ahead. We'll wait for you.

Oh, and one more thing. The only other constant in scorekeeping is the use of the letter "K" to denote a strikeout. A forwards "K" means a strike out swinging; a backwards "K" means a strike out looking.

Now that we've discussed the box score for the Pirates-Reds game, let's take a look at the scorecard I kept for that same game and see what it shows us. First of all, I hadn't scored a game in decades, so I had to refresh my memory by quickly rereading Dickson's book, then looking at the instructions in the scorecard binder that I bought from a local sporting goods store, and the instructions that came with a scorecard I bought at a Yankee game. Needless to say, outside of the strikeout "K" and the number system used to identify the fielders, the instructions in the scorecard book and in the Yankee scorecard were completely different. Far from being problematic, however, the lack of clear guidance only adds to what Dickson correctly calls the joy of keeping score. I had forgotten how much fun and how engaging it is.

Between my two sets of scorecard instructions and throwing in what I relearned from Dickson's book and what I vaguely remember from my own dim past, here's what the Reds half of my scorecard looked like:

In the scorecard, we see the Reds half of the game unfold as it was played. We see that Pirates pitcher Liriano was perfect for the first three innings: nine up and nine down. Then, in the fourth, he hit lead off batter Shin-Soo Choo and then, perhaps a bit rattled after that, gave up his first hit to Ryan Ludwick, a single. After the next two batters made outs, Todd Frazier's single scored Choo from second. After that, the Reds bats were pretty quiet for the rest of the game, excepting Choo's homer in the eighth.

I knew the Pirates pitchers threw a great game. Only six hits, only two runs. Not bad against a strong team like the Reds. But I didn't realize just how great a game they threw until I noticed something in my scorecard the morning after the game. A 7, 8 or 9 on the scorecard by itself means the batter flied out to left, center or right field, respectively. With that in mind, how many fly ball outs to the outfield did the Reds register during the game? Take a look. Look again. As hard as it is to believe, the Reds registered only two fly ball outs to the outfield during the entire game. That means that the other 25 outs were either strike outs or ground outs or, perhaps, a pop up out or two to an infielder. Add their six hits, all of which were hit into the outfield, and that means that the Reds hit the ball into the outfield only eight times during the entire game, or less than once an inning. Wow.

Why do I say, "Wow?" Take a look at the infield in any ballpark. Six fielders defend the infield. Now take a look at the outfield. Much bigger, right? And yet, only three fielders patrol the outfield. Where do you think you should hit the ball if you want to generate some hits and runs? The outfield, of course. But the Pirate pitching kept the Reds off balance all night long, preventing the Reds from getting good wood on the ball and limiting them the vast majority of the time to ground balls in the infield.

Pretty cool, right?

Two other noteworthy facts about the scorecard. First, you can see that outside of starting pitcher Johnny Cueto, who grounded out in the third, none of the other Reds pitchers had an at bat. It's the playoffs, after all! Also, four times the Reds grounded out directly to the first baseman, as indicated by a "3" along with my own addition of "GB" as in "ground ball." A "3" by itself only indicates an unassisted putout by the first baseman, but doesn't in itself tell you whether that unassisted putout was a ground ball that he caught and then stepped on first to get the batter, or a pop up that he caught on the fly for the out. Adding "GB" was my own way of noting ground balls.

Keeping score is a way that a fan can stay involved in the game, stay focused on the game, and keep up with the progress of the game. When a fan keeps score, he can immediately refer to his scorecard to see, for example, what a batter did in his previous at bat, who's up next, what pitchers have been used to far, and so on. If you see a fan at a ballgame keeping score, he's a serious fan.

But if you see a fan at a ballgame keeping score, take their picture. He or she is rare breed, and, sadly, a breed that seems to be on the verge of extinction. Nowadays, you can walk around an entire stadium looking over the shoulders of thousands of seated fans and you're lucky if you find four or five keeping score. On your way into the stadium you can buy a program, and the middle two pages will be a scorecard just waiting to be filled in, and if you ask the guy who sells the program, he'll even give you a little pencil to fill in the scorecard with, but nowadays people buy the program as a souvenir, or to look at the pictures, but, it seems, not to use the scorecard.

The reason no one keeps score at ballgames anymore is simple: the scoreboard does it for them. In the old days, scoreboards were simple affairs: Workers hung numbers on hooks in little windows to show the score, inning-by-inning and cumulative, as well as the total number of hits and errors for each team. But that was it. If you wanted any more information than that, for example, how many strikeouts a pitcher had so far in a game, it was up to you to maintain a scorecard so that you could keep track.

Nowadays, giant electronic scoreboards wrap around a good portion of the outfields in most Major League ballparks. They are massive and I can't imagine how much electricity they eat up. They are ever-changing and provide completely current, up-to-the-minute statistics and standings and the scores of games in progress all across the country. They show color instant replays in breathtakingly clear screens that are two stories high. They will tell you who's up, what he's done so far that day, what he's done so far that season, and they will give you a picture of his smiling face to boot.

And they never shut up. In addition to useful statistics, they will provide a constant bombardment of quirky and, in my opinion, completely unnecessary entertainment. It's as

Franklin SCORECARD © 2010 Franklin Sports Inc.

DATE ___ BALLPARK PNC WEATHER fine UMPIRES ___ SCORER Me!

START 8:05 END

	1	2	3	4	5	6	7	8	9	R	H	E
REDS	0	0	0	1	0	0	0	1	0			

#	PLAYERS	POS	1	2	3	4	5	6	7	8	9
1	CHOO	CF	K			HP	1-3			I?	
2	LUDWICK	LF	6-3							I?	
3	VOTTO	1B	3-1			K		K	3GB		
4	PHILLIPS	2B		4-3		4		4-3	3GB		
5	BRUCE	RF		K				3GB		K	
6	FRAZIER	3B		6-3		K			7		
7	COZART	SS			6-3		8-3	6-3	4-3		
8	HANIGAN	C			5-3		9	5-3			
9	CUETO	P			3GB						
10	MASEROCO	PH							4		
11	HELSEY	PH					5-4-3 DP				
12	MARSHALL	P									
13	HOOVER	P									
14	SIMON	P									
15	PARRA	P									
16	ONDRUSEK	P									

#	PITCHERS	W/L	IP	K	BB	H	R	ER	HB	PITCH COUNT
	Cueto	L B,N	0	1	8	3	4	0		
	MARSHALL	-	0	0	1	2	0	1	0	
	HOOVER	-	.2	0	0	0	0	0	0	
	SIMON	-	1.0	0	0	1	0	0	0	

if the lords of baseball, taking into account the short attention spans that made Twitter popular and Shakespeare less so, have decided that baseball fans, if let alone for even a few minutes, will get instantly bored to death and go home. Therefore, the scoreboard will go from useful statistics to animated applause meters that urge the crowd to cheer, to animated train races that prompt fans to choose one of three or four trains and root it on loudly as it travels around a race course and toward a finish line, to animated three-card-monte games where a baseball is put under a baseball hat and you are encouraged to keep track of it as the hats are shuffled around and shout out which hat you think the ball is under once the shuffling stops, to, and this is the most astounding, a "guess the baby" game where a player's baby picture is put up on the scoreboard and you are then given a multiple choice as to which player it is and, again, shouting out your choice on cue.

But enough of that. I promised myself when I started writing this book that, as tempting as it is, especially for middle-aged men talking about baseball, I would avoid romanticizing the past, the world we grew up in, at the expense of the present, the world our replacements are growing up in. Everything changes, even baseball scoreboards, and with every change, something is gained and something is lost. Let's just leave it at that.

One reason the scoreboard is so important in baseball is that among the wealth of information it constantly bombards us with are what are called the **out of town scores**, which are scores of every other game in baseball that is currently underway. In the old days, the out of town game matchups were listed on the scoreboard this way:

41   3 StL   2
38   Cin   0

In this game, the Cardinals are playing at Cincinnati (home team on the bottom, since they bat in the bottom of the inning). The "3" just to the left of the "StL" indicates that the Cardinals are at bat in the top of the third inning (when the Reds come to bat in the bottom of the third, the "3" will drop down next to the "Cin") and the "2" to the right of the "StL," along with the "0" to the right of the "Cin," means the Cardinals are leading 2–0. The "41" and the "38" in the first column are the uniform numbers of the pitchers. (A list of pitchers and their uniform numbers is usually contained in the baseball program.)

The frustrating thing about the old system was that the score would only be changed after each half-inning ended, which meant that you were completely in the dark while the half-inning was being played. The only indication you had that something might be going on, was if a half-inning took an exceptionally long time, which might mean that the team at bat was putting runners on base and, possibly, scoring runs, resulting in, possibly, pitchers being changed, resulting in, possibly, pinch hitters coming to bat in response to those changes and so on. All of that *could* be going on, but you wouldn't know for sure until the half-inning was over and an updated score was posted. If the game you were trying to keep track of on the scoreboard was important to your team, coping with the intervening silence meant could drive you batty. I remember sitting in the stands, looking at Red Sox scores and saying to my friend: "Darn! The Red Sox have been up for the last twenty minutes. This isn't good!"

Nowadays, the suspense is removed. With a few tweaks made possible by modern technology, scoreboards have moved past the primitive score keeping of yore and now contain all the information you need, as it happens. Now, for example, you might see something like this on a scoreboard:

41   StL   2
38   3**   Cin   0   ◊

The two asterisks next to the "3" would mean that not only are the Reds up in the bottom of the third, but there are two outs in the bottom of the third. The diamond next to the Reds replicates the infield. If there was a Reds runner on first, for example, the right-most point of the diamond would be lit up. If there were runners on first and second, the right-most and top point of the diamond would be lit up. No lights on the diamond means bases are empty. You might find the pitcher's number in the left hand column suddenly changes halfway through an inning, indicating a relief pitcher has been brought in. And, of course, the score would change instantly as appropriate.

FOUR
Major League Baseball Overview

OK, you are almost there. You have your tickets in hand, you have your favorite team's cap on your head, and you are ready to head off to the stadium. But hold on just a little bit longer while I introduce you to the world of Major League Baseball. I will do this by walking you through a calendar year in the Majors, beginning with January's Hall of Fame nominations and ending with the team owners' all-important Winter Meetings, which are held every December. First, however, a brief introduction to structure of the Major Leagues.

The Majors and the Minors

Stop right there. Did I say the Major *Leagues*—as in the plural? Yes I most certainly did, and let the lessons begin here. In 1903, when professional baseball was skyrocketing in popularity and independent, unregulated leagues were springing up all over the United States, fourteen baseball leagues sat down and entered into something called the National Agreement, by which the strongest two, the older **National League** (sometimes called the **Senior Circuit**) and the younger, upstart **American League** (sometimes called the **Junior Circuit**), were recognized as the Major Leagues, with all the other leagues being relegated to the status of **Minor Leagues** (the **Minors** for short), which were basically feeder leagues for the Majors.

To this day, the Majors are comprised of the National League and the American League. Both leagues have fifteen teams, with each league subdivided geographically into three divisions of five teams each: the Eastern, Western and Central Divisions. Only New York, Chicago and Los Angeles have teams in both leagues.

The first thing you need to know about the two leagues is that they play exactly the same game, and they play by exactly the same rules with the exception of the DH rule, which, we know, is used in the American League but not the National League.

The second thing you need to know is that teams from one league play teams from the other only on a limited basis. Starting in 1903, coinciding with the signing of the National Agreement, the first place finishers in each league met annually at the end of the season in a playoff series called the **World Series**, to decide the championship of Major League Baseball, but teams played the entire regular season exclusively within their own league. This arrangement lasted until 1997, when **interleague play** began, by which teams from each league now play twenty games a season against teams from the other.

As of this writing, there are 19 Minor Leagues located across the country and, unlike the Majors, most of them are regional, as indicated by their names, such as the Gulf Coast League, the Northwest League, and the South Atlantic League.

Each Major League team is affiliated with its own hierarchy of Minor League teams—sometimes called **Farm teams**—which the Major League team, the parent team, either owns outright or with whom they have entered into a Player Development Contract which gives them certain rights with regards to the players on those teams.

Here's how the Minor League hierarchy works. After signing a brand new player fresh out of college, for example, the Major League team will most probably place him on their lowest tier Minor League team, which will play in what is called a **Single A** or **Class A League** (sometimes subdivided into a **Short Season Class A League** and/or a **Class A Advanced League**). If and when that player has matured and sharpened his skills enough, the parent club will promote him to their team in a **Double A League**, and if and when that player has further

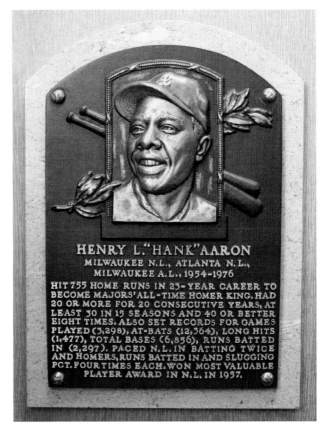

Hank Aaron's Hall of Fame plaque. Aaron started his career in the Negro Leagues. Major League scouts were initially skeptical because the young Aaron batted "cross-handed" – meaning that although he was a righty batter, he batted with his left hand on top of his right. Eventually Aaron abandoned the practice and went on to become one of the greatest players of all time, surpassing Babe Ruth in career home runs in 1974 (National Baseball Hall of Fame Library, Cooperstown, New York).

improved and grown to the point where they are Major League material, the parent club will move him up to their team in a **Triple A League**, which is the highest and final rung of Minor League baseball, the last stop before the Majors.

Minor League teams are located by and large in smaller towns and cities throughout the country and they are intimately tied to the communities they are located in. Their fan bases are extremely loyal, their stadiums are small, their seasons are short, and their tickets and concessions are priced much lower than the Majors. For all these reasons and more, the Minor Leagues are a great deal of fun.

At the start of this book I told how I spent most of 2009 unemployed. I will add now that my family also spent a good part of that summer visiting every Minor League ballpark within 150 miles or so of my home in Queens, New York. It was a great, low budget source of entertainment and each of the seven or eight ballparks we visited had a charm and a personality and a refreshing unpretentiousness all their own. I could give a hundred examples, but just let me say that for many years the Trenton Thunder in New Jersey, the Yankees Double A affiliate, had a loveable old golden retriever named Chase that ran out onto the field during breaks in the action to collect bats and balls that had been left by the players. I mean, can it get any cozier than that?

A Year in the Major Leagues

JANUARY

Every January, designated members of an organization called the **Baseball Writers Association of America**, or **BBWAA**, get together and cast their votes on that year's nominees for induction into the **National Baseball Hall of Fame and Museum**, most often referred to as just the **Hall of Fame**, or **the Hall**.

The Hall of Fame, which opened to the public in 1939, is housed in the beautiful little town of Cooperstown, New York, which was chosen for the site because it was believed that the game of baseball was invented there in 1839 by a Civil War general named Abner Doubleday. The website for the Hall of Fame defines it as an "educational institution dedicated to fostering an appreciation of the historical development of baseball and its impact on our culture by collecting, preserving, exhibiting and interpreting its collections for a global audience as well as honoring those who have made outstanding contributions to our national pastime."

Shoeless Joe Jackson. When he was first drafted into the Majors, Jackson became so homesick on the way to Philadelphia that he snuck off the train and made his way back home. When the team's managers went and retrieved him, he ran back home again after his teammates taunted him because of his illiteracy (Chicago History Museum).

The first half of that definition—"collecting, preserving, exhibiting and interpreting its collections for a global audience"—is fulfilled by the Hall of Fame's role as the definitive museum of all things baseball. However, it is the second half of that definition—"honoring those who have made outstanding contributions to our national pastime"—that the Hall of Fame is truly known for. Those select few who are inducted annually into the Hall by the BBWAA for their outstanding contributions to the game, are honored by having a bronze plaque bearing their likeness and a summary of their achievements installed in the Hall of Fame Gallery.

Of all the thousands of people associated with the game over the decades, as of this writing, only 300 have been inducted into the Hall of Fame. The high honor it is for a ballplayer to be so selected is reflected in the fact that for the rest of his life (and after), his status in the Hall will become a kind of regal title forever attached to his name. Former White Sox first baseman Frank ("The Big Hurt") Thomas for example, as of his induction into the Hall of Fame in July 2014, will now and forever be first and foremost known as "**Hall of Famer** Frank Thomas." Many of the players I have referred to in these pages are Hall of Famers, including Reggie Jackson, Jackie Robinson, Juan Marichal, Warren Spahn, Willie Mays, Joltin' Joe DiMaggio, Yogi Berra, Hammerin' Hank Aaron, Ted Williams, Tom Seaver, Wade Boggs, Nolan Ryan, Bill Mazeroski, Phil Niekro, Johnny Bench, Dan Driessen, Joe Morgan, George Brett, Rod Carew, Ty Cobb, Carlton Fisk, Lou Gehrig, Mickey Mantle, Joe Torre, Tony La Russa and, of course, the Sultan of Swat, the pride of St. Mary's Industrial School for Boys, Babe Ruth.

Normally, only ballplayers who played in the Majors for at least ten seasons, and who have been retired for at least five years before the vote takes place, are eligible for nomination to the Hall. Once nominated by the BBWAA screening committee, a player must receive 75 percent of the vote to be admitted to the Hall, but if he falls short, as long as he receives a minimum of 5 percent of the votes cast, he can be nominated again in succeeding years for up to the 15th year after his retirement. One of the 2010 inductees, Bert Blyleven of the Twins, was elected to the Hall the 14th time his name appeared on the ballot.

The Hall of Fame has not been without its controversies. Per Rule 3E of the BBWA Hall Election Rules, "Any player on baseball's ineligible list shall not be an eligible candidate." The ineligible list, maintained by the baseball commissioner, includes Pete Rose, one of the greatest baseball players of all time and the Major League's career leader in hits, who retired in 1986. Rose has been banned from baseball for life and denied induction into the Hall of Fame because he gambled on his team's games while he was the manager of the Reds. Eight players from the 1919 Chicago White Sox, who were paid off by gamblers to play poorly in the World Series in the notorious "**Black Sox Scandal**," are also on the list, though probably only one of them, outfielder Shoeless Joe Jackson, was good enough to be nominated to the Hall.

Shoeless Joe Jackson has become something of a cult figure in recent years, and there has been a persistent movement among some baseball historians and fans to have his ban from the Hall of Fame lifted. To some extent, the sympathy for him arises from the fact that he was the child of a South Carolina sharecropper, was raised in extreme poverty, and was illiterate his entire life.

His supporters contend that his illiteracy and his naïveté in the face of big city treachery led to his being taken advantage of, first by ruthless gamblers and, later, by overzealous prosecutors. They also point out that Shoeless Joe's fielding during the 1919 World Series was flawless, and his batting average in the Series (.375) was actually much higher than his batting average during the season (.351), casting doubt, they believe, on whether he actually participated in the fix. Still, he took the money ("They promised me $20,000," he testified, "and paid me five") and his brilliant career came to a crashing halt as a result.

The movie *Field of Dreams* (1989), thought by some to be the best baseball movie ever, was about Shoeless Joe and his teammates appearing as ghosts to play one last redemptive ballgame in an Iowa farmer's cornfield. "Getting thrown out of baseball was like having part of me amputated," says Shoeless Joe, played by Ray Liotta, in the movie. "I've heard old men wake up and scratch itchy legs that have been dust for over 50 years. That was me. I'd wake up at night with the smell of the ball park in my nose."

On the way out of Cook County courthouse after being indicted for defrauding the public, the man who Babe Ruth said was the best natural hitter he ever saw, was approached by a fan, a little boy, who grabbed him by the coat sleeve and famously pleaded, "Say it ain't so, Joe!" Shoeless Joe, who got his nickname because he once played in a Minor League game without shoes rather than let his blistered feet keep him on the bench, reportedly looked down at the lad and said, "Yes, kid, I'm afraid it is."

The controversy facing the Hall of Fame these days involves the use by ballplayers of **Performance Enhancing Drugs (PEDs)**, such as anabolic steroids and human growth hormones, in violation of both baseball policy and federal law. Beginning in 2004, ballplayers have been subjected to random urine tests to check for PED use, and those who test positive are penalized with lengthy suspensions from the game. Tragically, many of the best players in baseball over the last 20 years have now either tested positive for PEDs, admitted to using PEDs, or have otherwise been linked to PED use or to PED users and suppliers.

Until recently, widespread PED use was thought to be a thing of the past, confined mostly to the so-called **Steroid Era** of the late 1990s. The 2013 baseball season, however, was rocked when fourteen players were suspended after it was found they had been provided with PEDs by a sketchy Florida "health clinic." Subsequently, beginning with the 2014 season, the suspensions for PED use were increased from 50 to 80 games for the first offense, from 100 to 162 games for the second offense, and a life-time ban remains in effect for the third offense.

In my opinion, the abuse of PEDs in professional baseball has undercut the integrity of the game far more than Pete Rose's gambling and at least as much as the Black Sox scandal. It has gotten to the point where almost every above-average performance by a player is, by default, suspect. Hopefully, the increased penalties will help stop PED abuse from damaging the reputation of the game any more than it already has.

No player has been placed on the ineligible list for PED use. On the other hand, none of the players implicated with PED use—a list which, again, includes some of the most prominent names in the game for the last two decades—has to date received enough votes to be elected to the Hall. Clearly, the BBWA, at least for now, is using its voting powers to penalize PED-abusing ballplayers and take a stand against PED use. Remember, however, that as long as a nominee receives 5 percent of the votes tallied, they can be nominated for the Hall again and again for up to 15 years. The last chapter on how the Hall will treat PED abusers therefore remains to be written.

I'll end this discussion of the Hall of Fame on a more positive note. As discussed, prior to 1947, when Hall of Famer Jackie Robinson broke the color barrier by becoming the first African American ballplayer to play in the Major Leagues, African Americans were excluded from the Majors and played instead in what were called the Negro Leagues. In his induction speech to the Hall in 1966, Ted Williams expressed the hope that some of the great Negro League players of the past would someday be recognized and honored for their contribution to the game by being elected to the Hall of Fame. Since that speech, the Hall of Fame has reached back and inducted 35 players who played either exclusively or predominantly in the Negro Leagues. Included in the Negro League inductees have been such immortals as catcher Josh Gibson, who was reportedly the only player of any color to hit a home run ball clear out of the old Yankee Stadium, outfielder Cool Papa Bell, who was so fast it was said that he could turn off the lights and be in bed before the room got dark, and Satchel

Paige, who was considered by many to be the best pitcher who ever lived and who pitched until he was, well, pretty darn old. Paige's real age always remained a mystery. "Age is a question of mind over matter," he once said "if you don't mind, it doesn't matter."

One other baseball-related event happens in January: the countdown to **Pitchers and Catchers**. When I was a kid, in the *Daily News*, in the dead of winter, from out of nowhere a small box would appear in the corner of the daily sports pages. "30 Days 'til Pitchers and Catchers," it would read. And then the next day: "29 Days 'til Pitchers and Catchers," and so on. Nowadays, on the MLB website, there is an actual real time clock that during the winter months counts down not only the days, but the minutes and seconds until "Pitchers and Catchers."

The term "Pitchers and Catchers" refers to the opening of the baseball training camps that precede the start of a new baseball season. Pitchers and catchers are required to report to their team's training camps, all of which are located in the warm weather states of Arizona or Florida, a few days before the other players. The anticipation surrounding Pitchers and Catchers, therefore, is really anticipation for the start of training for the next baseball season, called **Spring Training**, which, in turn, goes hand and hand with anticipation of the arrival of spring and the end of winter. And that's why it feels good, in the dead of January, to open your newspaper (or your favorite sports website) and see that the countdown to Pitchers and Catchers has begun.

FEBRUARY

Pitchers and catchers will report to their team's training camp in early February, with the rest of the team following from four to seven days later.

Each team's training facility has a small ballpark, usually of a few thousand seats, and during Spring Training the teams will play practice games against each other to get ready for the season and to give coaches a chance to assess players and decide who will make the team. These preseason schedules are sometimes referred to as the **Grapefruit League** (those games played between teams whose training camps are located in Florida) and the **Cactus League** (those games played between teams stationed in Arizona).

MARCH

Spring Training lasts through March. Everyone on the previous year's team will have been invited to Spring Training, as well as any promising Minor Leaguers who the coaches just want to take a look at (or who have Spring Training invitations written into their contracts). There will also be many **non-roster invitees**, such as ballplayers who were let go by their previous team, who are not under contract to any team and who are, basically, looking for a job. Before the season begins, every team's roster must be reduced to twenty-five players, and these are the players who will start the season with the team.

APRIL

The baseball season starts in either the very last days of March or the first few days of April. Each team's first home game of the season is celebrated as **Opening Day**. It is one of the biggest days of the season, a day of hope and optimism and new beginnings; a day that begins, it is said, with every team tied for first place. On Opening Day dignitaries and celebrities inaugurate the festivities across the nation by **throwing out the first pitch**, meaning they actually come onto the field and throw a ceremonial opening day pitch to the home team's catcher. Since April 14, 1910, when President William Taft inaugurated the tradition, many a sitting president has thrown out the first pitch on opening day.

Once it begins on Opening Day, the baseball season is a marathon that will see teams play with a frequency unmatched in any other professional sport in the world. The season lasts about six months and during that time, teams will play every Saturday and Sunday and the vast majority of weekdays as well. Specifically, each team will play 162 games in about 180 days.

Of the 162 games, each team will play eighty-one games in its home stadium as the home team, and 81 games in other teams' stadiums as the visiting team. The season is broken down into **home stands,** periods of up two weeks at a time where a team will play a sequence of games at home, followed by **road trips**, during which a team will travel to other parts of the country and play a sequence of games in other teams' stadiums. Each home stand and road trip is further subdivided into **series** of games called, as applicable, **two-**, **three-**, or **four-game series** during which the same two teams play each other multiple times over consecutive days.

It should be noted that the 162 game schedule is called an **unbalanced schedule**. Each team does not play each other team in its own league an equal number of times. Again, each league is divided into divisions, called the Eastern, Central and Western Division. Within each league, to promote competitiveness within the divisions, each team plays teams in its own division about twice as often as it plays teams from the other two divisions.

An important event that occurs every April 15 is **Jackie Robinson Day**, which commemorates the breaking of the color barrier in baseball by Jackie Robinson. In every game played on Jackie Robinson Day, all players honor Robinson by wearing his uniform number, 42, and pre-game ceremonies honor his legacy and his meaning to the game. Some ceremonies will even be graced by the presence of surviving members of the old Negro Leagues.

Jackie Robinson's number 42 is now a **retired number** throughout the Major Leagues, which means that, in his honor, that number is permanently retired and no new players will be permitted to wear it. Mariano Rivera, who retired after the 2013 season, was the last active player to wear it.

May

As the baseball season leaves the cold days of March and April behind and starts to pick up momentum through the warmer days of May, you will more and more find yourself contemplating visits to the local ballpark. As you scan the schedule of the local team to choose a date, you'll find your decision on when to attend may be influenced by what are called **promotional days**, which are games in which either some special event is held or free mementos are given out to fans in attendance.

Among the special events commonly held are post-game fireworks displays, nights honoring those who served in the military, or nights celebrating one ethnic group or another. Among the free give-aways might be anything from home-team caps to bats to

President Obama, whose place of business is Washington, D.C., throws out the first pitch for the Nationals' 2010 home opener. As noted previously, the president is a White Sox fan, and as he took the mound he pulled out and put on a White Sox cap, as can be seen in this photograph. Per one spectator, "boos ensued from the sellout crowd" (photograph by Scott Ableman).

oven mitts to magnetic schedules to seat cushions to tote bags. **Bobble-heads** are big on promotional days. A Bobble-head, in case you are lucky enough not to know, is a little plaster figurine of a ballplayer or a manager whose oversized head, on a spring, bobbles when the figurine is shaken. Only special players and managers are honored with a Bobble-head day.

As might be expected, the Minor Leagues are notorious for their bizarre and often hilarious promotional days. In recent years one team held a "Pre-Planned Funeral Night" where one lucky fan went home with a guarantee that his funeral and burial would be completely paid for by the local funeral home that sponsored the event. Then there was "Toilet Plunger Giveaway Night," sponsored by a local plumbing company. And then there was "Ugly Sweater Night," where the fan who wore the ugliest sweater was awarded with a free shopping spree at the local Goodwill Thrift Shop. The best promotional date that I ever heard of is held annually by the Wilmington Blue Rocks, the Class A affiliate of the Royals. The event is called "Cowboy Monkey Rodeo Night" and during breaks in the game, I kid you not, professionally trained monkeys dressed as cowboys ride dogs around the field, herding rams.

Now let me stop right here for a moment, because I know there are going to be a lot of sports purists who are shocked, if not downright offended, by our toilet plunger giveaways and our cowboy monkeys. Let me say this about that: you can't look at baseball with your soccer glasses on, or your hockey glasses, or any other glasses for that matter. Baseball is different. It's a summer game. It's relaxed. There are a lot of breaks in the action. Have a old beverage. Take it easy. Chat with the stranger in the seat next to you. If your team gets their butt kicked today, don't worry, there will be plenty other games to make it up. Just remember that in the Majors a team can lose 62 games in a year—think of it, *62!*—and if they win the rest they will have had a great season and are all but guaranteed a first place finish.

June

In early June, baseball executives will be kept busy with the **First Year Player Draft**, also called the **Rule 4 Draft**. In the Rule 4 Draft, young prospects who meet certain age and eligibility requirements are invited by Major League Teams to join their organizations. College players are the usual targets of the draft, but high school graduates and players over 17 who don't attend any school at all are eligible as well.

Meanwhile, the baseball season marathon will be rolling on. As discussed, teams play almost every day, and as the season progresses, players invariably begin to fall to injuries and will be unable to play for varying periods of time.

If an injury is severe, if a player will miss more than a game or two, then, depending on the severity of the injury, the team can elect to put him on the either the **15-Day Disabled List** or the **60-Day Disabled List**, each of which is known for short as a **DL**. Teams with an injured player face a choice. On one hand, a player on either DL can removed from the roster and a player can be brought up from the Minors to replace him, which is good. On the other hand, that player cannot come off of the DL until either the 15-day or 60-day time period is up, which, if he heals faster than expected, can be bad.

As June 1 rolls around, teams will have played about 55 games each, meaning about one-third of the season will have passed. Unlike April and May, when you had the luxury of just enjoying games for what they were, come June, you will start to pay more attention to your favorite team's position in the **standings**, the day-by-day record of which teams are in first place, second place, third place, and so on, based on their won-loss records.

When you look at the standings, here's what you'll be looking for. Again, remember that each league is divided along geographic lines into a Western, Central and Eastern Division. Within each league, the teams that will qualify for the post-season playoffs are the teams that finish first in each of the three divisions, plus the winner of a one-game post-season elimination match between the two best non-first place teams, regardless of division, called the **Wild Card Teams**. You will be looking at the standings, therefore, to see not only how your team is measuring up in the race for first place in its division, but if that's being a bit overly optimistic, you'll also be looking to see how your team is measuring up in the race for the Wild Card spots.

In baseball standings, the first four columns you will see are (i) Wins, (ii) Losses, (iii) Percentage (short for **winning percentage**) and (iv) **Games Back**. The first two are self-explanatory, and the third column, percentage, simply represents the percentage of games a team has won out of the total games it has played.

Games Back is a bit more complex. Games Back, or **games behind**, means how many games the first place team has to lose and how many games any other given team in the division has to win in order for that other team to catch up to, to tie, the first place team. Suppose, after thirty games, the standings look like this:

	W	L	Pct	GB
1. Team A	20	10	.667	–
2. Team B	16	14	.533	4

Team B is four Games Back, because Team A has to lose four games and Team B has to win four games before Team B catches up to Team A, as both teams will then be even with 20–14 records.

Games Back is easy to follow when, as in the above example, the first place team and the team trying to catch them have played the same amount of games. The problem is that, until the very last day of the season, this will almost never be the case in the Majors. Over the course of a Major League season, different teams are scheduled to have days off at different times. Also, games can be postponed because of weather, to be replayed later on in the year. As a result, there will be several times during the year when some teams will have played up to four or five more or less games than the other teams in their division. That's when calculating Games Back can get tricky.

For example, suppose, Team B had played one less game than in the above example, and had one less win. The standings (leaving off Games Back for a moment) would look like this:

	W	L	Pct
1. Team A	20	10	.667
2. Team B	15	14	.517

If Team A lost the next four games and if Team B won the next four games, the standings would look like this:

	W	L	Pct
1. Team A	20	14	.588
2. Team B	19	14	.575

At this point, Team B is no longer one game behind Team A, because it is not necessary that Team B win *and* Team A lose in order for Team B to catch up to them. It is only necessary that Team B win *or* Team A lose.

Let's break that down. If, today, Team B is not scheduled to play, but Team A is, and it *loses*, Team B will overtake Team A by virtue of winning percentage:

	W	L	Pct
1. Team B	19	14	.575
2. Team A	20	15	.571

Or, instead, if Team A is not scheduled to play today, and Team B is, and it *wins*, Team B will catch up to Team A and tie it for first place:

	W	L	Pct
1. Team A	20	14	.588
2. Team B	20	14	.588

When Team A has to lose *or* Team B has to win for Team B to catch up to Team A, it is said that Team B is only a **half game** behind Team A. Thus, at the beginning of this example, the Games Back column would have looked like this:

	W	L	Pct	GB
1. Team A	20	10	.667	—
2. Team B	15	14	.517	4.5

You usually don't need a calculator to figure out Games Back, but if you want to impress your friends, the formula is as follows:

$$\frac{(difference\ in\ number\ of\ wins)\ PLUS\ (difference\ in\ number\ of\ losses)}{2}$$

OK, we're done with Games Back. Now for its evil twin.

Take a look at these two sets of standings and tell me which second place team has a better chance of overtaking the first place team:

Example 1

	W	L	Pct	GB
Team A	40	15	.727	—
Team B	37	17	.685	2.5

Example 2

	W	L	Pct	GB
Team A	40	15	.727	—
Team C	40	20	.667	2.5

Team B and Team C are both 2.5 games back, but clearly Team B is in much better shape. Team B, after all, has a game at hand on Team A. All that needs to happen for Team B to overtake Team A is for Team B to win two, Team A to lose two, and then Team B to win its game at hand.

Team C, on the other hand, has played five more games than Team A and lost them all. For Team C to overtake Team A, it has to hope Team A loses all of its five games at hand. Team C, as the saying goes, is not in control of its own destiny. It can only sit back and keep its fingers crossed.

The difference between Team B and Team C, some would say, can quickly be found just by looking at the **loss column**. Team B is 2.5 games behind, but it is only two games behind in the loss column. Team C is also 2.5 games behind, but, on the other hand, it is five games behind in the loss column. Therefore, in Team C's case, the Games Back column may be a bit deceptive. To be further back in the loss column (five games, in this case) than in the Games Back column (2.5 games) means your chances of catching up may be more difficult than the Games Back column indicates.

The loss column...

Every time I hear the words "loss column" I hearken back to the summer of 1973. I was in high school, and I was working a summer job at the *Daily News* on East 42nd Street in Manhattan. That summer I was working with a guy my age named Bob who was a rabid Mets fan, and whose Mets were involved in an amazingly tight battle for first place in the National League's Eastern Division against four other teams: the Cardinals, Pirates, Cubs and Montreal Expos (who, in 2005, moved to Washington, D.C., and became the Nationals).

Every morning, as we had breakfast in the News cafeteria, Bob would spread out his newspaper on the table like it was an IRS spreadsheet and he would study the previous night's scores and the standings intently. And as the summer began to wind into late August, and the race for first place among those five teams in the NL East went from close to razor-thin close, even though the Mets never seemed to rise above fourth place, Bob would always talk at length, every morning, about the secret meanings of the loss column and how, as a Mets fan, he found comfort in what it revealed to him.

This is what the loss column revealed to Bob: that year, as the race for first came down to its final weeks, the distance the Mets were from first place was due more and more to the unevenness, among all of those five teams, in the number of games each of them had played so far that season. Bob knew that the Mets were actually never as far behind first place as the Games Back column indicated. He knew, once each of the contending teams made up its games at hand, that, given the number of games, and given the opponents the other teams in the race were scheduled to face in those games, the Mets had a chance. Just a chance. "Ya gotta believe!" Bob would tell me, echoing what had become the Mets' rallying cry that year.

The summer job ended before the season did, but I thought of Bob every day for the rest of the season as the Mets shocked everyone and not only finished first, but made it all the way to the World Series. Shocked everyone, that is, except Bob and his loss column.

Bob, by the way, went on to become a sports announcer for the leading sports radio station in New York City. In fact, the leading sports radio station in the country.

Pretty cool, right?

JULY

Outside of the games themselves, three important events happen in July.

First, in mid–July, roughly halfway through the season, there is a break in the schedule, called the **All Star Break**, during which all teams have four days off and one of the Major League cities will host the annual **All Star Game**, also known more poetically as the **Mid-Summer Classic**, in which the best players in each league—as chosen mainly by fan vote—play a game against each other that showcases their talents and recognizes them as the best in the business.

The All Star Game does not affect the standings, but it is very important in a different way. In 2003, the lords of baseball ruled that the league whose team won the All Star Game would be the home team for the World Series. The World Series is a best-of-seven-games affair, with the home team hosting four of the seven games: the opening two games and, if either or both are necessary, the final two games. (Prior to 2003, the two leagues alternated as the home team for the Series.)

In the World Series, there is more to the home field advantage than the usual amenities of home cooking, sleeping in your own bed at night and having a huge, partisan crowds supporting you. The Designated Hitter rule holds that in the World Series, and in regular season interleague games as well, the Designated Hitter will be in effect when the American League team is the home team, and it will not be in effect when the National League team is the home team. Thus. having the home-field advantage in the World Series also means that you will play one more game by the rules you have used all season and that you have built your team around.

The second of the three important July events is the annual induction ceremony at the Hall of Fame, when the players who were voted into the Hall in January actually have plaques bearing their likeness and a brief synopsis of their accomplishments installed in the Gallery. The induction celebrations take place over the course of a weekend and festivities include a Legends Parade and the Hall of Fame Classic, a ballgame played by former Major Leaguers, including many of the previously inducted Hall of Famers.

You might say that while the All Star Game is a celebration of the stars of today, the Hall of Fame Induction Ceremony is a celebration of the stars of yesterday and of the enduring place the game of baseball has held in the identity and the history of this country.

The third important event that occurs during the month of July is the one that most affects the teams on a day-to-day basis. Come the end of July, some 110 games or so of the 162 game season will have been played, and most teams will have a pretty clear idea of whether they have a chance at making the post-season playoffs or not. Those that have a chance might want to make some personnel changes to address any weaknesses on their team that the season has revealed so far; those that do not, might want to make changes to build for the future, even if in the process they are, in effect, writing off the present.

The most dramatic type of personnel change occurs when a team **trades** a player, or **makes a trade**, with another team. It's a simple concept: you have a pretty good reserve shortstop that you're not using, but you need a right fielder; I have a pretty good reserve right fielder that I'm not using, but I need a shortstop. Easy. We trade your reserve shortstop for my reserve right fielder, and everyone's happy. The deadline for making a straight trade of players between teams in this manner, called a **non-waiver trade**, is July 31.

AUGUST

Trades can be made after the July 31 deadline, but they will fall under the auspices of the **Trade Assignment Waiver** rule. In brief, if a team wants to trade a player after the July 31 deadline has passed, it must notify the baseball commissioner, the word will go out around baseball and for the next two business days every other team in the league has the opportunity to basically intercept that player and **place a claim** on him. If a team claims the player, then the original team can only try to work out a trade with that team and no other. If no one places a claim the player, the player is said to have **cleared** trade waivers and off he goes unimpeded to the intended team.

The Trade Assignment Waiver rule was put in place to prevent winning teams from swallowing up all the good players just as the postseason playoffs are coming into sight, and, at the same time, to give teams with losing records a chance to improve their teams for the future.

SEPTEMBER

Somewhere within the first week or so of September, the last full month of the season, teams will start to be mathematically eliminated, one by one, from playoff contention, which means their "Games Back" will exceed the number of games left to play. At about the same time, you will start to hear more and more talk of a **Magic Number**, which is kind of Games Back in reverse. It refers to how many games a first place team or a Wild Card team will need to win to **clinch**, or mathematically ensure, its place in the playoffs.

You'll also start to hear more and more about a **pennant race**. A pennant is a small flag that is traditionally flown in ballparks to commemorate league championships won. In the old days there was one AL and one NL, in the sense that they were not yet subdivided into Divisions, and the team that finished first in each was said to have **won the pennant** in their respective leagues. Nowadays, since each league is subdivided into three Divisions, you'll often hear the term pennant race used for races in one Division or other, even though each Division's pennant race is technically only one-third of a pennant race, or a race for one-third of the pennant. But let's not be picky.

OCTOBER

October means only one thing to baseball fans: the World Series, often known as just the **Series**, or, more poetically, the **Fall Classic**. Now, of course, October also means the two rounds of playoffs leading up to World Series.

Here's how the Major League playoff system works:

Again, four teams make the playoffs in each league, the first place finishers in each of the three Divisions and the winner of the one-game elimination game between the two best non-first-place teams, regardless of Division, called the Wild Card teams.

There are three playoff rounds. In the first round, called the **American** and **National League Division Series** (the **ALDS** and **NLDS**), in each league the team that finished with the best winning percentage of the three first place teams plays the surviving Wild Card team, while the two remaining first place teams play each other, each in a best-of-five series. The two LDS winners then play each other in the best-of-seven **American** and **National League Championship Series** (the **ALCS** and **NLCS**), with the two LCS winners then meeting in the World Series.

To the players on teams who make the playoffs, October means the march to the World Series. To all the other players, October means one of two things. To the established players, it means the start of the **off-season** and the chance to go home, rest and recharge. To the players who are not yet that established, or to Minor League players—the players, in short, still fighting to earn a living as baseball players—it can mean the start of **Winter Baseball**, as they go off to warm weather professional baseball leagues in places like Australia, the Dominican Republic, Mexico and Venezuela, where they will continue to play, continue to hone their skills and dream of the day when they, too, can take the off-season off.

NOVEMBER

Within 15 days after the last World Series game ends, any player who has been in the Major Leagues for at least six years and whose previous contract has just expired, can declare himself a **free agent** and is now free to sell his services to whatever team he wants.

There is no end-date to free agency. Between now and next season's Opening Day, however, many big stars will find new homes, untold millions of dollars in contracts will be signed, and some fans will be left feeling a little alienated, a little torn, as they head off to work on the subway, wondering what it is they ever thought they had in common with these mega-millionaires they root so hard for almost every night for seven months out of the year.

But the perceived excesses of the free agency system are best viewed within the context of the system that preceded it, and which controlled baseball from the signing of the 1903

National Agreement right up until the mid–1970s. During that time, baseball was governed by the notorious **Reserve Clause**, a standard provision in player contracts which forced a player to negotiate new contracts with his team and with his team only. His only bargaining power was that he could choose to hold out, to not play, until the team came closer to satisfying his demands, but very few players had the kind of clout that could make a hold out work.

The perceived excesses of free agency should also be considered within the context of the unglamorous reality behind the headlines. First of all, again, a player is only eligible for free agency after six years in the Majors. The majority of players don't make it that far and thus never get the chance to sell their talents on the open market to the highest bidder. For those players, the Reserve Clause never went away.

Second of all, the sad reality is that to many free agents, the expiration of a contract with a team means just that: the end of work, the end of a paycheck. When one of the better players declares free agency, that player's team has a short exclusivity period in which they can try to work out a last minute deal with the player before the bidding opens. Other players, however, walk away from their team without an offer, and those players float through free agency waiting for a phone call that sometimes doesn't come. Then, like the rest of us who look up one day from their desk and find two glum bosses standing in the doorway, they are forced to dust off their resume and hit the pavement.

As a final word on the subject, it would be remiss of me not to at least mention that the decades-long dominance of the Reserve Clause came to an end and the right to work where you want to work, for as much as you can get, came to baseball only after years of very difficult and contentious and costly labor struggles between players and team owners. That right, as represented by the establishment of free agency and the settlement of related issues such as compensation for the team that loses a free agent, team salary caps and binding salary arbitration, came to baseball only after a total of eight owner lockouts and player strikes, beginning with a 12-day player strike in 1972 over pension plan issues and culminating in the 232-day player strike of 1994. That strike, precipitated by such issues as team salary caps and revenue sharing, resulted in the cancellation of the last two months of the season, the post-season playoffs and the World Series.

Another important November baseball event is the announcement of awards for individual player achievements during the previous season. The **Most Valuable Player Award**, or **MVP**, is given to the player in each league considered the most valuable, or best all around player. The **Cy Young Award**, named after Hall of Famer Cy Young, goes to the best pitcher in each league. The **Rookie of the Year Award** goes to the best first year player in each league, and finally, **Manager of the Year Award** is given out to the Manager who makes the most of the talent on his team. Awards are decided on by vote of the Baseball Writers Association of America, the same group that elects players into the Hall of Fame.

The **Gold Glove Awards** are also very prestigious. They are voted on by managers of the Major League teams, and are awarded to the best defensive players in each League. One Award is given for each defensive position in each league.

December

We know now that a player who has six years in the Majors and whose contract has expired is eligible for free agency. Conversely, a player who has less than six years in the

Majors and whose contract has expired is still forced to deal with his team, and his team only, for a contract extension. However, if he has at least three years in the Majors (two, in some rare instances) and if certain other preconditions are met, he has the option of requesting **binding salary arbitration**.

Early in December, teams release a list of players who are eligible for binding salary arbitration. They will also announce which of these players have been offered, or **tendered**, a new contract, and which ones haven't. A player who has been offered a new contract can accept the offer or he can request that his team enter into binding salary arbitration. A player who has not been offered a new contract becomes what is called a **non-tender free agent**, and, like the post-six year free agents, he is free to sign with any team.

One of the year's final activities is the annual **Winter Meetings**, in which the general managers from each team meet for three days and make some trades, sign some free agents, and conduct the **Rule 5 Draft**, which, briefly, allows teams to troll the minor league rosters of other teams and steal a player—just one player each—who, is still wallowing in the minors (depending on his age) four or five years after signing with the team.

The Rule 5 draft, like the trade waiver rule, is best understood if you keep its purpose in mind, which is to prevent Major League teams from stockpiling talented players in their Minor League systems for an extended period of time. Use them, or risk losing them, the Rule seems to be saying.

Are future stars ever found in a Rule 5 Draft? I'll answer that question with two words: Roberto Clemente. Hall of Famer Clemente, who was plucked from the Brooklyn Dodgers farm system by the Pirates in 1954, went on to play 18 years with the Pirates before he died in a plane crash while flying relief supplies to earthquake victims in Nicaragua. Clemente is widely considered to be one of the best and most important players in the history of the game.

Baseball will start to recede from the headlines after the Winter Meetings. To fill the void, baseball fans, baseball columnists, baseball bloggers, baseball writers, baseball podcasters and baseball radio talk show hosts, all join in something called the **Hot Stove League**. The Hot Stove League is really not a league of any kind, but more an informal and unofficial and completely unorganized network of baseball enthusiasts who survive the winter months by engaging in endless discussions about the previous season, by speculating and making predictions about the next one, and, of course, by counting down the days 'til Pitchers and Catchers.

FIVE

Final Thoughts

I think we're done now.

The little notes have finally stopped coming.

Over the last few years, as I was writing this book, I was forever writing or texting or emailing to myself little notes and reminders about issues and topics and factoids that popped into my mind during the course of the day and needed to be covered in this book, or that I needed to look into further. Sometimes several little notes in a day: "Explain why righty batters can't drag bunt," "Explain 'around the horn' double play," "Explain why catcher, not pitcher, calls pitches."

Baseball is an amazingly rich game. There just seemed to be no end to the strategies, the possibilities, the terminologies. And, correspondingly, there seemed to be no end to the little notes I wrote to myself. Just last week I was listening to the radio when the announcer said that a certain pitcher had **struck out the side** in the fourth inning. Struck out the side? I hadn't put that in the book yet! I grabbed a piece of paper and a pen, scrawled "struck out the side" and shoved it into my pocket. I would have to make sure that the reader knew that "struck out the side" meant that the pitcher faced the minimum three batters in an inning, and struck them all out.

But that was it. Since then, not one little note.

As this book began to wind its way slowly to a close, I thought of several ways to end it. One way, which I found myself gravitating towards time and again, had less to do with baseball, but, ending where I began, had more to do with my getting laid off and trying to provide for a family of six, while, at the same time, trying to reconcile all the unanswered emails and all the unreturned phone calls with my absolute certainty that I still had so much to offer.

That particular ending for this book focused on how the challenge of writing this book was one way of verifying, for myself, that I could still produce, still take on a difficult, multi-layered task and master it. "Dad," my daughter said to me one day as I typed away, baseball books piled high on either side of the keyboard, "you're always up to something, aren't you?" I thought for a moment about what she said. Yes, it was true. I was always up to something, because, especially then, for my own sanity, I had to be.

"Caroline," I responded after a pause, "I'm like Mariano Rivera."

"Who?" she said.

"Child," I exclaimed, "you cut me to the quick! Have I taught you nothing over the years? Mariano Rivera! The great Yankees relief pitcher! And, since you ask, here's how I'm like Mariano Rivera. Mariano, if he came into the ninth inning with the Yankees up by a run and the bases loaded and no one out would strike out two batters and get the third to pop out and in a few minutes, the game would be over. But sometimes, if Mariano came into a game with the Yankees up by three runs, he'd give up a run or two before buckling down and getting the three outs. It's almost like, if there wasn't a worthy challenge ahead of him, he would lose focus a bit, get a little careless."

"OK."

"Mariano, they say, was at his best when his best was called for."

"OK."

"Me too."

"OK."

She started to walk away, then turned and said, "Dad, what does 'bases loaded' mean?"

She's a football fan.

My book may be finished, but, thankfully, great challenges still lie ahead.

Bibliography

Books

Aaron, Hank, with Lonnie Wheeler. *I Had a Hammer: The Hank Aaron Story*. New York: Harper-Perrenial, 1991.

Adair, Robert K. *The Physics of Baseball*. New York: Perrenial, 1990.

American Baseball Coaches Association. *Baseball Strategies: Your Guide to the Game within the Game*. Champaign, IL: Human Kinetics, 2003.

Asinof, Eliot. *Eight Men Out: The Black Sox and the 1919 World Series*. New York: Henry Holt, 1963.

Bagonzi, John. *The Act of Pitching*. Woodsville, NH: Pitching Professor Publications, 2001.

Bernstein, Ross. *The Code: Baseball's Unwritten Rules and Its Ignore-at-Your-Own-Risk Code of Conduct*. Chicago: Triumph Books, 2008.

Bissinger, Buzz. *Three Nights in August: Strategy, Heartbreak, and Joy Inside the Mind of a Manager*. Boston: Houghton Mifflin, 2006.

Blewett, William. *The Science of the Fastball*. Jefferson, NC: McFarland, 2013.

Bondy, Filip. *Who's on First?* New York: Doubleday, 2013.

Brock, Lou, and Franz Schulze. *Stealing Is My Game*. Englewood Cliffs, NJ: Prentice Hall, 1976.

Canseco, Jose. *Juiced: Wild Times, Rampant 'Roids, Smash Hits and How Baseball Got Big*. New York: Harper, 2005.

_____. *Vindicated: Big Names, Big Liars and the Battle to Save Baseball*. New York: Simon Spotlight Entertainment, 2008.

Carew, Rod, with Frank Pace and Armen Keteyian. *Rod Carew's Hit to Win*. Minneapolis: MBI, 2012.

Clark, Dave. *The Knucklebook*. Chicago: Ivan R. Dee, 2006.

Cobb, Ty. *My Twenty Years in Baseball*. Mineola, NY: Dover, 2002.

Costa, Gabriel B., Michael R. Huber, and John T. Saccoman. *Understanding Sabermetrics: An In-troduction to the Science of Baseball Statistics*. Jefferson, NC: McFarland, 2008.

Darling, Ron. *The Complete Game: Reflections on Baseball and the Art of Pitching*. New York: Vintage, 2009.

Dickey, R.A., with Wayne Coffey. *Wherever I Wind Up: My Quest for Truth, Authenticity and the Perfect Knuckleball*. New York: Blue Rider Press, 2012.

Dickson, Paul. *The Dickson Baseball Dictionary*. New York: W.W. Norton, 2009.

_____. *The Joy of Keeping Score*, New York: Walker and Company, 1996.

_____. *The Unwritten Rules of Baseball: The Etiquette, Conventional Wisdom and Axiomatic Codes of Our National Pastime*. New York: HarperCollins, 2009.

Euchner, Charles. *The Last Nine Innings: Inside the Real Game Fans Never See*. Naperville, IL: Sourcebooks, 2006.

Fainaru-Wada, Mark, and Lance Williams. *Game of Shadows: Barry Bonds, BALCO, and the Steroids Scandal that Rocked Professional Sports*. New York: Gotham Books, 2006.

Feinstein, John. *Living on the Black*. New York: Little, Brown, 2008.

Feller, Bob, with Burton Rocks. *Bob Feller's Little Black Book of Baseball Wisdom*. Chicago: Contemporary Books, 2001.

Frankie, Christopher. *Nailed! The Improbable Rise and Spectacular Fall of Lenny Dykstra*. Philadelphia: Running Press, 2013.

Freeman, S.H. *Basic Baseball Strategy*, New York: McGraw Hill, 2006.

Galarraga, Armando, Jim Joyce with Daniel Paisner. *Nobody's Perfect: Two Men, One Call and a Game for Baseball History*. New York: Atlantic Monthly Press, 2011.

Gooden, Doc, Jeff Johnson and Ellis Henican. *Doc: A Memoir*. New York: New Harvest, 2013.

Halberstam, David. *The Teammates: A Portrait of a Friendship*. Hyperion: New York, 2003.

Hall, Donald, with Dock Ellis. *In the Country of Baseball*. New York: Fireside, 1976.

Helyar, John. *Lords of the Realm: The Real History of Baseball*. New York: Villard, 1994.

Hernandez, Keith, and Mike Bryan. *Pure Baseball: Pitch by Pitch for the Advanced Fan*. New York: HarperPerennial, 1995.

James, Bill. *The New Bill James Historical Baseball Abstract*. New York: Free Press, 2001.

Jeter, Derek, with Jack Curry. *The Life You Imagine: Life Lessons for Achieving Your Dreams*. New York: Crown, 2000.

Johnson, Randy, with Jim Rosenthal. *Randy Johnson's Power Pitching*. New York: Three Rivers Press, 2003.

Kahn, Roger. *The Head Game: Baseball Seen from the Pitcher's Mound*. New York: Harcourt, 2000.

Kaplan, Jim. *The Greatest Game Ever Pitched*. Chicago: Triumph Books, 2011.

Lane, F.C. *Batting*. Cleveland: Society of American Baseball Research (SABR), 2001. Originally published in 1925.

La Russa, Tony, with Rick Hummel. *One Last Strike: Fifty Years in Baseball, Ten and a Half Games Back, and One Final Championship Season*. New York: William Morrow, 2012.

Lau, Charlie, with Alfred Glossbrenner. *The Art of Hitting .300*. New York: Hawthorn, 1980.

Leventhal, Josh. *Take Me Out to the Ballpark: An Illustrated Tour of Ballparks Past and Present*. New York: Black Dog & Leventhal, 2000.

Lewis, Michael. *Moneyball*. New York: W.W. Norton, 2003.

Mathewson, Christy. *Pitching in a Pinch*. New York: Penguin Classics, 2013.

McCarver, Tim. *Baseball for Brain Surgeons and Other Fans*. New York: Villard, 1998.

McKelvey, G. Richard. *All Bat, No Glove: A History of the Designated Hitter*. Jefferson, NC: McFarland, 2004.

Miller, Stuart. *Good Wood: The Story of the Baseball Bat*. Chicago: Acta Sports, 2011.

Montville, Leigh. *The Big Bam: The Life and Times of Babe Ruth*. New York: Broadway Books, 2006.

Morgan, Joe. *Baseball for Dummies*. Hoboken, NJ: Wiley, 2005.

_____, and David Falkner. *A Life in Baseball,* New York: W.W. Norton, 1993.

Official Baseball Rules. Major League Baseball Official, 2013.

O'Keeffe, Michael, and Terri Thompson. *The Card: Collectors, Con Men and the True Story of History's Most Desired Baseball Card*. New York: Harper, 2008.

Okrent, Daniel. *9 Innings: The Anatomy of a Baseball Game*. New York: Houghton Mifflin, 2000.

Olney, Buster, *The Last Night of the Yankee Dynasty*. New York: HarperCollins, 2004.

Pearlman, Jeff. *Love Me, Hate Me: Barry Bonds and the Making of an Antihero*. New York: HarperCollins, 2006.

Piazza, Mike, with Lonnie Wheeler. *Long Shot*. New York: Simon & Schuster, 2013.

Prager, Joshua. *The Echoing Green: The Untold Story of Bobby Thomson, Ralph Branca and the Shot Heard Round the World*. New York: Vintage, 2006.

Remy, Jerry, with Corey Sandler. *Watching Baseball*. Guildford, CT: Insiders' Guide, 2004.

Report to the Commissioner of Baseball of an Independent Investigation into the Illegal Use of Steroids and Other Performance Enhancing Substances by Players in Major League Baseball. George J. Mitchell, DLA Piper U.S. LLP, December 13, 2007.

Robinson, Jackie. *I Never Had It Made*. New York: HarperCollins, 1995.

Rose, Pete, with Rick Hill. *My Prison Without Bars*. Emmaus, PA: Rodale, 2004.

Ruth, Babe. *Playing the Game: My Early Years in Baseball*. Mineola, NY: Dover, 2011.

Ryan, Nolan, and Tom House. *Nolan Ryan's Pitcher's Bible*. New York: Simon & Schuster, 1991.

Seaver, Tom, with Lee Lowenfish, *The Art of Pitching*. New York: Quill, 1994.

Seymour, Harold. *Baseball: The Early Years*. New York: Oxford University Press, 1960.

_____. *Baseball: The Golden Age*. New York: Oxford University Press, 1971.

Silva, Deirdre, and Jackie Koney. *It Takes More Than Balls: The Savvy Girls' Guide to Understanding and Enjoying Baseball*. New York: Skyhorse, 2008.

Sokolove, Michael Y. *Hustle: The Myth, Life, and Lies of Pete Rose*. New York: Simon & Schuster, 1990.

Southworth, Stu. *The Complete Book of Baseball Signs and Plays*. Monterey, CA: Coaches Choice, 1999.

Thorn, John, and Pete Palmer. *The Hidden Game of Baseball*. New York: Doubleday, 1986.

Torre, Joe, and Tom Verducci. *The Yankee Years*. New York: Doubleday, 2009.

Turbow, Jason, with Michael Duca. *The Baseball Codes: Beanballs, Sign Stealing, & Bench-Clearing Brawls*. New York: Anchor Books, 2010.

Tygiel, Jules. *Past Time: Baseball as History*. New York: Oxford University Press, 2000.

Vaccaro, Mike. *The First Fall Classic: The Red Sox, The Giants and the Cast of Players, Pugs and Politicos who Reinvented the World Series in 1912*. New York: Doubleday, 2009.

Vincent, Fay. *It's What Inside the Lines That Counts*, New York: Simon & Schuster, 2010.

_____. *The Only Game in Town: Baseball Stars of the 1930s and 1940s Talk About the Game They Loved*. New York: Simon & Schuster, 2006.

Wakefield, Tim, with Tony Massarotti. *Knuckler: My Life with Baseball's Most Confounding Pitch*. Boston: Houghton Mifflin Harcourt, 2011.

Weaver, Earl. *Weaver on Strategy*. Washington, D.C.: Potomac Books, 2002.

Weber, Bruce. *As They See 'Em: A Fan's Travels in the Land of Umpires*. New York: Scribner, 2009.

Williams, Ted, and John Underwood. *The Science of Hitting*. New York: Simon & Schuster, 1970.

Wojciechowski, Gene. *Cubs Nation: 162 Games, 162 Stories, 1 Addiction*. New York: Doubleday, 2005.

Zumsteg, Derek. *The Cheater's Guide to Baseball*. Boston: Houghton Mifflin, 2007.

Websites

Ask the Umpire. http://www.baseball-fever.com.

The Atlantic. http://www.theatlantic.com.

Ball Parks of Baseball. http://ballparksofbaseball.com.

Baseball Almanac. http://www.baseball-almanac.com.

Baseball Prospectus. http://www.baseballprospectus.com.

Baseball Steroid Era. http://baseballsteroidera.com.

Baseball Writers Association of America. http://bbwaa.com.

The Biz of Baseball. http://bizofbaseball.com.

Bloomberg. http://www.bloomberg.com.

Boston Red Sox. http://boston.redsox.mlb.com.

Brew Crew Ball. http://brewcrewball.com.

CBS News. http://www.cbsnew.com.

The Complete Pitcher. http://thecompletepitcher.com.

Cubbie Baseball http://www.cubbiesbaseball.com

ESPN. http://sports.espn.go.com.

Grantland. http://grantland.com.

Hard Ball Times. http://hardballtimes.com.

Historic Baseball: Bringing Baseball History to Center Field. http://www.historicbaseball.com.

Los Angeles Times. http://latimesblogs.latimes.com.

Major League Baseball. http://mlb.com.

MikeScottBaseball.com.

Minor League Baseball. http://milb.com.

National Baseball Hall of Fame and Museum. http://baseballhall.org.

NBC Sports. http://nbcsports.msnbc.com.

Negro League Baseball Players Association. http://www.nlbpa.com.

NESN. http://nesn.com.

New York Daily News. http://nydailynews.com.

New York Times. http://nytimes.com.

Purple Row, a Colorado Rockies community. http://www.purplerow.com.

SABR: Society for American Baseball Research. http://sabr.org.

St. Louis Cardinals. http://stlouis.cardinals.mlb.com.

San Francisco Chronicle. http://sfgate.com.

Sports Illustrated. si.com.

USA Today. http://usatoday.com.

Washington Post. http://washingtonpost.com.

Yogi Berra website. http://www.yogiberra.com.

Periodicals

The Baseball Research Journal, published by Society of American Baseball Research (SABR).

Memories and Dreams. published by National Baseball Hall of Fame and Museum

Index

Page numbers in **bold italics** indicate pages with illustrations.